Feeding the Ghost 1

Feeding the Ghost 1:

Criticism on Contemporary Australian Poetry

edited by
Andy Kissane, David Musgrave,
& Carolyn Rickett

To Greg McLaren, who first cooked this crazy idea up

PUNCHER & WATTMANN

© Andy Kissane, David Musgrave & Carolyn Rickett 2018

This book is copyright. Apart from any fair dealing for the purposes of study and research, criticism, review or as otherwise permitted under the Copyright Act, no part may be reproduced by any process without written permission. Inquiries should be made to the publisher.

First published in 2018
Published by Puncher and Wattmann
PO Box 279
Waratah NSW 2298

http://www.puncherandwattmann.com
puncherandwattmann@bigpond.com

A catalogue record for this book is available from the National Library of Australia

ISBN   9781922186966 (print)
        9781925780116 (ebook)

Cover design by Miranda Douglas
Printed by Lightning Source International

Editorial Advisory Board: Judith Beveridge, Peter Kirkpatrick, Michael Sharkey

We would like to thank Deakin University for supporting the production costs of this collection, and Avondale College of Higher Education for assisting with editing costs.

This project has been assisted by the Australian Government through the Australia Council, its arts funding and advisory body.

Contents

7
Chapter 1
"Seeing what the hunger is": current criticism on Australian poetry
ANDY KISSANE, DAVID MUSGRAVE & CAROLYN RICKETT

16
Chapter 2
"Bypassed Years": TimeSpace and stasis in
Gorton's 'Press Release' sequences.
CASSANDRA ATHERTON

36
Chapter 3
Mez Breeze Between the Centuries
A.J. CARRUTHERS

59
Chapter 4
Philip Salom: Feeding Time to the Contemporary
TOBY DAVIDSON

85
Chapter 5
Sentimental Educations: The Poetry of David Malouf
MARTIN DUWELL

112
Chapter 6
"Singing in my careless hand": Dorothy Porter's verse novels
ANDY KISSANE

148
Chapter 7
John Watson and the Comedy of Landscape
MARTIN LANGFORD

168
Chapter 8
Pam Brown's Ghostly Signature: "Half here/Half gone"
Lyn McCredden

190
Chapter 9
Randolph Stow's "Hungry Waiting Country"
Caitlin Maling

214
Chapter 10
Les Murray's Mannerist Grotesque
David Musgrave

250
Chapter 11
Matters Invisible: J. S. Harry's Lyrical Poems
Kerry Plunkett

280
Chapter 12
"The final subject has been set. I'm concentrating hard on death":
The poetics of loss in Philip Hodgins's *Blood and Bone*
Carolyn Rickett

311
Chapter 13
"But with a general groan": Public and Private Voices in
Jordie Albiston and Melinda Smith's Poetry
Tegan Schetrumpf

337
Chapter 14
Between Housework and Carrying Her Home:
Natalie Harkin's Reparative Poetics
Ann Vickery

Chapter 1

"Seeing what the hunger is": current criticism on Australian poetry

ANDY KISSANE, DAVID MUSGRAVE & CAROLYN RICKETT

This book is aimed at providing criticism of contemporary Australian poetry in a form that is accessible to general readers of poetry. It is intended to be the first in a series which will grapple with the bewildering diversity of the contemporary poetry scene. Part of the need for this scholarly collection is remedial; as we will argue, poetry review culture often lacks critical bite and the exigencies of academic research often bypass critical evaluation. The recent publication of *Contemporary Australian Poetry* (2016) highlighted the strength and vitality of the art form in Australia over the last quarter of a century. *Feeding the Ghost 1: Criticism on Contemporary Australian Poetry* is intended to complement that body of work which has surprised so many readers with its vigour and depth.

This introductory chapter explains the circumstances leading up to the present day where we see a palpable decline in poetry criticism. The great seismic shift in contemporary Australian poetry was comprised of three more or less contemporaneous events in the mid-1990s: the dropping of poetry lists by Harper Collins (Angus & Robertson), Oxford University Press, William Heinemann, Penguin and Collins; the rise of short run digital printing which had begun with the arrival of the first Gutenberg machine in 1990 and accelerated rapidly until it became the preferred mode of printing for poetry presses (to be supplanted later by Print on Demand); the rise of the internet, and later, social media. In addition to this, or perhaps as a consequence, the number of outlets which regularly reviewed poetry declined. Whereas it may not have been unusual for a single book of poetry to attract up to 17 reviews in the 1980s (Salom 2017), the maximum number of reviews achieved by a single poetry book in 2013 was nine.[1] Broadly speaking, the situation Australian poetry finds itself in is that there are a large number of poetry titles being published each year, there is enormous range of styles and modes within that large number of titles and it appears that there is a corresponding paucity of critical discussion, by which we mean discussion that is evaluative and not merely descriptive, as well as being disinterested.

In many ways this situation was predicted by Mark Davis in his 2006 article "The Decline of the Literary Paradigm in Australia". Davis claims that "Literary fiction will otherwise become the preserve of independent publishers and self-publishing"(104) and that "literature might become a do-it-yourself culture that will operate, for the time being, at least partly outside mainstream publishing culture, having cleared itself a space for experimentation and the development of new paradigms" (105). The same argument can be applied to poetry, perhaps even more so. Poetry publishing in Australia is largely the preserve of small operations which turn over less than one million dollars per year. The mainstays of poetry publishing in Australia are Puncher & Wattmann, Giramondo, Pitt Street Poetry, Five Islands, Fremantle, UWA, UQP, Vagabond, Cordite, Wakefield, Walleah, Hunter, GloriaSMH, Black Inc, and the now-defunct John Leonard Press. It is tempting to assume that all of these outfits remain small (or at least, the turnover of their poetry lists remains small) because the size of the readership of poetry is roughly equivalent to the number of poets. For as long as we can remember, this has been one of the charges against the relevance of poetry to mainstream Australian literary culture.

Two of the editors of this volume are associated with Puncher & Wattmann, and an analysis of our sales indicates a substantial amount of poetry sales (in some cases up to one third) go to libraries, schools and university bookshops. Income from Public Lending Rights and Educational Lending Rights indicates a significant readership beyond other poets. An analysis of our sales database does not support the argument that it is largely poets who buy and read other poets' books. Nevertheless, it is difficult from this data to form a profile of the general reader of poetry. Most likely such a person does not exist, given the wide range of poetry being published in Australia. It is more likely that there are specific readers of poetry who read with a desire to write themselves, who read following a (manageable) handful of reputations, who read based on a coincidence of interest (e.g. poems about science, poems about a particular person etc).

Another issue to consider when postulating the existence of the general reader of poetry is that there is very little in the way of a broad critical overview to guide them. Reviews, as Ben Etherington and Emmett Stinson argue, are an imperfect guide. Ben Etherington, in his essay "The Poet Tasters" undertook a survey of poetry reviews published in 2013. He found that there were "247 reviews covering 159 volumes authored or edited by 142 poets (66 women and 76 men) by 134 reviewers (62 women and 72 men)". It is fair to generalise from this sample that it would also apply to the present day. Surveying all these reviews, Etherington identifies a common approach which he calls "the compliment sandwich". Typically, reviewers quote two or three poems in an approving manner, express reservations about one or two poems, but nevertheless affirm the worthiness of the volume. Etherington argues that "when reviews are long on praise and short on criticism, it weakens the praise. There is no sense that it has been won from a determinedly critical disposition … The quantum of praise does not add up." Ultimately, there is no reliable guide for the general reader of poetry, no discussion of the huge range of poetry being published that consistently moves beyond description, nowhere to go to find an intelligent, unaligned reading of poetry that is evaluative, thoughtful and critical. Etherington's conclusion is unsettling:

> … it seems that the criticism of poetry is falling short of its civic responsibility. We see the profile of a community turned inwards which can forget that there might be a broader readership curious to know about what is going on.

The reasons for this state of affairs have been widely speculated on, but perhaps Emmett Stinson's notion of the "prosumer" comes closest to providing a convincing argument. The term "prosumer" refers to readers who have some kind of creative investment in the literary work they consume. Borrowing the term from Alvin Toffler's *The Third Wave: The Classic Study of Tomorrow*, Stinson understands the term as "the adoption of practices in service industries that blur consumption and production" (35), with the "service industry" he has in mind being literary publishing, and that "this contemporary form of literary "prosumption" resembles the mode of literary production of the avant-garde as described by Pierre Bourdieu;" (23). Assuming that the term "prosumer" applies to readers of poetry, it is clear that disinterestedness is hardly likely to be a feature of engagement in critical discussions outside the academy.

What, then, of criticism that comes from the academy? Poetry criticism does appear from time to time in the form of research, but it should be kept in mind the difference between the two. Research is often guided by research funding, which is in turn governed by a complex set of criteria determined by the Australian Research Council and other academic funding and regulatory bodies. One consequence is that some research can be empirical, or some can be concerned with examining poetry within a broader political or sociological context, especially as it might relate to identity; there might also be the subordination of criticism of poetry to broader theoretical aims, often employing highly specialised language. As academic researchers ourselves, we are thoroughly familiar with these paradigms of academic research, and while much, if not all academic research is available to the determined general reader of poetry through libraries, it must be admitted that a great deal of the research on poetry that we are familiar with is not criticism in the sense that it is a disinterested, critical evaluation of the literary qualities of the work. And we freely admit that this is where it gets difficult: what is disinterestedness? what is literary value? Who decides how these terms are to be defined?

"Disinterestedness" is the concept Matthew Arnold developed to describe how curiosity, or "the free play of the mind" might allow the mind to engage, without an agenda, with works of literature (26). It is naïve to think that one can be free of an agenda; the social and ideological construction of subjectivity is more or less a truism, and we do not pretend to think that "pure disinterestedness" is at all possible. After all, Arnold's concept is over 150 years old, and does appear to have been jettisoned quite regularly from time to time in the years since. Fully aware of this difficulty, we have tried to commission essays which pair a critic with a poet with whom there are no especially strong ties of friendship or enmity, ideally placing a critic outside their "comfort zone" in the hope that their insights might be unblinkered by social or political allegiances. We also have an interest in promoting critical discussion of poets who we consider to be important but relatively neglected in critical discussions: Mez Breeze, Natalie harkin, Philip Salom, Melinda Smith and John Watson are examples. Finally, where we have included criticism on well-established poets, we have sought to include only that which makes an original contribution to knowledge of that poet's work, rather than recycling the platitudinous party lines with which we are all too familiar.

A number of anthologies compiling Australian poems have performative functions that seek to address forms of exclusion. For example, Susan Hampton and Kate Llewellyn reveal part of their motivation in the introduction of their anthology of *Australian Women Poets*:

> In fifteen well-known collections of Australian poetry published since 1970, the average of female authors selected was 17 percent ... This may not be a problem of deliberate critical neglect, but a problem of consciousness — until recently most anthology editors, literary historians and critics have been male, and their gaze was unconsciously focussed on other men" (2).

Other editors of anthologies constellate poems around particular and invested themes, Mark Tredinnick's selection of *Australian Love Poems*

2013 is one such example. Samplings of other anthologies reveal a variety of motivations for their origins as indicated by their editors' introductions; see Wallace-Crabbe, 1981; Leonard, 1998, 2001, 2009; Kinsella, 2009; and Adamson, 2010 as exemplars.

While the practice of anthologising Australian poetry has over the past several decades produced various oeuvres, we believe there is an increasing gap between the practice of producing collections and anthologies and the practice of timely "reflective, attentive consideration and analysis of a literary work" (Murfin & Ray 78). We are seeking to redress this situation by focussing on criticism as a means to directly address the problems Etherington and Stinson identify in reviewing culture. We think that the review form is too short to allow the elaboration of disinterested criticism: it is more the domain of the review essay or the critical essay. On the question of "literary value", we prefer an approach to criticism that comes from literary studies, and while not devaluing the contribution of cultural studies to the literary domain, we prefer to leave that for others.

The editors of *Contemporary Australian Poetry* contend that

> Somewhat astonishingly, and while no-one was looking, Australian poetry has developed a momentum and a critical mass such that it has become one more luminous field in the English-speaking imagination. Increasingly, anyone who seeks to explore the perspectives or music available in English will also have to consider the perspectives and music which have originated here—Australia having turned itself, too, into a place in the mind. (xii)

We take this contention as a starting point for reconsidering how criticism should address and complement contemporary Australian poetry. And we posit that Australian poetry deserves a criticism that accompanies the astonishing momentum and luminosity that has developed, a criticism that both elucidates the scale of poetic achievement and is also not afraid to evaluate that achievement through a critical lens that is rigorous, disinterested and not hampered by the preference for praise that appears to restrict contemporary reviewing practices.

Peter Steele, an Australian critic offers this insight:

> To love the language, for all its curiosities and occasional vexations, is indispensable in a poet, since what he or she is doing is in part a 'magnifying' of that very medium (205).

We also see this kind of 'magnification' at work in effective criticism. In this book, there are varying approaches to 'magnifying' aspects of poets' work: Cassandra Atherton investigates Lisa Gorton's treatment of the compression of TimeSpace; A.J. Carruthers argues for the importance of the post-digital avant-garde in examining the work of Mez Breeze; Toby Davidson suggests that the critical neglect of Philip Salom's poetry might be due to his exuberant changes of style and subject matter; Martin Duwell charts the diverse sources that lead to the expansion and education of the self in David Malouf's poetry; Andy Kissane argues that an interrogation of love and desire lies at the heart of Dorothy Porter's verse novels; Martin Langford writes about John Watson's innovative exploration of landscape through the comic mode; Caitlin Maling departs from the critical emphasis on landscape in Randolph Stow's poetry to chart the inner landscapes of his love lyrics; Lyn McCredden appraises Pam Brown's linguistic wrestle with disappearance; David Musgrave evaluates Les Murray's work in the context of theories of the grotesque and mannerism; Kerry Plunkett looks at the way the notion of egolessness informs J. S. Harry's lyrical poems; Carolyn Rickett explores the thanatological impulse in selected poems from Philip Hodgins' *Blood and Bone*; Tegan Schetrumpf discusses how the public and private voices adopted by Jordie Albiston and Melinda Smith are harnessed to present stories that are seldom told; and Ann Vickery examines the work of Natalie Harkin in the light of literary interventions in the colonial archive.

Finally, we would like to thank Philip Salom for allowing us to re-use the title of his 1993 collection *Feeding the Ghost*. In the poem

"Cryptographs" Salom writes:

> Looking for a title
> then seeing what the hunger is
> and what all art is:
> feeding the ghost. (22)

The "ghost" in question ultimately derives from Salom's time in Singapore when he witnessed the Buddhist-Daoist Hungry Ghost Festival. Australian poets have been feeding the ghost with extraordinary energy and acumen over the last quarter of a century; it is now time for Australian poetry criticism to catch up.

Notes

1. Etherington finds that Lisa Gorton's *Hotel Hyperion* received nine book reviews in 2013, followed by Jennifer Maiden's *Liquid Nitrogen* (8), Geoff Page's *1953* (7) and Alan Wearne's *Prepare the Cabin for Landing* (6). Less than a handful is the norm, although as Etherington freely admits, this data may be flawed as reviews can often appear in following years.
2. This precedes the publication of Fred D'Aguiar's lyrical third novel *Feeding the Ghosts* (1997).

Works Cited

Arnold, Matthew. "The Function of Criticism at the Present Time." *Selected Essays*, Oxford University Press, 1964.
Adamson, Robert (ed). *The Best Australian Poems 2010*, Black Inc, 2010.
D'Aguiar, Fred. *Feeding the Ghosts*, Chatto & Windus, 1997
Etherington, Ben. "The Poet Tasters" *Sydney Review of Books*, 30 January 2015. www.sydneyreviewofbooks.com/australian-poetry-reviewing.
Hampton, Susan & Kate Llewellyn (eds). *The Penguin Book of Australian*

Women Poets, Penguin Books, 1986.

Harwood, Gwen. *Selected Poems*, Penguin Books, 2001.

Kinsella, John (ed). *The Penguin Anthology of Australian Poetry*, Penguin Books, 2009.

Langford, Martin, et al. *Contemporary Australian Poetry*, Puncher & Wattmann, 2016.

Leonard, John (ed). *Australian Verse: An Oxford Anthology*, Oxford University Press, 1998.

---. *New Music: An anthology of contemporary Australian Poetry*, Five Islands Press, 2001.

---. *The Puncher & Wattmann Anthology of Australian Poetry*, Puncher & Wattmann, 2009.

Murfin, Ross & Supryia M. Ray. T*he Bedford Glossary of Critical and Literary Terms 2nd Edition*, Bedford/St Martins, 2003.

Salom, Philip. *Feeding the Ghost*, Penguin, 1993.

---. Personal Interview, August 18, 2017.

Steele, Peter. *Braiding the Voices: Essays in Poetry*, John Leonard Press, 2012.

Stinson, Emmett. "Small Publishers and the Emerging Network of Australian Literary Prosumption" *Australian Humanities Review*, 59. April-May 2016. www.australianhumanitiesreview.org.

Toffler. Alvin, *The Third Wave: The Classic Study of Tomorrow*, Bantam, 1980.

Tredinnick, Mark (ed). *Australian Love Poems 2013*, Inkerman & Blunt Publishers, 2013.

Wallace-Crabbe, Chris (ed). *The Golden Apples of the Sun: Twentieth Century Australian Poetry*, Melbourne University Press, 1981.

Chapter 2

'Bypassed Years': TimeSpace and stasis in Gorton's 'Press Release' sequences.

CASSANDRA ATHERTON

The compression of time and space, coined "TimeSpace" by Wallerstein[1] (1991) in his modern world-systems analysis, aims to eliminate dualisms and highlight the interdependency or indissolubility of time and space in human geography. Building on Fernand Braudel's (1980) identification of three social times, Wallerstein argues, "time and space are not two separate categories but one, which I shall call TimeSpace" (139). Indeed, moving from Structural TimeSpace to a melding of geographical concepts and metaphors with conceptualisations of time play, Jon May and Nigel Thrift suggest that removing the space or hyphen between these two words is an attempt to eliminate any possible prioritization of one over the other, to focus instead on the ways in which "time and space are inextricably interwoven" (2). Their interdisciplinary edited collection of essays, *TimeSpace Geographies of Temporality* (2001), highlights the relevance of TimeSpace to Geography, Sociology, Gender Studies, International Studies and English Literature (2). This essay is an analysis of the relevance of TimeSpace to poetry, specifically an examination of imaginative geographies in Gorton's poetry. It is a response to the way in which the imaginative realm has been identified as of "considerable importance to our understandings of TimeSpace and hence, in turn, to how we subsequently act in TimeSpace" (May and Thrift 20). This chapter takes as its starting point, May and Thrift's assertion, "the issue of slowness has perhaps failed to gain the attention it deserves" to explore stasis in representations of the futuristic in Lisa Gorton's "Press Release" sequences in her two poetry books, *Press Release* (2007) and *Hotel Hyperion* (2013).

The significance of the poem "Press Release" is evident from its status as the title poem of Lisa Gorton's first book of poetry and the starting point for the poetry sequence "Hotel Hyperion," which is the centerpiece and title of her second book of poetry. The poem, set in 2020, is a dramatic monologue where a mother outlines her final goodbye to her son who has been chosen as the "*first / Hibernation Astronaut for the missile, 'After Life'*". He is in, what appears to be, a cryogenically frozen state, "backed with ice" (*Press Release* 21). The question of the relevance of TimeSpace to Outer space is an important consideration that has been largely overlooked. Historical geographer Nuala C. Johnson opens her essay, "From Time Immemorial" with a discussion of C.S Lewis' *The Lion, the Witch and the Wardrobe*, discussing "other worlds" and the difficulties of "imagining times" (89) other than our own. However, her essay is concerned with national space and its link to the past, rather than imagining the compression of time and space in the future. Despite this, Johnson acknowledges the possibility for TimeSpace studies of the future in her concluding statement:

> If understanding times past can be likened to entering a foreign country, predicting times future is no less an alien universe and perhaps best explored through the literary rather than the social scientific imagination (105).

In "Press Release", Gorton is also "imagining time" that is not her own, but in this poem she is imagining two future TimeSpaces: the year 2020 from which the mother delivers her monologue and the mother's projection of her son's future in his "New Life on Titan." "Press Release" is the second poem in a sequence of three poems titled, "Sci Fi" in Gorton's poetry book, *Press Release*. Indeed, both Gorton's poetry books include futuristic references and appeals to Science Fiction. TimeSpace in the Science Fiction genre has been largely overlooked, despite writers such as Edgar Allen Poe in his essay,

"Eureka: A Prose Poem" (1848) arguing that "Space and duration are one" (118) and mathematician Hermann Minkowski's appeal to experimental physics to posit "space, by itself, and time by itself, are doomed to fade away into mere shadows, and only a kind of union of the two will preserve an independent reality" (qtd in Blankson 217). Time and space are compressed in Science Fiction, not least because the future is a new frontier that has not been traversed or experienced in human geographic terms; it can only be constructed through the imagination. While a similar argument could be made for the past, or history more generally, the important difference is that the past has been inhabited and the future can only be imagined. Therefore, Science Fiction "explores the possible, its territory ranges from the present Earth we know, to the limits of the possible universes that the human imagination can project" (Franklin), which demonstrates its relative boundlessness. Perhaps because of this, Gorton's "Sci Fi" sequence prioritises slowness. This should not be read as any kind of commentary on future TimeSpace lacking dynamism. While speed is often viewed as preferable to slowness, for its emphasis on progress and productivity (Shaw 137), Gorton's "Sci Fi" sequence promotes weightiness, thought and caution as byproducts of slowness. This ponderous and careful exploration of eugenics, patriotism and duty is signaled in the seeping cold and the way it is twinned with the epigraph's emphasis on perfection and beauty. The focus on physical perfection is presented as "cold" in the way it excludes human imperfection as unique and valuable:

> *To honour the Year of Perfected Vision, in 2020*
> *the PDK-4 Corporation signed up its first*
> *Hibernation Astronaut for the missile, 'After Life',*
> *launching its Perpetual World campaign:*
> *'Preserving Our Most Beautiful Offspring for the New Life on Titan …'*

They chose my child. I visit him
daily in the tiled room. His naked skin
looks backed with ice. I see his heart
beat hourly on the screen. He is safe,
I know, for his will be an innocent world,
conquered in peace.
He does not breathe
more than once a heartbeat. My own
small breaths haunt the cold when I speak
into the audiofile they have contracted to play
across his light years on repeat. 'Don't be afraid,'
I say. (*Press Release* 21)

In these opening stanzas, the coldness of the room is established with the image of the son's "naked skin" and the way it "looks backed with ice." Furthermore, the "tiled room" in which he lies is a sterile chamber, devoid of character: a cold space. In this futuristic cryogenic chamber, the mother appears not to touch any of her surroundings nor have physical contact with her son, it only "looks" to her like he might be lying on the ice. By contrast, the mother states she "knows" her son will be "safe" in his colony "light years" away. Her faith is undercut by the oxymoron that his futurist colony has been "conquered in peace." Indeed, the word "conquer" is not easily paired with peace and her reference to an "innocent world" being defeated is also problematic; generally a place loses its innocence when it is colonized. This new colony, Titan, will be built on beauty and perfection as part of a "Perpetual World," thus suggesting that it is these attributes that are worth perpetuating at the expense of qualities like intelligence, uniqueness and a strong character. These clever contradictions indicate that the mother no more "know[s]" her son is safe than she "know[s]" whether he lies on a slab of ice.

In this futuristic scene, her son's heart beats only "hourly on the screen" and he takes a single breathe each hour. The enjambment of "He does not breathe / more than once an hour" emphasizes his lack of respiration. It is a statement that first appears qualified as the reader experiences a delayed understanding that he is breathing at all. His solitary, hourly breath is juxtaposed with his mother's "small breaths" that "haunt the cold" when she records her message to her son on the "audiofile." These specters, formed from her hot breath in the cold chamber, are evidence of her living warmth as she inhabits a kind of future-present. If the rapidity of her heartbeat also mirrors her breath, then her heart is similarly beating fast but possibly shallowly.

Gorton's manipulation of TimeSpace in this poem is a sophisticated response to concepts of future pace and place. Jenny Shaw in her essay, "Winning Territory: Changing place to change pace" argues, "changing pace [is] part of the search for a better quality of life and the growing tendency to equate the good life with the slow life" (120). Gorton slows time in the chamber with the numbing cold. The icy temperature preserves her son as his body experiences hibernation; his vital signs are slow. The TimeSpace in this chamber is constructed to emphasise the weightiness of these years in the future-present (termed for its future for the reader and the present for the mother). The cold, scientific space evokes seriousness and underlines the importance of the son's mission and his mother's ultimate sacrifice.

The mother imagines her son's future and projects herself into that TimeSpace with the recording of her voice. In this way, Gorton is imagining what the future may hold for the human race and, more specifically, for women. This illustrates Shaw's sentiment,

> The process of projection enables places to serve a range of symbolic and imaginative functions – evoking or containing feelings, triggering memories or promising fresh starts, offering solace of inducing recuperation (144).

The future-present and distant future in "Press Release" are places of unrest, while the compression of TimeSpace highlights the polyvalence of stillness. In "Press Release" the mother is inert in a very different way from her son. While his stasis is passive, hers is an inferred immobility from which she speaks her rousing words into the "audiofile." The mother demonstrates the way in which "Stillness punctuates the flow of all things" (Bissell and Fuller 3). In this poem, Gorton explores the power of stasis over movement for its ability to preserve and encourage reflection. Indeed, the mother's stirring words become a meditation on defeat, as she must ultimately relinquish her son. The juxtaposition of his vital signs with his mother's demonstrates two very different kinds of living. When she looks at her son, she is trying to project herself into his future TimeSpace, which she cannot bodily inhabit. In this way she is attempting to "accommodate a different tempo," his tempo, which Shaw argues "challenges what is expected and can produce intense feelings of dislocation in those forced to march at an unfamiliar pace" (137). Instead, she can only breathe with the rhythm of her words, which further alienates her from her son's hourly heartbeat and breath.

Much like the room, her words of love are set against a more formal and distant frame of duty and patriotism:

> Like a handshake, palm to palm,
>   A gentleman's agreement,
> Your heartbeat tenders you – Are you cold?
> Listen, out of these bypassed years,
> silence in your mouth, you will amass such –
> Only to think of you, falling from your name for the sky
> in this astonishing vessel!
>   Press release, my darling,
> and do not sorrow. Do not once sorrow.
> If you will think of me, think only of these years
> I held your unfailing present in my empty hands. (*Press Release* 21)

The language is stark and pared back in this poem; the mother is sparing in her descriptions and in her final message to her son. To her, every word is considered as her message is recorded and will play "across his light years on repeat" (21). Her words must be weighty in order to sustain her son's future TimeSpace.

In "Press Release," future TimeSpaces are poised between two different concepts of speed, grounded in the imagined quality of life in the future. On the one hand, the desire for a slower pace is reflected in the yearning for leisure time and rest. Her son is in artificial hibernation, an enforced rest, which is preparing him for his future mission. On the other hand, future TimeSpaces are often presented as faster than their present counterparts because technology's speed increases productivity, allowing a faster experience of life. If, "the pace of life …var[ies] geographically" (Shaw 122) then it also varies in the past, present and future TimeSpaces. The mother in "Press Release" mentions the present, her son's future and the "bypassed years" in between these two points, which are "light years" away. Her voice plays across all of these TimeSpaces but effectively she only experiences his "unfailing present", imagining his symbolic fall as she urges him to "press release". Her "empty hands" are juxtaposed with the "palm to palm … handshake", demonstrating her enduring loss as she sacrifices her son to the future TimeSpace. The mother's message to her son, played repetitively is meant to be calming, as repetition can induce a "calm state" (Shaw 141). However, the question "Are you cold?" coupled with the silence and the repetition of the word "sorrow" and "years", intensifies the experience of emptiness and isolation. The son cannot respond to his mother from his hibernation. His stillness connotes a kind of peace – a counterfeit deep sleep. While the son's stasis is unnerving for his mother, she understands that he is safe in this chamber.

The poem, "Evolution 3000" follows "Press Release" and is the concluding poem in this "Sci Fi" triad. The two stanzas in this poem, with their hanging indents, mirror the poetic structure of "Press Release" and suggest an unwillingness to let go of the past. The hanging indents create a pause in the poem, exacerbated by the em dashes, which in "Press Release" represent a break in thought and in "Evolution 3000" link the past, present and future TimeSpaces. Indeed, Gorton's appeal to history evokes environmental scholar Theodore R. Schatzki's argument for "the existence of the past in the present," or "historicity as the prolongation of the past into the present" (202). In this way, the past in Gorton's poems "press ... the future" (Schatzki 202).

In "Evolution, 3000," the opening line negates the interpretation of history as something that falls away or becomes irrelevant. Instead, "In case you see history as sheer loss" (*Press Release* 23) is a line demonstrating the way in which the past, present and future TimeSpaces are irrevocably connected. Rather than viewing the past as negatively impinging on present and future TimeSpaces, or as presenting unwelcome surprises from its receding position, Gorton suggests that discoveries from the past are always relevant and illuminating. In two important ways, she extends Schatzki's argument that "the gap between past and present is an illusion. The past is in the present. It has not fallen away behind the present, consigned to inertness, irrelevance or inexistence" (202). First, she demonstrates in her appeals to Science Fiction that the past is equally important to future TimeSpaces. Second, in Gorton's poems, "inertness" is not a pejorative word, instead, it offers the opportunity for reflection. Even the reference to the "speeding ticket" in the first stanza of "Evolution 3000" demonstrates that it's a crime to speed. Coupled with the point that it takes "two weeks" for the fine to reach its recipient in the "mail", the poem prioritises slowness. In "Evolution 3000", New Titan – the planet to which the narrator's son is being sent to colonize in "Press Release"– is explored in an imagined future TimeSpace. The narrator imagines the "alum in a human skeleton" from her present, might be identified as the "Missing Link" fossil of the Cenozoic Age on New Titan:

> In case you see history as sheer loss –
> a speeding ticket two weeks later in the mail –
> the future's visiting bearded archeologist finds

alum in the fossil jaw of your Cenozoic skeleton.
'The Missing Link?' makes headlines
on New Titan. (*Press Release* 23)

Indeed, the missing link between the past, present and future TimeSpaces is presented as the understanding of their overlap and interdependency. This is underlined in the concluding stanza where the narrator reminisces about an earlier time and, in doing so, illustrates the Schatzkian historicity – defined as "the presence of the past (in current activity), according to which past phenomena circumscribe, induce-orient, and underwrite the public manifestation of – but do not cause or antecedently pin down – present activity" (x). In this way, the past has presence in the present and future TimeSpaces:

But do you remember
How we swatted flies in the balding shade
a morning's walk from the launch?
Their ships made a mirage fall,
our ozone crashed about our ears and we stood
mesmerised in all that falling light. (*Press Release* 23)

The "mirage" and "mesmeris[ation]" at the heart of this poem are pitted against the repetition of "fall" , "falling" and "crashing", suggesting both an enchantment and a hard hitting awakening. The poem ends on an exhilarating note by intermeshing these oppositions to demonstrate how one polarisation is infused with and invested in its other.

Gorton returns to these concerns in the "Hotel Hyperion" sequence of her 2013 book of poetry of the same name. "Press Release" is reprinted in this collection "because it forms the starting point for the 'Hotel Hyperion' sequence" (*Hotel Hyperion* 48). Indeed, it is divided into two sections: the first is a five-part suite beginning with "Press Release" and it is followed by the second section, which comprises two poems entitled "The Futures Museum." The relevance of Hyperion to this sequence is paramount. The title of the book and the name of the hotel at the centre of it, references the titan of light, "Hyperion" or "High One," which can loosely be translated as "one who watches from above." This is reminiscent of the falling light that concludes "Evolution 3000" and references "Titan," Hyperion's race, as well as the planet being "conquered in peace" in "Press Release." In "Hotel Hyperion," Gorton undercuts the omniscient Hyperion figure to suggest the past infiltrates present and future TimeSpaces; there is not one, monolithic perspective. This is reinforced in the epigraph to "Settlement, Titan," which quotes from John Keats' "The Fall of Hyperion": "Fanatics have their dreams, wherewith they weave a Paradise for a sect ..." (*Hotel Hyperion* 22). The reference to Keats' fragment poem, "The Fall of Hyperion," further undermines Hyperion's omniscience while simultaneously introducing the Keatsian metaphor of human life as a "Mansion of Many Apartments." This metaphor references John Donne's[2] "Prayer":

> O Eternal and most gracious God, who is in thy upper house, the heavens, though there be many mansions, yet art alike and equally in every mansion, but here in thy lower house, though thou fillest all, yet art otherwise in some rooms thereof, than in others, otherwise in thy church, than in my chamber, and otherwise in thy sacraments, than in my prayers; so though thou be always present, and always working in every room of this thy house... (qtd in Alford 549)

This, in turn, references the Bible, specifically, John 14:2-3, "In my Father's house are many mansions: if it were not so, I would have told you, I go to prepare a place for you." It is a metaphor Gorton adapts when she describes the Titan Settlement as, "rooms within a room" (*Hotel Hyperion* 22) and she similarly suggests that not all rooms are accessible.

The "Hotel Hyperion" sequence is ostensibly about a futuristic hotel where a Fowlesian collector amasses artifacts from the history of failed space settlement. Johnson in her discussion of national space has argued, "to think about time for many of us is paradoxically to think both in our own time and yet to attempt to step outside of it" (89). In this sequence, Gorton introduces museums and repositories to the exploration of TimeSpace compression. Indeed, while Johnson identifies "Historians, museum curators, filmmakers, biographers" as those who "are acutely aware of the dilemmas attendant on narrating and imagining times other than the one in which they are located" (89), poets and writers can easily be added to this list. Gorton writes the "Hotel Hyperion" sequence aware of the multiple TimeSpaces she is traversing. TimeSpaces press on one another as her futuristic narrator is employed to collect relics from "failed outposts of [space] settlement." Poignantly, one of these settlements is Titan, the planet referenced in "Press Release," which lends pathos to the re-reading of this poem in "Hotel Hyperion." While the mother's hopefulness is asserted in "Press Release" (2007), it is undercut in the "Hotel Hyperion" sequence when the failure of the settlement on New Titan is noted in the "wreck, its landing chute/ice-caught" (*Hotel Hyperion* 23). In this way, the narrator in "Press Release" and the narrator in "The History of Space Travel" demonstrate the way in which "pasts continue to act in the present" (May and Thrift 39). Gorton extends this idea by exploring the way they resonate in future TimeSpaces, including "lost future" TimeSpaces (*Hotel Hyperion* 28). Indeed, the "history" referred to in "The History of Space Travel" is a future TimeSpace for the reader and yet is already the past for the narrator, demonstrating a sophisticated play and assertion of a "space-time prism" (May and Thrift 161).

In the opening lines of this poem, the narrator introduces her eleven years of 'collecting' when she "kept a room… in the Hotel Hyperion" (*Hotel Hyperion* 20). Johnson states, "For nationalist movements times past may … underscore the fluid ways in which interpretations of time's passage become the idiom and the accent of a nation's trajectory" (89). It is unclear if she is collecting the relics in a nationalistic documentation of the history of space travel or if it is a reminder of the inability to control, colonize, conquer or settle TimeSpace. Either way, the narrator's eleven years are punctuated by "anaesthetic sleep" and a long, drawn out mourning for the "forsaken places" and "abandoned voices" (*Hotel Hyperion* 20). The inert dream-like state of the narrator encourages the blending and blurring of TimeSpaces in the "Hotel Hyperion" sequence:

> In truth, the history of space travel
> Is a history of rooms
>   — I kept a room
> those eleven years in the Hotel Hyperion.
> It had been a prison, the first in orbit,
> and its guest rooms kept the old locks.
> The Futures Museum was paying me for the artefacts
> From the failed outposts of settlement. (*Hotel Hyperion* 20)

The referencing of prison and the "old locks" on the doors explores "carceral TimeSpace," which Dominique Moran argues, encourages reflection on "past and future" (Moran 55). Indeed, it is through the "now" that "both past and future and the passage of time are viewed" (55) in carceral TimeSpace. Gorton's narrator similarly reflects on the past and future TimeSpaces from her carceral 'now.' While she is not physically locked in the room, the fact that the "guest rooms kept old locks" is reminiscent of its original use as a contained Timespace (20).

Kevin Hetherington argues,

> Prisons, asylums, hospitals, schools, libraries, museums, housing estates and so on — all sites of some kind of social engineering — all are testament to this modern utopic expression of social ordering through new forms of spatial arrangement. (64)

Indeed, if doors liberate spaces, a locked door is confining. Andrew Metcalfe and Lucinda Ferguson argue in "Half-Opened

Being," "Space without doors evokes a terrifying condition of endlessness and pointlessness, but doors make space habitable" (240). While a locked door may similarly stop the physical flow of space, it is not always "terrifying" and as Moran suggests, can stimulate deep reflection across TimeSpaces. The narrator, in her solitary confinement in "Hotel Hyperion," grapples with important questions about human civilisation across TimeSpaces. This is also relevant to museums and the collection of artifacts, which introduce inertness and reflectiveness to the poetical narrative of colonisation. The relics are static objects and will be stored in The Futures Museum and presumably viewed by patrons. As Justine Williams, Jason Schuler, Patricia Faolli and Vanessa Gilbert have argued, "Artifacts in the Museum are immobile, untouchable, and often separated from the visitor by glass, giving a sense of stasis. This can make Museums' objects' stories feel fixed, at least historically, to visitors." To overcome the motionlessness of the fossils, Williams et. al. discuss a kind of "alchemy" between the viewer and object. In this way, multiple TimeSpaces can be interwoven through imagination. It is a point referenced by Gorton in her first poem on The Futures Museum where "Life-cast figures" are motionless, but brought to life through the reader's (and narrator's) imagination:

> In this display the artist
> has wrapped life-cast figures in a hand-
> made net of fishing wire – Figures
> painted with a one-hair brush and true
> even to the number of their eyelashes, the blind
> sheen of their nails – so much like life
> they bring home the strangeness of things
> being motionless. (*Hotel Hyperion* 25)

Furthermore, while the title "Futures Museum" houses future and past TimeSpaces, it also points to Gorton's play with TimeSpace consciousness where "Rooms [are] so familiar/they complete themselves in me" (*Hotel Hyperion* 26) and images "detail by detail… install themselves in me" (*Hotel Hyperion* 21). "The Futures Museum" poems, which conclude the "Hotel Hyperion" sequence, take up the Keatsian metaphor of entry to rooms as representative of entry to a higher consciousness. In a letter to J.H. Reynolds in 1818, Keats stated, "I compare human life to a large Mansion of Many Apartments, two of which I can only describe, the doors of the rest being as yet shut upon me" (Keats). Like Keats' mansion, the hotel, in the "Hotel Hyperion" sequence has many doors, chambers and "corridors turned into themselves" (*Hotel Hyperion* 21). While Gorton ultimately comes to the same conclusion as Keats – that many doors are closed, out of reach or invisible – she extends this to comment on the accessibility and multiplicity of TimeSpaces. In this way, Gorton suggests the understanding of the interaction of TimeSpaces will continue to evolve. Indeed, Williams et. al. suggest this evolution of TimeSpace might eventually lead to an understanding of "a hybrid metaverse" and beyond.

These rooms can also be likened to a camera obscura as the first examples were small, darkened rooms with a tiny hole in the wall to let in light. This is significant because the epigraph to the poetry book *Hotel Hyperion* is a quote from *Vita Anomina*, written in the mid-fifteenth century and points to Gorton's awareness of shifting perspective, both parallel and linear, and its application to TimeSpaces:

> By looking into a box through a little hole one might see great plains and an immense expanse of sea spread out till the eye lost itself in the distance. Learned and unlearned agreed that these images were not like natural things but like nature itself. (*Hotel Hyperion*)

Samuel Y. Edgerton in his book, *The Mirror, the Window, and the Telescope: How Renaissance Linear Perspective Changed Our Vision of the Universe* (2009), states of the *Vita Anonima* quotation, "Do we have here an early imitation of the optical telescope, actually a "perspective tube" just like Alberti's camera ottica. The "window" effect of which is simply extended and expanded by magnifying lenses?" (132). The identification of the camera ottica in this quotation, coupled with the accepted view of it as roughly "synonymous with the camera obscura" (qtd in Tavernor 22) and "a forerunner to the camera" (Fossi 174), underlines their common ability to use light, passing through an aperture, to compress and capture a range of TimeSpaces, including the viewer's own Timespace. In addition to this, Lev Manovich, a professor of computer design points out, "in one of the earliest depictions of the camera obscura, in Kircher's *Ars magna Lucis et umbrae* (Rome, 1649), we see the subject enjoying the image inside a tiny room, oblivious to the fact that he had to imprison himself in this 'dark chamber' in order to see the image on the screen" (Manovich 107). This imprisonment and ultimate immobility of the viewer connects with the "old locks" on the doors in the Hotel and similarly encourages reflection across TimeSpaces. This is significant, given that Gorton appeals to the camera ottica, camera obscura and cameras in the "Hotel Hyperion" sequence. The first is mentioned in "Settlement, Titan":

> It is so orderly and strange. A sort of camera obscura
>   that would teach how to make
> the illusion of depth on paper, which is to say
>   they lived their whole lives here – (*Hotel Hyperion* 22)

In this poem, Gorton emphasizes the power of the "illusion of depth", which the camera obscura-like device "teach[es]" the viewer. This same "illusion" and reference to the camera's ability to distort perspective is also explored in "Screen Memory." In this poem, the "trick of memory," "cameras that made each thing/speak itself in light" and the failed "vanishing point" refer to forced perspective and the way in which the camera "expands our perception of time beyond our position in it" (Caporlingua, iv):

> – technicolour galaxies
> fitted to the room, cameras that made each thing
> speak itself in light. They had no vanishing point.
> Only detail by detail they installed themselves in me,
> (*Hotel Hyperion* 21)

It is a process also referenced in "The Futures Museum: Night Guard":

> Even the simplest fact is
> at each instant folding itself in light, is
> opening out into false perspectives the way
> in each glass pane the doubling reflection
> of a thing stands farther off and smaller,
> farther off and so far gone into a trick of longing. (26)

The "false perspective" refers, again, to the optical illusion presented to the viewer through the pinhole in the camera obscura, or the viewfinder in the modern camera. Like an Ames room, things in the TimeSpace appear to be different sizes. Referring to this manipulation of human visual perception, this poem explores the way objects appear further away to the narrator. Once again the viewer's fixed and prime position is undercut by these "tricks" which undermine his/her comprehension. "Screen Memory" extends this metaphor to focus on "cameras on delay" (*Hotel Hyperion* 21). This slowness references the camera's ultimate ability to freeze TimeSpaces. As Hockney theorizes about the camera, since its inception in 1839, "The ability of the camera-apparatus to produce a frozen moment, as it appeared before the lens" (qtd in Chappell 10). It connects with the ice and cold of the Titan settlement and the boy in hibernation, "His naked skin... backed with ice" in "Press Release" (*Hotel Hyperion* 19). This "delay" is another form of slowness, one that is captured by the eye. Indeed, linear perspective "presents the world as seen by a singular eye, static, unblinking and fixated" (Manovich 106). This points to the way in which in "Alberti's window, Dürer's perspectival machines, camera obscura photography, cinema – in all of these screen-based apparatuses, the subject had to remain immobile" (Manovich 109). In this way, Gorton suggests that slowness and immobility encourage important rumination that is otherwise lost in more harried approaches and understandings of the future TimeSpaces. Most importantly, in "Discovery", the grave importance of stasis is explored in the final image:

> That instant I see them
> in my mind as they will be found, unwaking,
> stored in the machinery of patience,
> in their Perspex coffers
> blindly face to face and nothing decayed –
> Only, on their ice-backed skin
> this filigree of ice
> the machine is breathing them, resembling
> the mechanism of a clock copied in snow. (*Hotel Hyperion* 24)

This poem acts as a sad postscript to "Press Release." The collector of relics finds the ultimate artifact of failed space settlement: the astronauts "in their Perspex coffers". They lie frozen across TimeSpaces and the narrator imagines their "ice-backed skin" and the image of a caliber duplicated in the snow. Indeed, metaphorically "the mechanism of a clock copied in snow" indicates that just as the astronauts' decomposition has been arrested, so, too, has the narrator's immediate Timespace, from which she makes her grisly discovery for the Futures Museum. Most importantly, the numbing stasis in this futuristic TimeSpace is not presented as inferior or lacking. Instead, Gorton demonstrates that thought – and in this sequence, grief – are most effective from a slow and considered futuristic TimeSpace.

Gorton's "Sci Fi" and "Hotel Hyperion" sequences in her poetry collections, support Thrift's argument that "There is little sense to be had from making distinctions between space and time – there is only space-time" (93). Her appeal to cameras and rooms in a Science Fiction frame, foreground a series of TimeSpace projections in which she provides commentary on the integrity of coldness, slowness and stillness. Gorton breaks new ground in TimeSpace scholarship for her focus on stasis and reflection as progressive in futuristic Timespaces.

Notes

1. Bahktin's theory of the chronotype, translated as 'time-space', predates Wallerstein's TimeSpace but it is built on very different assumptions. Bahktin uses it to develop organizational processes and to demonstrate the differences between literary genres or categories. Wallerstein's theory is more applicable in an analysis of Gorton's poetry as it focuses, instead, on social spaces and moral choice, two tropes identified in Press Release. Furthermore, Wallerstein's theory focuses on moving away from equilibria, which are temporary.
2. Significantly, Lisa Gorton completed her doctorate on the poetry of John Donne at Oxford, when she was a Rhodes Scholar. She was awarded the John Donne Society Award for Distinguished Publication in Donne studies.

Works Cited

Alford, Henry. *The Works of John Donne, D.D., With a Memoir of His Life*, Vol 3, London, John W. Parker, 1839.

Bissell, David and Gillian Fuller. "Stillness Unbound" *Stillness in a Mobile World*, edited by David Bissell and Gillian Fuller, Routledge, 2011.

Blankson, Samuel K. K. *Time in Science and Life the Greatest Legacy of Albert Einstein: Challenging Minkowski's Theory of Space-Time*, Practical Books, 2009.

Caporlingua, Christopher Michael. *The Place of the Viewer's Expansion in Optical Systems: The Use of Time in Media and its Spatial Applications*, MA Thesis, University at Buffalo, State University of New York, 2012.

Chappell, Danica. *A Constructed Composition from a Darkroom Haptic,* MA Thesis, Victorian College of the Arts, The University of Melbourne, 2012.

Edgerton, Samuel Y. *The Mirror, the Window, and the Telescope: Renaissance Linear Perspective Changed Our Vision of the Universe,* Cornell University Press, 2009.

Fossi, Gloria. *The Uffizi: The Official Guide,* Ministero per i Beni e le Attivita Culturali, 1999.

Gorton, Lisa. *Press Release,* Giramondo, 2007.

---. *Hotel Hyperion,* Giramondo, 2013.

Franklin, H. Bruce. "What is Science Fiction – and How It Grew." Gunn, James, Marleen S. Barr and Matthew Candelaria, *Reading Science Fiction,* Palgrave MacMillan, 2009.

Hetherington, Kevin. "Moderns as Ancients: Time, Space and the Discourse of Improvement." *Timespace: Geographies of Temporality,* edited by John May and Nigel Thrift, Routledge, 2001.

Johnson, Nuala C. "From Time Immemorial: Narratives of Nationhood and the Making of National Space." *Timespace: Geographies of Temporality,* edited by John May and Nigel Thrift, editors. London and NY, Routledge, 2001.

Keats, John. "On Axioms and the Surprise of Poetry: Letter to John Taylor, 27 February, 1818." *Selections from Keats's Letters,* Poetry Foundation. https://www.poetryfoundation.org/articles/69384/selections-from-keatss-letters

Key Concepts in Geography 2nd edited by Nicholas J. Clifford, Sarah L. Holloway, Stephen P. Rice and Gill Valentine, Sage, 2009.

Manovic, Lev. *The Language of New Media,* MIT Press, 2001.

Moran, Dominique. *Carceral Geography: Spaces and Practices of Incarceration,* Ashgate, 2015.

Poe, Edgar Allan. *Eureka: A Prose Poem,* Project Gutenberg, 2010 (1848). http://www.gutenberg.org/ebooks/32037

Schatzki, Theodore R. *The Timespace of Human Activity: On Performance, Society, and History as Indeterminate Teleological Events,* Lexington Books, 2010.

Shaw, Jenny. "'Winning Territory': Changing Place to Changing Pace." *Timespace: Geographies of Temporality*, edited by John May and Nigel Thrift, Routledge, 2001.

Tavernor, Robert. *On Alberti and the Art of Building*, Yale University Press, 1998.

Thrift, Nigel. "For a new Regional Geography 2". *Progress in Human Geography*, vol.17, no.1, 1993, pp. 92 -100.

Timespace: Geographies of Temporality, edited by John May and Nigel Thrift, Routledge, 2001.

Wallerstein, I. *Unthinking Social Science: The Limits of Nineteenth-Century Paradigms*, Polity Press, 1991.

Williams, Justine, Jason Schuler, Patricia Faolli, Vanessa Gilbert. "Metaverses – Merging Time, Space, and Content through Augmented Reality." *Digital Underground*, Metropolitan Museum of Art.

Chapter 3

Mez Breeze Between the Centuries

A.J. Carruthers

I.

For well over two decades now, since the middle 1990s, Mez Breeze (born Mary-Anne Breeze), has remained at the forefront of digital and electronic poetics over a period of time in which its basic functions morphed or were variously updated. A full 'cyberbibliography' of her career, from older work with 'net.art' narratives, through what she has thought of as the "Golden Phase of Mezangelle," to her work on games like *#PRISOM* (2013), will turn up a vast and evolving ouevre with recurrent strands. Her most well-known invention is the generative language of "Mezangelle," which uses code, MUD (Multi-User-Domain), online chatlogs, avatars, JavaScript and HTML (Hypertext Markup Language) as procedural, linguistic and textural means, and ends, for poetics. The result is an absorptive and playful reworking of these into poems and, as I will pay special attention to here, sequences of poems. Breeze's writingways share *topoi* that interweave the digital and ethics, language and ecology, the abstraction of contemporary life and what she described to me in an email as "A sense of sP[l]ace collapsing + concertinaed comprehension-nesting, of contractions and expansions." Such writing is situated in spatial locales both matrixial and fractal; "shaped by my own personal intrigue with language and the land, of openings within openings, of lingual whorls and patterns that blossom + contract."

Two of the major book publications Breeze has produced this century, *Human Readable Messages* (2011) and *Attn: Solitude* (2016) support an expansive poetics that is at once radically outside convention and familiar to literary criticism. This is poetry that works with the defamiliarisation of language and a poetics of contraction and expansion that transforms the verbal textures of the digital, in sound and in sense. A foremost thinker of the post-digital C.T. Funkhouser, in *New Directions in Digital Poetry* from 2012, has noted the significance of Breeze's invention in that while she is not the first poet "to invent her own form of language"

> she is certainly among the first, along with [Alan] Sondheim and [John] Cayley, to adopt verbal constructions emerging from the digital era into literature [...] One way of looking at the work is to see it as an expression of how alteration, confusion and types of ruin play a heightened role in our lives, conditions easy to reflect in texts utilizing digital media's heightened verbal and visual extensions that, apart from other qualities, invite excessive use of representative symbols [...] Mez works this possibility — with her application of language, and by using images as prefix and suffix — to extreme ends; by doing so she metaphorically hits two, three, or more notes with a single gathering of letters in ways previous generations of writers could not. (164)

Funkhouser is not saying that what gets applied to language at the level of the text itself — in Breeze's case a verbal and visual excess of representative symbols, the compaction of image to prefix and suffix — then means that New Media and digital media with their ensuing aftermath of alteration, ruin and confusion becomes some kind of antithesis to the poetry. It is, rather, that these "extreme" things in the graphic and phonic field of the poem, something her peers were unable to do, occasions a poetics quite representative of life under contemporary conditions. Bring the laws of life into the gathering of letters we call literature, in other words, and the result can indeed be excessive, even estranging.

It is difficult to make an assessment of Breeze's poetry, which is certainly significant both inside and outside an Australian context, which situates it *without* recourse to judgement, but that I will try to do. This will only serve poorly as an exhaustive introduction to Breeze's work or a total review of its worth. I will therefore spend more time opening the writing up to critical readings, pursuing resonances in the writing, before briefly situating her work in Australian poetry at large. I can read her poetry as taking digital utility into fields of heightened verbico-visual expression, something Breeze, in her preface to her book of Mezangelle, *Attn: Solitude,* calls that microtextual work "at the cusp of code and poiesis" (ix). Breeze's work, especially her codework, which Rita Raley calls "the use of the contemporary idiolect of the computer and computing processes in digital media experimental writing" ("Interferences"), we can read closely in the context of Australian poetry and theories of literary history. There are ways to read Breeze that are fruitful to our understanding of the poetics of form, and of contemporary style in the broadest of senses.

II. Postdigital Historicity: Theories, Continuities

The first extended study based on the term "postdigital," by Robert Pepperell and Michael Punt, *The Postdigital Membrane* (2000), imagined the aftermath of the digital revolution as, precisely, a kind of membrane. Their aim was to show that the digitisation of information had been conceptualised too much along reductionist lines; they insisted that the "continuum" between art, computing, philosophy and science" had been reduced to discrete binary units which could not describe the "stable yet dynamic" reality of the postdigital age (2). The power of the membrane metaphor — a metaphor with clear posthuman resonances — they then argued, was its "dual and contradictory function" as a transparent wall and "lubricating sheath" that both connects and divides the form of these complex phenomena. The "digital revolution" in some ways was no revolution at all; in this respect, theorists, they enjoined, needed to take into account continuities as much as cuts in the operation of digital technology and the conceptual/intellectual models used to process it.

In his introduction to Mez Breeze's 2017 book of Mezangelle, *Attn: Solitude*, Florian Cramer, theorist of the post-digital and digital poetics, begins with a blunt qualification: "Don't mistake this for an experimental poetry book. This is a five-year archival snapshot of text-streaming transmissions; a recording that documents continuity" (xi). In what sense would mistaking it for an experimental poetry book detract? Nay, in what sense add? What pits experiment against continuity? Cramer goes on to sketch out some historical and technological contexts adding that:

> In the 1990s and early 2000s, Mez Breeze's *mezangelle* language needed explication. People who were unfamiliar with internet and New Media culture did not get the references. Those who were already immersed in this culture often considered it a separate realm, a cyberspace, and thus had difficulties with the blending of the digital and the physical, technology and embodiment, code and subjectivity in Mez's writings. Their stripped-down medium of plain text didn't speak to them either. (*Attn: Solitude*, xi)

The nearsighted view of this might be to point out the importance of "sticking to one's vision," sustaining a certain practice and seeing it through, and so forth, but the message here is really one of historicity. The actuality Breeze brings forth is both historical, and historically reflective against, the textures of contemporary readership; the history is one of histories of reading and the limit-cases of readability. In fine, cyberspace was at once the nub of the New Media milieu and its historical contemporaneity, and a present oddity: that the digital would be something embodied, physical and in this sense subjective, did not yet fully make sense. Mezangelle, that is, was at once extremely contemporaneous and too much on the nose for its contemporaries. Funkhouser would find a theoretical way through these historical contradictions by positing the digital and the electronic literacies that came before it as comprising a "prehistoric" poetics, one whose beginnings can be found in the historical avant-gardes and those second or third wave iterations of them in OuLiPo and the likes of Jackson Mac Low who worked with computer programs in several of his works (*Prehistoric Digital Poetry*, 43-82). We might add, then, that for there to be a postdigital age we need also to imagine a predigital age.

The reality, though, is that Breeze's work is not just on the page, even if that is where some of it has ended up, and another continuity in Breeze's poetics is its politics. Kent Aardse takes Breeze's place in electronic literature as one which raises questions of biopower and its resistance (in biopolitics) as key to her code and codework. The matter of the body, subjectivity and the relation of these to power Aardse reads into works _*the data*_[*b!*]*[bleeding texts*_ (2000). Aardse provides a passage that requires his own input; the popup box asks the reader or author-reader enter their childhood nickname, in Aardse's case, Kenton, into the dialogue box. The result:

> /me waits, wanting the n.des to catch on/up,
> comprehending nothing, regurgitating everything][please][
> /me had thoughts uncoded by the sanctity of the network. The sanctity was profound, the data-traffic lost. The rhythm broken. How to convince the nodes of their existence/resistance?
> [Clue insert:You, Kenton , dear c.-auth.r and reader, are the nodepoint. The point in the fluid. The point that flows between, behind, before….comprehension critical/crucial.]

Aardse's reading of the passage, one that in effect both Breeze and himself generated, is not only that nodes are activated subjects, "both network and people" but that Breeze's question: "How to convince the nodes of their existence/resistance?" means 'we' will be both interpolated, knotted into the system and encouraged to think of resistances against the network. Key here, one may add, is the very fluidity of the subject, if pitched against the sanctity of the network, which leads from the 'me' of the text to the insert of the 'You' (author-reader), an in between which, crucially, is marked by a break in rhythm. Node is *nodus*. Coming from the Latin, the reader acts with or against difficulty; the node is also, via late Middle English, a 'knotty swelling.' We can read a literary node, by extension, as nominative; not only a knotting the subject into the network, but one that knots the literary into itself (and if this analogy can be pushed a step further, we may imagine the very point of contact between author and reader as some bumps enrhythming a swelling of 'literary' knots).

The resistance, Aardse claims, is "active" because it is a resistance pitched against the digital-capitalist enterprise. Precisely through the reinvention of language through "physical and digital bodies" such an engagement brings the inventive language of the resistant body (biopolitics) against biopower. In the final, and sixth, part of _the data] [h!][bleeding texts_ a fixed text appears in which the node or nodepoint, is codeword for authorreader:

> [thizz is the tumble of graffiti, the smear of thort.flit and markologiez
> bound, the colour of the hip N the rhythm ov the hop.....a unit reversed N
> atom broke, rejoined @ the lip ov sense N the t[aste]ongue ov sound without the music tag N lab[ia]elle]
>
> [my wurds r the misheard, songz played N lyrics chewed in2 the wrong,
> non-lit[t]er[s ov young 1s]al...cut up wurds from pulp mags N muze, paste
> em in2 a youthful clutch of terms N breaks...grab ah crayon N scrawl,
> breaking the nub N pointte N gettin it all]
> ("_][jus][texts_: email performance remnants_")

What we might take from this is that the notion of being led by error, where what gets misheard shows something different in the graffiti "smear of thort." What trips up, or gets citationally pulped, forms blockages from node to "nub," to the author in a kind of resistant "markology" in which the lettristic is subjective in its base of the vocal apparatus (sound and sense), with "N" as ampersand and conjunctive, the coordinating nub of node. The nodal in this case does not seem the kind of smooth equipment that can link the reader up to a known network. In other words, the poem is both a redistributive node for linking up with other networks of meanings and a terminus, an endpoint in distributive, lettristically charged meaning. Another way to say it is that Breeze's poetry, even though it might not always look like it, is quite like any other poetry in some very fundamental ways; it is a poetics marked up in rhythm and through sound, and sense, the semantic clutch and tumble of thought.

The same work has caught the attention of N. Catherine Hayles, who offers a close reading of the following two lines from _the data] [h!] [bleeding texts_ : ".a mezzian flesh-mote enters. .the libr][bin][ary is cold. a s[]l][i][ver glint pulls the / mote 4wards. .4warding][ing of the datadervish][in2 the][comp][lab lair." For Hayles it at first appears that the "prose of the plaintext has been converted into poetic lines, a transformation that brings into play the traditional poetic tension between the ending of one line and the beginning of another" ("Deeper into the Machine"). The enjoining and forbidding of this running and slacking back of lines leads less to agglutination, the compaction or clumping together of particles, as infixation, even Tmesis (insertion of whole morphemes or whole words inside words). Some questions follow us at this juncture: How does the Tmetic function rhetoricise her poetics? Given the textual particulars — periods and brackets, which indicate more string than line — Hayles links lineation and segmentivity through Perl, the programming language released in 1987:

> In the programming language Perl the dot is a concatenation operator used to add strings together, so the lines now exist both as discrete units and additive lines, with the dot signaling division when read as a period ending a sentence, and addition when read as a concatenation operator preceding the string. The second line, typical in its use of interjected square brackets, shows how

mezangelling works. "Library" can be recovered as a word, but only after encountering "][bin][ary," the binary code still largely missing from this "cold" library. "Binary" is in a sense now hidden or found to be concealed within "library," a form of reading that anticipates the coming transformation of this institution as it creeps into the information age, a process already begun in its primitive word-processing laboratory.

The library, at least in the way we automatically tend to theorise it after Borges or, indeed, the internet, is not a laboratory because it contains several binaries; it has claims to the infinite and an immense finitude, things taken in and taken out, disorder and order. A laboratory produces something where a library does not; it produces nothing except, perhaps, a binary, what it catalogues and what it does not catalogue. So much is going on in these lines in ways that pertain to *readings*. The relevant literary result is the work and play of punning chorality in the binary that has crept into the library of the 'information age,' something Hayles is then willing to read further into the brackets][which also appear in the title of the work in a reading that might feel a little less familiar:

> Despite its violation of normal syntax, "][" has a polysemy that draws MEZ to it, for it resembles "I," the nomination of selfhood, and also "H," which by back-formation can often be read as "I" in her texts. Although the brackets can be broken apart, "][" often functions as a symbol in its own right. That the "bin" of binary should be surrounded by this symbol suggests the implication of the subject "I" in the discovery of the binary within the library, an association that the plaintext makes clear in other words.

Here is a way of reading Breeze's work which may remind us of the importance of the lettristic in the subjective aspects of her work; and it may remind us of its ability to be read both as compacted, faceted in the "Mezzian" subject, and subjectively or psychosocially dispersed within or contaminated by the sociotextual library, the world. Not universe, but world. The world, that is, not only meaning reality but in the subjective work of language, word-worlds, vocabularies (given or constructed), syntax and code. These readings also allow us to maintain some distinction between code and language which, while interacting, transform each other at a distance; which is to say the critic can then pay close attention, as Hayles does, to the *work* of code in those microtextual elements of language, and to treat it as poetics, that is, as the work of words. Code leads us closer, that is, to a Mezzian *corpus*.

III. Breeze Between The Centuries

What constitutes Breeze's *corpus*? What is this work? What is a digital ouevre anyway? What is a digital ("Mezzian") subject? What is a digital *text* and how do we grasp it, read it, read it if it appears, as Breeze's poems sometimes do, in print books this century, or disappear off old links to defunct sites from the previous century? How may we read mezangelled texts as interpolated into "contemporary" contexts? What elements of the Antipodean can we find in Breeze's ouevre and how does it fare in its global-poetics reckoning? A digital ouevre has to engage multiple temporal vectors at a certain cusp: late century and new century political and aesthetic histories. Taking up such linguistic, rhetorical and discursive elements, and historicising them in light of post-digital historicity, we factor in those elements of the digital and physical, technology and the body; biopolitics, biopower, ecology, statehood, governance and surveillance. What are we to make of passages like this?

5.7   July

5.7.1   _s[p]erver[se]_: 404 poetry (2007-07-04 11:10)

> 925.has.d-tec[hy]ted:
> 404.poetry:
> that you
> redirect the
> request for
> this address
> in a way that will
> never complete.
> (*Human Readable Messages* 261)

Such a passage seems to operate on the proviso that whatever redirections or server-led requests inhibit the running of a poem, somehow a poem peeks, perversely, outside the mediatic curtain. From *Human Readable Messages [Mezangelle 2003–2011]*, published by the Vienna-based publisher Traumawein, Breeze's *magnum opus* to date, the sheer hybrid capacity of the work gives it the quality of a postmodern long poem. As a contemporary long poem the extended sequence of code comprises a 323-page book, collecting her Mezangelle works over an eight year period, chronologically organised and complete with the exact date and time of writing. The appearance is code, but it has to a large extent exceeded its function. If as Mina Loy put it "poetry is prose bewitched," so too this poetry is code betwitched, a codework poeticity replete with the segmenting of words — full stops, underscore, colons, and the use of brackets which in code delimit code blocks, an elementary unit in code's lexical structures — which in turn create puns, missteps, errata slips and semantic slippages. Hence "_s[p]erver[se]" gives us perverse, server, and potentially *per se* and verse. The poem, 404, is unable to communicate with the server, but of course, the poem is right there, and whatever redirection it might have taken to reach the reader, this process of displacement, removal or coincidence is "never complete."

There is a certain openness to Breeze's text. What and where the poem is, where it has escaped to or how we are to read it, gives itself to this sense that this is a poem with the hybrid capacity of a contemporary long poem. The long poem begins with interviews and poetics (in prose, serving as an interpolated quasi-introduction), suggesting an immediate self-reflexivity and an interest in the critical poetics of the work that would then unfold. Lineated poetry will not appear until page thirty. Yet despite all this, this poetry, for that is what we must call it, can be characterised like any other poetry, conventional or not: line breaks matter, as does the segmenting of words into syllables. It is a syllabic poetics, one in which textual encryption, Tmesis, and notariqon-like, etymological findings of words-in-words emerges from the digital environment that it has become and vice versa; the language reflects back on these environs. For Northrop Frye, context is similarly vital in any discussion of what goes on in verbal creation itself, which "begins in associative babble ... sound and sense are equally involved. The result of this is poetic ambiguity" to which Frye then adds that the poet is not one to define words but rather one to "establishes their powers by placing them in a great variety of contexts. Hence the importance of poetic etymology, or the tendency to associate words similar in sound or sense" (334).

The difference, perhaps, is that Breeze engages not an enthrymed, encrypted poetics alone but rather a hybrid mish-mash of styles and genres including life writing. In some capacity these are collagistic life poems, albeit outside that formal tradition. Present in earlier works like _the data][h!][bleeding texts_ there are excerpts from correspondences and the emailing list "performances" Breeze has maintained that offer glimpses into the the management and moderation of these lists and the communities around them. One discussion titled "2.8.4   Fwd: [-empyre-] Re; [empyre] nettime and alan, mez, nn" dated August 2004 revolves around discussions of criticism and the "cultural politics of the nets" particularly in "experimental presentations" (120). Other sections engage in self-citation and reflection, which can result in a highly analytic, critical poetics:

> ■Thus, when I
> ■think about 'digital writing' I have to do with a doubled or better:

a
- self-referential notion.
>
> self rif.f[lings+ego=arrowings]>construction ripplings _
>
- Aesthetically, digital writing – for me – is
- concerned with the processes, conditions and potential of writing in its
- pure sense.
>
>
>processes
>conditions
>potentionals
>*
(*Human Readable Messages* 196)

Including judgement, aesthetic judgement, and incorporating this language of assessment and adjudication whilst redacting some detail, Breeze's works take on socioliterary citationality. It's peculiarly contextual, but not unusual; a poem that includes its poetics. Over, and well after the period that the extended sequence was written, what remains remarkable is how consistent the underlying characteristics of the poetry are, including its sense of the citational *in poetics*, despite the changes that occur in the history of the digital through that time. In what reads as a premonition of Twitter, created in 2006, one section dated 2005-06-19 refers to the "twittering cutsie output of a blogger" (167), but by 2008 Breeze begins refering to "Twitterwurk" (282). In Chapter 7, which runs through 2009, the inclusion of Twitter in "[twitte[reality_fiction" dated between 17/7/09 and 28/7/09, could not, of course, have appeared when the poem began, showing that what Breeze's work is in some senses a long poem as a kind of book-repository of digital and then post-digital histories. Some of this stems from an online residency "Twitterwurking," which was commissioned by New Media Scotland for July 2008, where Breeze produced poems in the form of tweets using her account @netwurker. Thinking Twitter through New Media meant that, even if stylistically and formally the works stay predictably hybrid, media's historical shifts would issue change in content more than in form. In "[twitte[reality_fiction" a reply to @botgirlq reveals she has been "using 'twittering' a year b4 Twitter." An historical Twitter would take up one part of an expansive poetics though. What appears on the page, subject to happenings underneath, (processes, conditionals, potentials) gives us writing in its "pure sense." The result: constructed ripplings of writing's digital historicity.

IV. Megaliteracies

I want to interrupt this discourse by saying that, wherever these or other readings can or will in the future go, we can, heeding digital historicity, read *Attn: Solitude* as a companion or subsequent volume of the Mezangelle long poem sequence, collecting her Mezangelle works from 2011 to 2016, taking off from the end of *Human Readable Messages*. There is a continuation at work across these two books; a "[socially_mandated_word]g[r]abbing" (33) that is as much an open, multivalent text as that Hayles described, and as unpredictable: "All megaliteracy will be wildly experimental" (191).

The remarkable continuity of style in the later book *Attn: Solitude* begs the question, I argue, of what a post-digital long poem looks and reads like, and of whether the work can now be read as a lifelong or modular epic; or whether this is now a megaliteracy, a new kind of writing machine distinguishable both from the modern and the contemporary long poem. "Attention" and "solitude" might seem to be two opposing things if we are to read attention as renown, critical or popular attention. On the other hand one seeks solitude in the meditative. Solitude might be that which conjures the Romantic:

"white dab sky" – 2011-10-21 14:06

– no results found for "white dab sky".
Results for white dab sky (without quotes): []
–
Your search – "porcelain dabs" in an "azure sky" – did not match any
documents.
–
Showing results for "sky
Search instead for "sky dabb[l]ings"
–
Showing results for sky *[eyed]stabbings*
Search instead for sky [eye]d[st]abbings
–
Showing results for *skype*]
Search instead for sky[pe]
(7)

But something is missing other than results. For if there is lyric manner in these failed searches, missing the sky and hardly subterranean, what doesn't quite turn up is the poem as a machine for representation. Megaliteracies, like megacities, offer both unceasing attention and utter solitude. Sky turns into skype; the failure of the search is a kind of egoic and ecological exhaustion. Postdigital too: there is no heaven, no utopia in the digital, save for the solitude of the postdigital subject. Meaning is trite, you might say, the sky flattened to a screen. It is not unmeaningful to suggest that there is often a sense that a screen is behind or somewhere outside a Mezzian page. We come to something like an Agnes Martin painting in several sections which seem to blank out the medium, flirting with the possibility that a page could either pixelate or go full blue screen:

:the:W[M]ild:[Wo||]Man: – 2013-09-02 10:16

… has t[(i)m]e[a]eth the size + shape of a broken d[w]inner_pl[f]ates.
… curves in human huddl[eS]ing_beneath_wHole(y)_memRra(i)ne_
w(h)ing(e)s.

_____
_____
_____
_____
_____
_____
_____
_____
_____
_____[vs]_____
_____

::::::::::::::::::::::unfurled translationing + com[a]mentary::::::::::::::::::::

(*Attn: Solitude* 42)

This is followed by a full page featuring the word "sheetetrite" repeated, which I approximate here, in which a page comes to undermine its mediatic presentation: there comes to be no medium for a poem such as this. The Tmetic function has crept into the title, infixed with nothing more cryptic than a question that, in this reading, I will provide no answer to:

2013 – 11

sheete[u_knok_wot_i_mean_by_this,_right?]trite – 2013-11-04 10:01

sheetetritesheetetritesheetetritesheetetritesheetetritesheetetrites he
etetritesheetetritesheetetritesheetetritesheetetritesheetetrites heete
tritesheetetritesheetetritesheetetritesheetetritesheetetritesheete tetrit
esheetetritesheetetritesheetetritesheetetritesheetetritesheetetrites h
eetetritesheetetritesheetetritesheetetritesheetetritesheetetrites heet
etritesheetetritesheetetritesheetetritesheetetritesheetetritesheete tri
tesheetetritesheetetritesheetetritesheetetritesheetetritesheetetrites
heetetritesheetetritesheetetritesheetetritesheetetritesheetetrites hee
tetritesheetetritesheetetritesheetetritesheetetritesheetetritesheete tr
itesheetetritesheetetritesheetetritesheetetritesheetetritesheetetrites
heetetritesheetetritesheetetritesheetetritesheetetritesheetetrites hee
tetritesheetetritesheetetritesheetetritesheetetritesheetetritesheete tr
itesheetetritesheetetritesheetetritesheetetritesheetetritesheetetrites
heetetritesheetetritesheetetritesheetetritesheetetritesheetetrites hee
tetritesheetetritesheetetritesheetetritesheetetritesheetetritesheete tr
itesheetetritesheetetritesheetetritesheetetritesheetetritesheetetrites
heetetritesheetetritesheetetritesheetetritesheetetritesheetetrites hee
tetritesheetetritesheetetritesheetetritesheetetritesheetetritesheete tr
itesheetetritesheetetritesheetetritesheetetritesheetetritesheetetrites
heetetritesheetetritesheetetritesheetetritesheetetritesheetetrites hee
tetritesheetetritesheetetritesheetetritesheetetritesheetetritesheete tr
itesheetetritesheetetritesheetetritesheetetritesheetetritesheetetrites
heetetritesheetetritesheetetritesheetetritesheetetritesheetetrites hee

tetritesheetetritesheetetritesheetetritesheetetritesheetetritesheetetri
tesheetetritesheetetritesheetetritesheetetritesheetetritesheetetritesh
eetetritesheetetritesheetetritesheetetritesheetetritesheetetritesheete
tritesheetetritesheetetritesheetetritesheetetritesheetetritesheetetrite
sheetetritesheetetritesheetetritesheetetritesheetetritesheetetriteshee
tetrite

(*Attn: Solitude* 43)

V. The Antipodal Avant-Garde

In Camus's *Le Mythe de Sisyphe* (1942) Sisyphus, whose task is to repeatedly push a boulder up a mountain, becomes an absurdist hero: not only does Camus posit the question of what one must do in the face of meaninglessness, he provides several answers that result in a materialist twist. Such a struggle — which begets revolt, freedom, passion — becomes a happy one; one must "imagine Sisyphus happy" in part because "Each atom of that stone, each mineral flake of that night filled mountain, in itself forms a world" (Camus 123).

If we can imagine being atomists in the face of meaninglessness, so too the avant-garde's textualist minerality, and conceptualist performativity, has opened itself to interpretations of its activity as a kind of ecstatic meaninglessness, from the death wails of Elsa von Freytag-Loringhoven, whose "career,"- and literal suicide, now sparks a belated recuperative fascination for contemporary scholars, to what Paul Mann calls the "theory-death" of the avant-garde, a theory itself tempered by Tyrus Miller's exploration of the misunderstood network of relations between theory and the avant-garde. The avant-garde, it so seems, cannot imagine, or give way to theorisations of, a future, because it has instated itself as the continuous future.

The problem is, the kinds of writing that theorists and critics can now pay close attention to are not as meaningless as originally thought, which has changed the questions we ask especially when we speak of the material text in avant-garde poetry and art after 1960, and ways in which experimentation or "innovation," as practice, has been incorporated, sometimes seamlessly, into digital age. In the case of digital texts it gets more complicated. We resist the historicisation of recent work; contemporary experimental poetry is frozen before an avant-garde past. Its historicity is absurd: Don't theorise *just yet*! Literary theory doesn't determine what will stand the test of time! There have been exceptions, challenges to such premises in theorisations of avant-garde literary history. In the work of Brian Reed, to take a notable example, "twenty-first-century avant-garde poetry" in a porous North American context can be said to continue, in contested forms, and in digital times, sometimes through the print medium (*Nobody's Business* xiv-xviii). But I suspect that sometimes we, and I mean readers but also authorreaders in the critical context of Australian poetics in global times, have often been forced to imagine a Sisyphean vanguard, or, antipodal rearguard, that labors "in solitude" — without hope of renown in this life — thus condemning themselves, happy or not, to the Sisyphean task of moulding the materials of art without end and, apparently, without purpose.

Some self-reflection is called for: Who mourns such impasses? Are such things, even if true, matters pertaining to literary criticism? Must the contemporary critic then commit to *enlivening* the vanguard, to less hang off it as push it forward? Does the avant-garde even need a critical industry behind it, a support network? More dire than this: do critical industries *kill* the avant-garde? In "Literary History and Literary Modernity," Paul de Man in 1969 suspected already that such an impasse had opened up, saying that

> Not so long ago, a concern with modernity would in all likelihood have coincided with a commitment to avant-garde movements such as dada, surrealism, or expressionism. The term would have appeared in manifestoes and proclamations, not in learned articles or international colloquia. But this does not mean that we can divide the twentieth century into two parts: a "creative" part that was actually modern, and a "reflective" or "critical" part that feeds on this modernity in the manner of a parasite, with active

modernity replaced by theorizing about the modern. (*Blindness and Insight* 143)

A problem with criticism arises when there is a perceived loss from a lack of participation in the creative act. There is no modernity without the avant-garde, but it gets complicated when we find that modernity is not reducible to the avant-garde, and further, no modernity without the theories and theorists that maintain it. Does the same go for postmodernity? In the historical present, can appeals to the postmodernity, and globality of contemporary poetics do away with all this binarising tonality, or for that matter, critical parasitism? J. Hillis Miller asks the same with reference to citation as practice:

> What happens when a critical essay extracts a "passage" and "cites" it? Is this different from a citation, echo, or allusion within a poem? Is a citation an alien parasite within the body of its host, the main text, or is it the other way around, the interpretative text the parasite which surrounds and strangles the citation which is its host? The host feeds the parasite and makes its life possible, but at the same time is killed by it, as "criticism" is often said to kill "literature." Or can host and parasite live happily together, in the domicile of the same text, feeding each other or sharing the food? ("The Critic as Host" 439)

Who cites? Who theorises? Who then critiques, "kills" literature? Or who *makes*, on the one hand, and who reflects, on the other, "hangs off" those doing the making? If we were to assign the name of Sisyphean vanguard to those with courage enough to confront, and form a frontline for, the contemporary world, in our times such a poetics "confronting the world" seems more like a rearguard, a mode of aesthetico-political defense, defense of a literary postmodernity that is a world-unto-itself, or in Breeze's language that is both world and underworld, a leading light and a preventative "firehose_of_the_nOw." We have a defensive model, a vision of a mediator, or the death of literature itself in its citational aftermath, nay grave.

To do readings of and cite Breeze in a book — whether or not readers wind up reading this on a screen — therefore registers something of a dark irony. Can we figure the Sisyphean vanguard as subterranean, an Underworld, one that moves between Romantic sky and the curved surface of the screen, between the historical avant-gardes and those no longer attached to any vanguard whatsoever? It goes from works to the promise of criticism. As Breeze herself puts it, we are "reordering.ur.bleached.+.Sisyphean.promise" (*Attn: Solitude* 65)? This now, the weight of the now, *this* contemporary cannot help but be some kind of warding-off of catastrophe, of failure and setback, some putting-out of the fires of the (rhizomezatic) Underworld. There is a certain conceptual clarity that pulls its own weight: no option but to convert the solitude of the digital poet into a form of expansion which goes somewhat against the vanguard as collective. This is the most mysterious thing about Breeze's work; the vanguard lacks an epical drive when it collides with postmodernity and the logics of capital and commercial culture, and yet the epical "attention" to solitude in Breeze is theoretically weighty in ways that defy these logics. We confront once again the rearguardism of our terms. The matter of digital poetry is still matter in time. Postdigital or posthuman, Breeze exhausts and seizes matter, is a materialist of some sort, both of the body, as Aardse and others have argued, one engaging a syllabic, lingual materialism whose messages are readable, an extension of the body, a lingual prosthesis. Again the issue seems to have become this: rather than a vanguardism that forges ahead or opposes, what experimental poetry risks doing in the twenty-first is precisely losing the risk, becoming a defence-guard, rearguard, something that defends itself rather than enlists a collective to form a frontline.

But a frontline beating back against what? Breeze's poetics has no truck for the Silicon Valley ethos or aesthetic; there is no idolisation of technocratic globalism, and little sense that proficiency needs to lead to the digital boutique. The work has its own ecologies, its whorls and steady, persistent moves. It takes its time between the centuries, as historical work, a kind of digital literacy that's up to taking in all sorts of fluxes while somehow retaining those forms of poetic expansion that mark its moves through time.

VI.

The antipodal avant-gardes, which have very often found themselves in contexts transnationally and hemispherically unhinged, temporally warped, timely, belated or already in the future, misplaced out-of-context or even throwing context into confusion in some Sisyphean task never fulfilled or continually resisted, are now reimagined as a series of crises in literary historicity.

We can here cite certain puncture-points in Australian literary modernity and postmodernity. To provide a pattern of contexts one recurrent example from an Australian poetics heritage is Christopher Brennan's *Musicopoematographoscope* (1897), rewriting Mallarmé from the same year. We may look to Harry Hooton's anarchistic materialism, or Jas H. Duke, who brought Dada to Melbourne in 1973, or Amanda Stewart's sounding poetics. There is something timeless in Lionel Fogarty's undoing of the English language and total remaking of poetics. And then in this (post)-digital moment, we can add Breeze's *Human Readable Messages* and *Attn: Solitude*. One constructs such histories through degrees of artifice: this is all some manner of speaking about theories of literary history, for if we can say that the work of Breeze, like those mentioned above — you may label them risk-takers, radicals or nonconformists — form part of a loose theoretical-historical network of antipodal avant-gardes, these are networks looming as some splendid appearances above critical *aporiae*. They may revolt or retreat; no matter, critics theorise. A vanguard that refuses to court convention or even directly show its face becomes a rearguard, and pursues languages of invention through guerilla means, means we have been familiar with, or that we have then become parasitically attached to because of a desire to travel down this path.

In closing I would like to say that we would be foolish critics not to include these languages of invention as part of the histories of Australian poetry and, in parallel, to borrow a phrase from Northrop Frye, the "critical path" we choose for such histories. Alongside New Media and critical languages adept at situating electronic literature historically, criticism might now begin to read Breeze's writings, first and foremost, as poetry. Better; *poetry in poetics*. Such a poetics, despite, or perhaps given its special use of the language of code and the digital, moves sound and line in myriad rhythms to (unbounded) sense.

Works Cited

Aardse, Kent. "The Biopolitics of Electronic Literature: On the Writings of Mez Breeze." *Digital Literary Studies*, vol. 1, no. 1, 2016. https://journals.psu.edu/dls/article/view/59648/59908
---. *Attn: Solitude*, Cordite Books, 2017.
---. *The Dead Tower*, 2013.
---. *Filtah*, 2000.
---. *Human Readable Messages (Mezangelle 2003-20011)*, Traumawein, 2011.
---. *Internal Damage Report*, 1997-1998.
Breeze, Mez. *#PRISOM*, 2013.
Camus, Albert. *The Myth of Sisyphus, And Other Essays*, Alfred A. Knopf, 1955.
Clemens, Justin. "No creation but through submission." *UnMagazine*, vol. 7, no. 1, 2013. http://www.unprojects.org.au/magazine/issues/issue-7-1/no-creation-but-through-submission/
Cramer, Florian. "What is 'Post-Digital'?" *Post-Digital Research*, 2013. www.aprja.net/?p=1318
de Man, Paul. *Blindness and Insight: Essays in the Rhetoric of Contemporary Criticism*, University of Minnesota Press, 1983.
Farrell, Michael. *Writing Australian Unsettlement: Modes of Poetic Invention*,

1796-1945, Palgrave Macmillan, 2015.

Frye, Northrop. *Anatomy of Criticism: Four Essays*, Princeton University Press, 2000.

Funkhouser, C.T. *Prehistoric Digital Poetry: An Archaeology of Forms, 1959-1995*, University of Alabama Press, 2007.

---. *New Directions in Digital Poetry*, Continuum, 2012.

Hayles, N. Katherine. "Deeper into the Machine: The Future of Electronic Literature." *Culture Machine,* vol. 5, 2003. https://culturemachine.net/index.php/cm/article/viewArticle/245/241

Hillis Miller, J. "The Critic as Host." *Critical Inquiry,* vol. 3, no. 3, 1977, pp. 439-447.

Mann, Paul. *The Theory-Death of the Avant-Garde*, Indiana University Press, 1991.

Miller, Tyrus. "Avant-Garde and Theory: A Misunderstood Relation." *Poetics Today,* vol. 20, no.4, 1999, pp. 549-79.

Pepperell, Robert and Michael Punt. *The Postdigital Membrane: Imagination, Technology and Desire*, Intellect Books, 2000.

Raley, Rita. "Interferences: [Net.Writing] and the Practice of Codework." *Electronic Book Review*, 2002. http://www.electronicbookreview.com/thread/electropoetics/net.writing

Reed, Brian. *Nobody's Business: Twenty- First Century Avant-Garde Poetics*, Cornell University Press, 2013.

Chapter 4

Philip Salom: Feeding Time to the Contemporary

TOBY DAVIDSON

One way to witness the futility of defining the contemporary is to read someone attempting it twenty years back. Geoff Page's *A Reader's Guide to Contemporary Australian Poetry* (1995) opts, after some vacillations ("does it include last year, last decade or even the last three decades?") to locate it in the poets of the late 60s, "whether they were later considered conservative or radical"—Tranter, Forbes, Adamson, Murray, Lehmann, Gray (1-2). While Page finds it "hard to think of any woman born between 1940 and 1950 who has rivalled the impact of most of the male poets cited so far", Jan Owen (b. 1940), Jennifer Rankin (1941), Joanne Burns (1945), Jennifer Maiden (1949) all are given entries of roughly the same length (8). The critical and commercial success of the slightly younger Dorothy Porter (b.1954) proved a little too contemporary for Page, with *The Monkey's Mask* reduced to "the verse detective novel she is now working on", even if, four lines below, his own bibliography gives the title and its publication date of 1994—the year prior (228). While the "general loosening up" caused by the "Woodstock generation", paperbacks and live performance has proven fruitful, Page concedes that the majority of his sixty-four chosen poets are no longer writing, with only twenty-four remaining active, the rest "lost to journalism, academia, early death, arts administration, the novel and the counter-culture of northern New South Wales" (2-3). *A Reader's Guide to Contemporary Australian Poetry* demonstrates the delay between what is deemed "contemporary" and what is actually being written, published or performed at the time. It is also representative of the significant state of flux Australian poetry found itself in during the mid-1990s with generational change in the canon, an evening up of gender representation and the reconfiguration of publishing to smaller scale publishers after the demise of Angus and Robertson.

This chapter traces the long-term reception of a poet who emerged in the 1980s, Philip Salom (1950–). I argue that Salom has been critically neglected beyond the initial review stage because his restless, exuberant changes in style and subject matter have outstripped the ability of peers, scholars and critics to keep pace with them. In particular Salom's enduring interests in postmodernity, hyperreality, transnationalism and intersections between youth and technology have not resonated with many critics of his own generation. The low level of post-review scholarship is one proof of this, another is his persistent anthologising as a poet of Gallipoli, the Bicentenary, barbecues and memories of his father, though there is wider diversity in the contemporary-minded selections of Page's *A Reader's Guide*, John Kinsella's *Landbridge: Contemporary Australian Poetry* (1999), John Leonard's *New Music: An Anthology of Contemporary Australian Poetry* (2001) and Martin Langford et al's *Contemporary Australian Poetry* (2016). In effect, Salom has been sanctioned for his obsession with the technological 'now' as it is experienced, especially by youth, in the seismic shift from the cinema to digital age. Perhaps, as a new generation of scholars emerges, these will be seen as prophetic depictions of our base reality and noses instead might be wrinkled or looked down at Salom's nostalgia for freeways and drive-ins (you watched a movie from your car?).

This chapter is structured around four types of 'betweenness' which, in my view, have led to Salom being underrated and under-interpreted. For expediency, I chiefly limit my analysis to *Feeding the Ghost* (1993), *The Rome Air Naked* (1996) and the three contained in 2015's *Alterworld—Sky Poems* (1987), *The Well Mouth* (2005) and *Alterworld*. Tackling Salom's entire career of (at last count) sixteen poetry collections and three novels would too easily result in the kind of gently-guided tour characteristic of Australian poetry reviews more generally, as Ben Etherington found in his exhaustive study "The Poet Tasters" (2015). Along the way, I aim to interrogate the poetic and critical faultlines which have facilitated and exacerbated Salom's various states of 'betweenness,' despite his two Commonwealth Poetry Prizes (one for best first book), two WA Premier's Prizes, two Newcastle Poetry Prizes and the 2003 Christopher Brennan Award for lifetime achievement in poetry. Under "Philip Salom, 658 works by", in the Austlit scholarly database, only two dedicated articles post-1995 appear: John Jenkins's "Provincial to Post-Modern: The Poetry of Philip Salom" (2002) and David Musgrave's "Poetry as Knowing: Philip Salom's *Keepers Trilogy*" (2014). There is nothing on Salom's grittiest and most accessible collection, *The Well Mouth*. By contrast, Dorothy Porter's *The Monkey's Mask* has been interpreted by over ten dedicated articles and a 2012 book, more when Anne Kennedy's film version is added. In order to understand Salom's relative exclusion it is necessary to first trace his career and its reception from 1980s Perth to present-day Melbourne.

Between Perth and the Divided East

Salom emerged out of the fecund 1980s Perth poetry scene and found most success with his third collection *Sky Poems*, from which "Seeing Gallipoli from the Sky" is still widely anthologised. In Dennis Haskell and Hilary Fraser's seminal 1989 anthology *Wordhord: Contemporary Western Australian Poetry*, he was the last of its ten featured poets after Fay Zwicky, Andrew Lansdown, Shane McAuley and ahead of a host of (then) minor poets such as David Brooks, Andrew Burke, Caroline Caddy, Michael Heald, John Kinsella, David McCooey, Mudrooroo, Mark Reid and Nicolette Stasko. Like many of his contemporaries, Salom wouldn't stay put in Perth. He lived briefly in Singapore and Rome, before permanently moving to Melbourne in 1997. Around this time, although he continued to appear in historical and contemporary anthologies, the trickle of critical enthusiasm that *Sky Poems* created almost completely dried up. Certainly there was a degree of regionalism in this, as well as the ongoing effects of the 1980s split between "Murray's lot" and "Tranter's lot" (as Salom himself one described it to me) which must have felt especially absurd to a poet raised on a dairy farm with a marked fascination for the urban and postmodern. There was, at least, some faint praise from Murray, who lauded the "remarkable" Salom in his erratic prose collection *Blocks and Tackles* and Tranter and Philip Mead's 1991 anthology *The Penguin Book of Modern Australian Poetry* found room for Salom's "Walking at Night" (Murray 166).

Since *Wordhord*'s fine essay by Haskell and Fraser, which claims Salom's work is "sharply different from that of any other Western Australia writer" and closer to that of Murray and Peter Porter, most anthologists have avoided Salom in their introductions (152). By contrast, the introduction to Kinsella and Tracy Ryan's recent *The Fremantle Press Anthology of Western Australian Poetry* really goes to town, describing him as "the great poet Philip Salom, a model for so many who followed ... His restless exuberance links with something sharp, even bitter, which makes for a poetry unlike any other, anywhere" (43). Yet this is the exception rather than the rule, and it is worth pointing out that both exceptions originate from the same most isolated city in the world. Salom's exuberance, for exuberance it is, met with a more mixed reception in the East. Geoff Page's *A Reader's Guide to Contemporary Australian Poetry* characterises Salom's poetry as crackling with an "intense verbal and metaphoric energy" reminiscent of Gerard Manley Hopkins and Dylan Thomas from his 1980 debut *The Silent Piano*. For Page, this intensity is thrilling but risks clashing images and "a constant danger of melodrama" where "things happen fast" and sex "is never far away" (257, 260). Salom's fifth collection *Feeding the Ghost* is especially singled out for its "'Look, Mum, no hands' kind of cockiness" which only apparently improves when he "decelerates" in his Singaporean poems (260).

It's hardly a revelation that I tend to be less conservative than Page, and that I'm not Robinson Crusoe in this regard. Nonetheless, I agree with him in regard to *Feeding the Ghost*'s second and third poems

("A Corporate Workout" and "Computer Games"), which pastiche current events and popular culture circa 1990. Time capsules rarely great poems make, even for one of Australia's most consistent poets. Yet as the collection proceeds, I fail to see the hurriedness. Perhaps it's my own contemporaneity? I was twelve at the change of decades. Did I learn to read faster, think faster (though not better) than a generation back, even prior to the internet? Or am I just personally excessive, risky (risqué?), melodramatic, cocky? Page has made no secret of his distaste for postmodernity, both thematically and stylistically. Back then, his conservatism fit the times: Salom noted, as early as 1988, that his own preference for multiplicity and surrealism was placing him at odds with a new orthodoxy around the lyrical 'I.' He admitted "I am a bit pissed off with the force that the lyric has taken. Australian poetry has become very conservative ... it's a reaction to the 60s and 70s" and suggested this had limited the expectations of poetry readers:

> People want poets to refer to their own immediate world. A lyric impulse has taken over; in contrast I set up strange, jarring effects for some readers. They say "The 'I's don't sound the same in this collection". Well, of course, they're not ... multiple personality is more a reflection of our experience. ("Interview" 64, 62).

As criticism around the lyric has evolved, it has finally found room for Salom on its fringes—David McCooey identifies *The Well Mouth* as an example of the "extra-lyrical mode ... large, idiosyncratic works that undermine the distinctions between lyrical and narrative poetry, poetic and non-poetic thinking" along with works by PiO, MTC Cronin, Jordie Albiston, John Kinsella and Ouyang Yu, among others (133).

Salom himself has reflected of late that he may be returning to a more complex version of the lyric, after discussing an 'oldie' of his with a school student:

For years I have not exactly resisted the lyric—I must [have] written a hundred lyric poems—but preferred to warp the I into various masquerades and othernesses, or simply write without it. There are traps in the lyric which many poets slip into and for all my wariness I must have too: the too-easy self-posturing, abstract propositions never argued into authority, the automatic assumption therefore of "authenticity" ... So even though the lyric dominates Australian poetry, and accounts for many successes, there are endlessly more poems of sop or phoniness ... The particular poem the student chose enacts an epiphany of sorts and this return has released another and different kind of epiphany in me—one to do with style and the latent elements of style which we carry with us through many experiments and innovations. And have perhaps forgotten the value of. (*Philip Salom Poet and Novelist*, pars 1-2)

How fascinating that Salom sees the kind of unrestrained posturing and abstraction in the lyric that Page sees in his departures from it! Yet underneath the ostracism for not following the conventional lyrical 'I' is, to my mind, an accusation of a lack of feeling, empathy or sincerity. Poet and poetry editor for *The Age*, Gig Ryan (1956–), suggests as much in her 1998 review of Salom's *New and Selected Poems* where the "public, bardic" tone adopted in the new pieces means 'these are doubt-free poems, and the pendulous "I think of ..." usually heralds an omniscient observer's superior compassion ... *Sky Poems* (1987), particularly "Bar Sonnet," looks better in retrospect, but many of the later dismissive tourist-in-Europe poems read like a patriotic suite" (10). The rest of the paragraph given to the book is peppered with further charges of obscurantism, "wandering construction", overwrought similes and "bitchy prose". Ryan's remarks, combined with those of Page, show that influential East Coast poets (from Melbourne and Canberra, respectively) found Salom too zealous, manic, self-aggrandising, ill-disciplined or obtuse. Others, like Adelaide's Jan Owen (1940–), concluded that while the uneven pace in *Feeding the Ghost* led to some risks that didn't come off, these were validated by "triple somersaults and much sleight of thought; Salom is a virtuoso of images ... In short: one helluva good poet" (581).

Between Exile and Transnationalism

In 1988, Salom confessed "I don't really read a lot of Australian poets. I'm familiar with their work here and there", adding he preferred to think of himself as a poet, rather than an *Australian* one ("Interview" 63). This preference for the universal translates well to the surreal and transnational worlds of *Sky Poems* and *Feeding the Ghost* and their shifting senses of (dis)embodiment and identity. There are masks, but not the heteronyms of the *Keepers* trilogy (which David Musgrave suggests may owe something to Beckett as well as Pessoa), but the masquerades of mental experiences which underpin *Sky Poems* in particular (Musgrave par 21). Interviewed shortly after the collection's release, Salom acknowledges the influence of the art of Fremantle-based artist Theo Koning as well as the Latin American magical realism of Jorge Luis Borges, Gabriel Garcia Marquez and Octavio Paz. The interviewer, Barbara Williams, draws a line from the last poem of *The Projectionist* to *Sky Poems*, a line which could now be extended to *Alterworld*:

> BW: In "Packing", the final poem, you say "... words, states / of mind ... perform, after leaving, masquerades." "Perform", "masquerade"—there's a distancing, a shift.
>
> PS: Experiences stay alive; we love to embellish, alter; we offset this against our terrible tendencies to oppression and savagery. The mind has this great power to take up its own experiences, play games with them, but I think we're always in control of it; it's mischievous: the masquerade, pretence, veils, dramas ... [in *Sky Poems*] those games then take their own shape, the coming to fruition of things that don't normally do so. (Salom and Williams 62)

National masquerades—Gallipoli and Bicentenary—are tailor-made for such mischief. As well as being regularly anthologised, "Seeing Gallipoli from the Sky" and "Bicentennial: Living Other Lives" have been compared to Latin American poetries for their "templates of national identity overwhelmed with alterity ... as reinscriptions of official History. His 'others' are both familiar and anonymous ..." (McCarthy 194-195). Tracing *The Silent Piano* through to *A Cretive Life* (2001), John Jenkins concludes that "Being a writer means, for Salom, a sort of psychic rebuilding, a reinvention of himself in personal and social terms" and that the sky realm in *Sky Poems* serves as a kind of "promised land for the untrammelled ego", though Salom in his 1988 interview explicitly states the ego must also have its limits (Jenkins 223; Salom and Williams 62). If reading outside Australian poetry as well as being geographically outside the major poetry factions and debates led to what some of the earliest *Sky Poems* scholars see as two intersecting traditions of exile, namely "social commentary and self-absorbed introspection" (Pedersen and Rutherford 68).

There is exile, too, in *Feeding the Ghost* and *The Rome Air Naked*, the latter as exile from his wife Meredith but also a sense of exile from self and the city, the dual dissociation of tourism. The final sequence of *Feeding the Ghost*, "In Residence: In the Month of the Hungry Ghosts, Singapore, 1989", while historically informed, is a meeting of cultures in the streets and classrooms in a more open manner, with a moment-by-moment sense of reciprocity. Though not transnational in an ongoing sense (as, for example, the Melbourne-Wuhan poet Ouyang Yu [1955–]), "In Residence: In the Month of the Hungry Ghosts, Singapore, 1989" pre-empts the 1990s turn towards Asia by both non-Asian and Asian Australian poets. (In 2014, Salom continued to innovate by reaching out to Chinese readers through a bilingual English-Mandarin volume *Between Yes and No*.) A recurrent theme of *Feeding the Ghost* is travel by train, boat or plane and its ability to take one out of oneself, be it mentally, culturally, sensually, paranormally. Twenty pages in, the middle section of "Cryptographs" explains the title:

4
Sunk into language you can swim
without moving. The currents sway you
as much as the sharks.

5
Or sit there in its armchair
as it stares coolly from the fireplace
and you go up in flames.

6
Looking for a title
then seeing what the hunger is
and what all art is:
feeding the ghost.

7
And having fed it I
in choosing words for what
did not at the time exist
make it our illusion. (21-22)

Other travels around Europe, the Middle East and Asia foreground wind and smoke imagery. In "Briefly at the Airport Lounge", it is at the threshold of travel itself where "Leaving is a death. Your life, like the rumour, / pulses in its ghost before you … it's jealous / of the other ghosts you feel arriving …" (85). Yet it is just as significant that feeding the ghost can take place simply by sitting still. There is a *kenosis*, an emptying of the self to a ghostliness that allows elemental and imaginative hungers of past and present to enter and combine, a process that "did not at the time exist" and is made more illusory, not less, by its subsequent naming. It is an honest, intimate response to the unanswerable question "Where does poetry come from?", while at the same time allowing the ghost metaphor to mask the brutal quotidian realities of artistic practice in favour of the inspired confluence and receptivity open to any artistic seeker at any age. If feeding the ghost is an illusion, it is one that works, and will lead time and again to realised creativity. It may be accessed in different ways in the jet age or computer age, but there is nothing innately contemporary about it—indeed, quite the opposite.

The hungry ghost metaphor, for all its universality, is one that is derived from the poet's real-life experience of a specific cultural phenomenon. *Feeding the Ghost*'s "In Residence" sequence of thirty-five sonnets of fluctuating line lengths and stanza breaks is set in the Buddhist-Daoist Hungry Ghost Festival, held in the seventh month of the Chinese lunar calendar. In Salom's Singapore experience, this is soon after the Tiananmen Square massacre:

> Offerings of food for the hungry ghosts—are wasting
> by platefuls outside houses, under beige walls of flats.
>
> Can't help the pun. Beige. Beijing. And Lee Kuan Yew's
> big-time condemnation of the tanks. (The hungry tanks ...) (110)

An outsider to both region's current politics and traditional rites, he chooses instead to feed the thin local cats while pondering his own ancestors whose names and faces "I am blind to, and cannot drink to, ignorant / of their burial high or low ground, in Australia, / or England, Wales, or as my father's mother liked / to think: Spain ..." (116). This poem is one antecedent for a later piece, "The Family Fig Trees". Old Asia, the British Empire, Japanese invasion and hypercapitalist transformation retract and spill like waves of humidity, waves of people, food and ghosts. Escapist devices like computer games are suddenly so proximate they need their own escaping. News from Australia of political corruption and Aboriginal deaths in custody warn against judging the Singaporean system, although "no critics / slam their talents against the wall, under the barred window, caught: 'Exaggerating problems of the poor.' Ours is not that kind of fear."

(129). As his teaching residency peters out, he is drawn once more to the exchange of ancient and modern in the ghostly thrall of TV:

> On the endless TV shows from China,
> the soap not the sung operas,
> there's this mad eternity again:
> half nostalgia, much more pain.
> China is front-stage, alive and dead
> as ancestors. The future cannot be fed
> from this, and the order's all wrong:
> ghosts should hunger for the mortal song. (135)

On the immediately preceding page, poetry is "inquiry, the old haggle / not for bargains or defeats, but for those forms / which get the matter lived through, or imagined, / nearly right" (134). At no stage does he hunger for Australia. Instead, he wonders at the impact of his advice to Singapore's over-behaved youth, especially "how / to question, how language must unearth, enliven":

> Are words remembered?
> Laughter, tremor, me the middle and cause of it:
> poet-and-joker ...
> The bite I want to leave in youngish hearts.
> All cut through me. I cannot say goodbye. (139)

In 2013, the year the groundbreaking anthology *Contemporary Asian Australia Poets* appeared, Salom was interviewed by Jaydeep Sarangi for *Mascara* online journal, a major forum from transnational and Asian-Australian poetries. Salom outlines his engagement with Indian poetry in English and Vedic culture (as in *Alterworld*'s "A Night-long Performance of Peter Brook's *Mahabharata*"), but his broader Asian influences extend back to Sufism in *The Silent Piano* and forward to the bilingual English-Mandarin collection *Between Yes and No* (2014). He also accepts that the "age of Facebook" could produce another

Keats "if there's enough time" for writing and reading, for repose, for *receiving*—he identifies the "knowings I receive" as a key motivation for his own work (Salom and Sarangi, "Interview," pars 9, 25 27). The ghost is not the only one fed.

Unlike the poets of the generation prior who either ignored or only briefly toured Asia (with a few key exceptions such as Harold Stewart), Salom actually lived and taught in Singapore at a time when Australia was grappling with its Anglophone past and its Asian destiny. Though not a radically transnational poet in the same way as many Asian-Australian poets who have since risen to prominence, he is a poet of his own transnational experience of airports, of living in a different culture and climate, of witnessing the legacies of a different arm of the British empire, of simultaneously seeing Singapore and Australia from the outside, of being many outsiders in one, of finding himself on multiple cognitive and metaphorical thresholds at once. Not only could many of the critics of his own generation not relate to this, but Australian academia of the era was still hypnotised by the Europhile wonderland of postmodernism and poststructuralism, despite the international turn to postcolonialism and narratology. For most Australian critics the postmodern was exemplified outside Australia or Asia, in Europe or the late capitalist hyperreality of the United States. The economic turn to Asia through the mining boom and the rise of China was still some years away. Next stop: hypertextual Rome.

Between Cinema, Video and Digital Ages

Salom knew his disruption of the lyrical 'I' would grate with the conservative forces of late twentieth-century Australian poetry, but his subject matter, particularly that of computers and changing technology, was possibly too contemporary for some and too obtuse for others. For Dennis Haskell in the 1998 *Oxford Literary History of Australia*, it was "casting about for possibilities" and suggestive of the poet's own "restless, jagged curiosity" (284). Salom's ventures into experimental forms associable with the postmodern (notably in *The*

Rome Air Naked and *Alterworld*) are preceded by an abiding interest in hyperreal, consumerist lives. For John Jenkins, "the condition of postmodernity is one in which he thrives" as a playful risk taker, who can exhaust as well as startle readers, "assertive, flashy, a poetic show-off" (225). Salom's active interest in postmodernity means almost anything can serve as subject matter, including aspects of youth culture, commercialism, globalisation and popular media shunned by more conservative, lyrical poets. I can only wonder what Page and others made of Salom's comparison of the male orgasm to bungee jumping in "The Man Who Mistook His Wife for a Hat". What about other pieces in *Feeding the Ghost* which reference pioneering arcade video games like Sega's driving simulator *Outrun* ("The Sex or Autostrada Driving") or the 3D beat-em-up game *Double Dragon* in "Living in a Time-Zone: Like a Race"? Few Salom critics and reviewers acknowledge the beginnings of what is now known as gamer culture. My own reaction was so intense I wrote a poem in response to "Living in a Time-Zone: Like a Race", published almost twenty years later in 2012, which prompted a critique of both pieces by Lachlan Brown, emerging poet and scholar of Australian computer game culture (Davidson 64-65, Brown). The kids in Salom's video game poems, who may possess nostalgic, even mythopoetic relationships to these games, are only now starting to respond poetically or critically.

Salom's interest in technological changes to communication and perception, especially through film and computers, has increased in keeping with the rate of change. His obsession with film is traceable to the projectionist character Benchley in *The Projectionist* (1983), who returns in *Alterworld*:

> The flat screen is strained, broken in dirty pixels
> the sensuous ripple-soles of bitumen lapping forwards in salvos of
> shadow or shockwaves of light-shot, from the projectionist's
> sullen bunker. Dead grass. Darkness. An iron gate.
> The smash of windows.

> Metal loudspeakers hang on stands like Darth Vader foreheads
> louvered with worry, tart-lipped
> as death. I trip and fall, my jeans tear open at the knee.
> A child. I am that child, bleeding beside his fallen bike.
> I stand and run from the figure behind me.
> It must be a man. I turn to see ...
> ("At the Disused Drive-in Theatre" 239)

Salom bears a youthful affection for film which marks and celebrates its evolutionary phases, the last evident in 'Visit to the Omni Theatre' in *Barbeque of the Primitives* (1989). Film serves as a way to poetry even (especially?) when it is blatantly facile, such as the "violent yuppie kingdom of designer sex" in "9½ Weeks—The Film" from *Feeding the Ghost* (55). No complaints of hypnotised youth or the decline of civilisation to be found here! Rather, under Omni's hemispherical megascreen, it is the Eighties/Nineties child who feels "lost" while their parents laugh at the "vertigo of dreaming, or laughing, or making love" (*Barbecue* 41).

In "Living in a Time Zone", Salom's own arcade nostalgia is interrupted by that of the screen-based present. At times his resentment resembles that of a silent film fan who has seen their hallowed ground ruined by the "talkies". At other times there is an Attenborough-esque fascination with on-screen versions of self as well as metabolic and biological realities of the young players:

> The arcade games were once hands-on.
> Upright as thin soldiers in a row:
> five soccer men on spindles we spun ...
>
> The clack and buzz rhythms of pin-ball
> grunted from the hips and sprang like sex.
> But all that steel. The game played cool,
> under Coke ads with breast, buttocks
> and the curvature of phoney surf. You had

to be fit to be a delinquent. Now it's
leaner, mental as a salesman, tapping the currency
of yes and no. All head and reflex system. (*Feeding* 61)

Table soccer (aka fussball), pool, billiards, pinball are all—like the drive-in—places of tactile prowess and sexual display, "And players / had hangovers, not needles in the arms." Lachlan Brown's "'The Beautiful Pixels': Computer Games and Two Contemporary Australian Poems" (2015) interprets Salom's poem as "a playfully ironic account of the computer game world from the perspective of a cantankerous baby boomer" (par 31).

"Playful" is the key word here, because Salom characteristically elects to interpret rather than disengage. As a result, he may well be the first (anti-)video game poet in Australia, decades ahead of the seven Brown identifies in James Stuart, Keri Glastonbury, Saxby Pridmore, Derek Motion, Jaya Savige, Connor Weightman and myself. While *Double Dragon* is the only game besides *Outrun* that Salom identifies, "Living in a Time-Zone: Video Prints" is almost certainly a denunciation of the infamously crass PC adventure game *Leisure Suit Larry in the Land of the Lounge Lizards*. Its 16-bit sleaze is rendered repugnant along with other adventure games which bombard his son with the same basic narrative: "The maid saved by some / little maggot with a big sword." (Salom 60). This is poles apart from his individual experience of soft porn in *9½ Weeks*, which is enjoyably trashy *and* erotic. Salom's satires of the digital age are just as prevalent in his later career, notably in "Ode Owed to Data" and "The Hotel of When-it-Was" in *Alterworld* and "A Cannoli Maker's Second-Person Selfie Metaphysic" published in *Eureka Street* in 2014. The technological targets of his satire are just as "contemporary" as they were in 1993, with arcade games replaced by metadata and wifi.

What credit will be given to Philip Salom by poetry scholars of the digital age? It may depend on their view of Salom's role as an early observer of computer technology and one who used this technology to create new poetic forms. The new forms come in the "concurrences" of *The Rome Air Naked* which remix his letters home using William Burroughs and Brion Gysin's famed cut-up method (famously used by Burroughs in his masterwork *The Naked Lunch*) reframed, literally, by Bill Gates's masterwork experienced by most Westerners on a daily basis from the mid-1990s. As Salom explains in his foreword to the collection:

> I had a new laptop computer ... I began by dropping one text (a poem) into the body of a letter [home] and applying text-wrap. It looked good and read strongly: the poem created a clear space for itself inside the enveloping prose of the letter and immediately suggested attractive cross-over readings. Anyone who uses a personal computer gets used to seeing several windows open at the same time while moving between files, documents, or cutting and pasting, etc. It alters the way we understand form. We are increasingly channel-changers and many of us are accustomed to rapid switching between different and often competing calls (demands?) on our attention. (*Rome* i)

Hypertext, multimedia, non-linear and simultaneous systems of reading all come into play in several "concurrences." Of these, "The Stone Operas" is the most Windows-like, with seven open "windows" across three pages. The second and third windows are especially noteworthy. The second is inset from another obscured window behind it. It reads "impossibility of fully describing a document or the intent of a request without ambiguity or needing to answer yet another question" (96). The third, below, is bordered only by space, suggestive of a physical or cognitive blindness, or, given its content, a splash or ripple: "the baby falls in / the pond higher in / moonlight / plop of the old frog." Behind these, an abstract letter babbles on as follows, rendered here with the window's lines in square brackets:

> The old world is heavy ... with witches from Macbeth, or Tasmania's blacks in nets of grieving ... The world's too small / too big: 20

million refugees [the baby falls in] the world hatched and won't take in at sea like travelling [the pond higher in] islands, their one compass shaking as a power-boat [moonlight] approaches, and like them runs no flag, but whose nation is [plop of the old frog] piracy and rape. Oh he is a pirate king not Christ upon the water. It's not the post-modern condition any more than abacus rattle like a reassuring sum, or computer mutter on each disk their tiny runes. Theory won't annul. [Oh Dear, what can the matter be? ...] (96)

Here, and in the final poem "Contraries and the Long Curving Back of Space-Time", the parallel typographic stagings of *The Well Mouth* are garishly prefigured. In an era when physical letters transmuted into emails, Salom's "concurrences" updated the Burroughs and Gysin's cut up method for the digital age and used Windows technology to open new non-linear collages of meaning. Salom was not the first Australian poet to experiment with writing programs or computer-based hypertext, nor was it his chief compositional method. Nonetheless, when the influence of digital culture on Australian poetry is ultimately documented, the post-Windows 95 release of these "concurrences" makes a strong case for Salom's inclusion as an 'early adopter' of information technology for the purposes of subject and form.

Between Mortal and Altered States: *The Well Mouth* to *Alterworld*

Salom's underwhelming critical reception owes something to confusion around his philosophical and religious underpinnings. He certainly respects religion as a spiritual practice, mindful of Christian mystics in Rome, Buddhism in Singapore, the Vedic epics and Sufism. To my mind, he usually practices a mystically-informed ecstatic humanism, but, like anyone, he can get distracted. In 1986, Les Murray included three early works, "Leonardo", "Day" and "The Execution of [the

Sufi] Hallaj" in *The Anthology of Australian Religious Poetry*. Eight years later, two pieces from Rome appeared in Dennis Haskell's *Tilting at Matilda: Literature, Aborigines, Women and the Church* and just one poem, "Inquiry of the Spirit Body" graces Kevin Hart's *The Oxford Anthology of Australian Religious Verse*. Yet anthologists' interest in Salom as a poet of religion and metaphysics has not translated into long-term critical interest, which languishes with the postmodern and the heteronyms Alan Fish and M.A. Carter. Perhaps when Salom tackles religious or metaphysical themes he covers too much to be safely aligned to any one school of thought, or faith. Regardless, some of his boldest theological statements can be found in states of "in-betweeness" in *The Well Mouth* and *Alterworld*.

By 2005, Australia had drastically changed. Interest in the postmodern was waning and cybernetically-enabled terrorism surged past the AIDS and the Millennium Bug as the next apocalyptic fear. Most Australians now carried a mobile phone with SMS, camera and internet capabilities. Changing tack himself, Salom turned to the local and the shockingly real through a hybrid of long poem and verse novel, with a play of voices undercut by a single lyrical 'I' at the foot of the page. Salom's adopted home of Melbourne is the location of this hybrid verse novel (Salom prefers "world of the newly dead") (*Philip Salom Poet and Novelist* par 6). Salom claims *The Well Mouth* originated from a combination of experiences of wells: first-hand as a dangerous no-go zone as a child in country WA, and second-hand from "recurrent stories of women (usually) who had gone missing, presumed murdered, and were dropped down wells or shafts" (par 4). He goes on to explain how *The Well Mouth* conceptually corresponds with *Sky Poems*:

> *The Well Mouth* began as a kind of answer to the desiring world of *Sky Poems* and then became darker and more of a Limbo. Desiring has ceased, and life does not progress so much as meditate upon itself ... The dead woman in the well, the [prophetic Greek] Tiresias figure, "hears" them for us. She is their medium, their cypher and

their sometimes commentator. Merged with their voices are the accounts of her own murder and those responsible for it. This aspect of the book is about criminals and corrupt police and the populist commercial ways media represent them.

It is a Dante-esque world, one of strangely poised levels of consciousness. It is lyrical yet dark, and grim but also oddly funny. It is also a world of mythical shifts through the shadows of Tiresias and Odysseus, parables of folly, narratives of want and fragments of phrasing, speaking, remembering. (pars 7-8)

There is also the shared imagery of sky (up through the well, "one disc / of light an optic fibre white angelic"), wells and fire, plus shared themes of limbo states and modern fame / notoriety and hope—to become "well", or better, by knowing, by finally having a chance to speak (*Alterworld* 88). *Sky Poems* ends with "Return from the Sky", where:

> The lift-well has grown
> a square and empty tower with cables for spine.
> A resuscitation machine is wheeling to a corner
> as the doctors shake their head. The lift light
> is approaching the bottom floor.
> Some celebrity
> appears in his penthouse, uppermost if not crust,
> wealthy as the modern gods are.
> The fire equipment
> reddens and waits. The city is back again, intact.
> And there—one thin trail of smoke above it
> like a line of ink.
> The whole city is suspended from it. (82-83)

What goes up must come down. And down, or half-way up again, ghosting each page of the newly departed. Finally, it is only thanks to the sudden nakedness of a *"burnt out treescape"* that *"one vehicle's / soft tyremarks pressing in continuous lines"*—another thin trail—finally approach and the woman's suspension may end, though she is far from intact (166). The suspension of others will continue, including among the living in the digital world of email or the offshore detention of asylum seekers, both prominent for the last doomed voice.

Death is the medium, but the truth is the motive: the truth more a stranger than death to the more ruined, corrupt or powerful. The untitled people and poems in *The Well Mouth* suggest a reality that is unproclaimed, unheadlined, but also, like some of the characters themselves, a law or voice unto themselves. This anonymity is shattered in the *Alterworld* section, living up to its name, in "By the Time They Found Adele". Here, the murdered transsexual prostitute Adele Bailey (1955–1978) is named as the voice of *The Well Mouth*. Her high-profile case, replete with allegations of police sexual impropriety, double-homicide murder and corruption, was the subject of a number of official inquiries, media reports and books in the decade prior to the publication of *The Well Mouth* after her skeleton was found down a mine shaft in February 1995 (Ambrose). Before Bailey disappeared in 1978, she wrote to her sister than she was having an affair with a policeman, Denis Tanner, and in 1984 Tanner's sister-in-law, also in the poem, was found by police to have "suicided":

> Yes, the cleverest ever of suiciders, who
> shot herself right through the palms of both
>
> hands, and who so amazingly outside herself
> shot herself twice in the head with a single-shot
> bolt-action rifle. Is she in the Guinness Book
>
> of the Dead? *Yes, yes*, the policemen said. (Salom 233)

Just under three months after Bailey's body was found in the Jack of Clubs Mine near Bonnie Doon in northern Victoria, the house Jennifer

Tanner died in was burnt to the ground. Since the publication of *The Well Mouth*, further evidence of a cover-up has come to light. Salom, however, prefers to leave the last word with Adele:

> Yeah I was belly-up before Underbelly, to be ID'd by what I was not. it takes imagination, my implants were the saddest eggs. but listen. like Tiresias small birds rise in my throat. this is what I see. everyone rises through the surface of the earth. (233)

But not absolutely everyone rises. In *Alterworld*, another Bailey appears, Adrian Ernest Bailey, who in 2012 infamously raped and murdered Jill Meagher a suburb away from Salom's home. In "At the Disused Drive-in Theatre", the mute projectionist Benchley switches scenes from a younger Salom watching Olivier's *Hamlet*, the tragedy of "a man who must murder", to a modified *Inferno* with

> The three-headed
> animal of Adrian Ernest Bailey (the lion the leopard the she-wolf)
> having been irrevocably introduced
> into the world of existing things.
> (240)

Bailey is bound upside down with the same ropes and chains he used, which lower him for near-drowning, a taste of both "gravity" and "mercy" for his eternal punishment. Intertextually, a great deal else is in play: Bailey's three heads being those of the three beasts which block Dante's path in Canto 1 (generally thought to symbolise lust, pride and avarice); Primo Levi's *The Drowned and the Saved* (Bailey is both) is cited to highlight the shame a just man feels at the seemingly unstoppable crimes of another. After Bailey come "killers and extortionists, the bent police, the QCs" and the "Dead eye politicians who punished and divided refugees and children ... split / in half to stare one-eyed, horrified upon their other half" (240-241). But even Pain and Hell are overwhelmed, *Inferno* "not a narrative / but a tense: all three at once" and the projector explodes on Benchley, burning him once again. The poet of past, present and future selves (and alter-selves) returns to the abandoned drive-in with Dantean stars on his face.

Even some individual poems in *Alterworld* operate in threes (and threes within threes). The collection deserves a comprehensive study of its poetic architecture, including how *Sky Poems* and *The Well Mouth* themselves have been altered and rearranged. Graeme Miles' *Cordite* review makes some initial observations, for example the shifting of one *Sky Poems* character closer to the front, possibly to emphasise his 'alter' poem, "Smithy Again Again" (par 3). Certain character types recur as well, such as the lone rogue criminal or their reanimated victims such as the "one done in" by Perth's first official serial killer Eric Edgar Cooke in "Through the Open Sky Window" (Salom 47). What else has been (re)connected or rearranged in *Alterworld*? Salom himself should not have to be entirely trusted here, subject as he is to his Shakespearean—yep, Shakespearean—propensity to integrate tragedy and comedy, corporeal and metaphysical, eccentric gravitas and well-founded farce. How else could one who has plumbed the darkness of twenty-first century true crime describe his own (semi-) Divine Comedy across the three volumes of *Alterworld* thus: "Despite their age differences—1987, 2005, 2015—they are in a relationship. A metaphysical ménage à trois." (*Philip Salom Poet and Novelist* par 8). Facebook parodies aside, does this indicate that *The Well Mouth* should be considered as metaphysical true crime? Whatever Dantean heights are reached, there also stark lyric mysteries, cosmic reciprocities to be found in the shadow of the most earthly cruelty and injustice:

> *three kilometres from here it has*
> *been raining: the water is rising*
> *from below. ocean swell Hildegard's*
> *migraine of God strobing up-brain*
> *tunnel and birthing the down-up Id*
> *death's other language, other poem.*

a poem full of irony: the doubleness
of life / death. a presence where is isn't.
a poem is becoming pauses inside story.

poems written alive with the eyes closed
by poets fearful alert because they know
well a poem is death with its eyes open. (*Alterworld* 141)

"the doubleness of life / death, a presence where is isn't", "a poem is becoming pauses inside story"—philosophers and theologians could happily lose themselves in such lyrics of metaphysical splendour, even treasure. Water, birth, God, death, language and the craft of poetry are all implicated philosophically but also conjoined with the corporeal tragedy of the murder victim who will never return to physical life. Twelfth-century German mystic Hildegard of Bingen, popularised in late twentieth century translations, is also implicated in this passage, especially so when her credentials as a poet and composer are taken into account. "Where is isn't" is also beautifully suggestive of Christian modes of the *via negativa* and negative theology, as well as Zen. While reviewers and critics were busily chasing the postmodern Salom, too many, it seems, lost sight of the medieval.

As we have seen, the 'contemporary' is its own ghost from the outset, so feeding it time makes a great deal of sense, and Salom has been thus sensible across the three and a half decades. Perhaps it is simply his wit and versatility which scares academia off, or could it be the erudition? "Epigrams for Performers in the Sky" gestures towards the future with a seamless amalgam of the computer age, metaphysics and the creative impulse:

> The sky is a computer. You had one text
> when you came and used it. Now you have
> infinite editing, a virtuoso set of nerves.
> Go loose among your incarnations. (33)

Questions of what is real, or ghostly, free or cruel, dance around these central lines. And so the contemporary might here be cut loose among the poet's and his readers' incarnations back as well as forward, down as well as up, exiled from the supercilious as well as the mundane. Salom reflects in "Writing through Heteronyms: How the Mask Reveals" (2014) that "Knowing through poetry is why I am a poet" (par 29). His beguiled and brilliant future readers, who may see their youth in his cutting-edge subject matter, are called to loosely or knowingly respond.

Works Cited

Ambrose, Teresa. "Copper in Trouble." *The Age*, 24 February 2003. 2017. https://www.theage.com.au/national/copper-in-trouble-20030225-gdva4i.html

Aitken, Adam, Kim Cheng Boey and Michelle Cahill, editors. *Contemporary Asian Australian Poets*, Puncher & Wattmann, 2013.

Brown, Lachlan. "The Beautiful Pixels: Computer Games and Two Contemporary Australian Poems." *Axon: Creative Explorations*, vol. 5, no. 2, 2015. Accessed 5 February 2017.

Davidson, Toby. "Double Dragon." *Beast Language*. Parkville, Five Islands Press, 2012, pp. 67-68.

Etherington, Ben. "The Poet Tasters." *Sydney Review of Books*. 30 January 2015. https://sydneyreviewofbooks.com/australian-poetry-reviewing/

Jenkins, John. "Provincial to Post-Modernism: The Poetry of Philip Salom" *Heat*, vol. 3, 2002, pp. 219-230.

Haskell, Dennis. "Poetry Since 1965," *The Oxford Literary History of Australia*, edited by Bruce Bennett and Jennifer Strauss, Oxford University Press, 1998, pp. 265-285.

Haskell, Dennis and Hilary Fraser. "Philip Salom." *Wordhord: Contemporary Western Australian Poetry*, edited by Dennis Haskell and Hilary Fraser, Fremantle Arts Centre Press, 1989, pp. 152-154.

Kinsella, John and Tracy Ryan, editors. *The Fremantle Press Anthology of*

Western Australian Poetry, Fremantle Press, 2017.

McCarthy, Bridie. "Identity as Radical Alterity: Critiques of Eurocentrism, Coloniality, and Subjectivity in Contemporary Australian and Latin American Poetry." *Antipodes*, vol. 24, no. 2, 2010, pp. 189-197.

Miles, Graeme. "Philip Salom's *Alterword* (Review)." *Cordite Poetry Review*, 17 December 2015.

McCooey, David. "Two Developments in Contemporary Australian Poetry." *Five Bells*, vol. 15, no.4, 2008, pp.131-141.

Murray, Les. *Blocks and Tackles: Articles and Essays 1982 to 1990*, Angus & Robertson, 1990.

Musgrave, David. "Poetry as Knowing: Philip Salom's *Keepers Trilogy*." *Axon: Creative Explorations*, vol. 4, no.1, 2014. http://www.axonjournal.com.au/issue-6/poetry-knowing

Owen, Jan. "Pomegranates, Persimmons and Pasolini." *Meanjin*, vol. 52, no.3, 1993, pp. 573-581.

Page, Geoff, editor. *A Reader's Guide to Contemporary Australian Poetry*, University of Queensland Press, 1995.

Petersen, Kirsten Holst and Anna Rutherford. "Sojourn in the Sky: Conventions of Exile in Philip Salom's *Sky Poems*." *Westerly*, vol. 33, no. 2, 1988, pp. 67-74.

Ryan, Gig. "Enterprise Requiring Shape and Subtlety." *The Age*, 22 August 1998, p.10.

Salom, Philip. *Alterworld: Sky Poems, The Well Mouth, Alterworld*, Puncher & Wattmann, 2015.

---. *Barbecue of the Primitives*, University of Queensland Press, 1989.

---. *Between Yes and No*, translated by Chris Song Zijiang and Iris Fan Xing, Flying Island Books, 2014.

---. *Feeding the Ghost*, Penguin, 1993.

---. and Jaydeep Sarangi. "Jaydeep Sarangi in Conversation with Philip Salom." *Mascara Literary Review*, vol. 14, 2013. http://mascarareview.com/jaydeep-sarangi-in-conversation-with-philip-salom/

---. and Barbara Williams. "Interview with Philip Salom." *Westerly*, vol. 33, no.4, 1988, pp.59-65.

---. "Metaphysical Selfie." *Eureka Street,* vol. 24, no.5, 2014, pp.18-23.
---. *Alterworld (Philip Salom Poet and Novelist),* 2001. http://www.philipsalom.com/
---. *The Projectionist,* Fremantle Arts Centre Press, 1983.
---. *The Rome Air Naked,* Penguin, 1996.
---. *The Silent Piano,* Fremantle Arts Centre Press, 1980.
---. "Writing Through Heteronyms: How the Mask Reveals." *Axon: Creative Explorations,* vol. 4, no.1, 2014.

Chapter 5

Sentimental Educations: The Poetry of David Malouf

MARTIN DUWELL

David Malouf's poetry, marvellous as it is, is only one, comparatively small, part of a literary output noted for the variety of his modes. It is difficult to name many other writers working in poetry, the novel, the short story, the memoir, the review, the play, the critical essay and even libretti. It's tempting to say that, as in Malouf's imaginative universe, the boundaries between these modes are more porous than usual. In fact it is not a matter of Malouf mastering and excelling in different modes, but rather one of his transforming the latent possibilities of existing modes in order to make them play a part in the unfolding and expansions of this universe. Nicholas Jose has made a similar point recently adding the comment that Malouf's transformations of modes might be seen as deliberately playing against them:

> He has written in most genres: poems, novels, short stories, essays, memoir, a play, libretti and all kinds of invited occasional prose. *Out of* most genres, I want to say, rather than in them, since so many of these works play against their category and resist pigeonholing. The essays move in and out of memoir; the stories and novels have meditative paragraphs and the logic of poetry; prose appears with poems that are both imagistic and discursive; criticism reaches to other art forms, and to cultural analysis; the libretti turn classic fiction into words for contemporary music. In this environment, unity becomes less a matter of form than

conceptual and self-defining, with a passing nod over the shoulder to tradition. (2)

Rich as this world is, it poses a lot of new problems for critical readers since the poems (or, for that matter, the novels and short stories) cannot be read as a group: they have too many tentacles extending deep into the other modes. And this of course requires that critics be at least partly polytechnic, as their subject so impressively is: poetry critics need to look into the strange world of narrative and, equally, critics of fiction need to become far more comfortable with lyric poetry than most of them are. At any rate, trying to describe Malouf's poetry involves deciding which thread to pull in an immensely complex thematic web.

My own, tentatively chosen, point of entry is to focus on the idea of the education of the poet's inner life by enormously complex and often surprising techniques. Instead of growing merely concerned with itself, this is a self which is required to abandon any comfortable self-conception in the presence of all the othernesses that hover around it, both inviting it into their world and simultaneously asking it to accept them. At heart – and with these reservations – it is an autobiographical approach and thus might begin with the author's own description of the broad shape of his life in the Author's Note to his third selected poems, the 2008 volume, *Revolving Days*, which replaces an ordering based on time of writing or publication with one organised by the period of the events which a particular poem eventually derives from:

> Part I deals with childhood and youth in Brisbane and its surroundings in and after the Second World War, Part II the 1960s, when I was teaching in the north of England and travelling in Europe, Part III the decade after, when I moved to Sydney. The poems in Part IV record the years since then, which until recently I spent moving back and forth between Sydney and a village in Southern Tuscany.

A good place to begin is with some fairly representative early poems. "At My Grandmother's" from "Interiors", Malouf's section of the 1962 collection, *Four Poets*, taps into two threads of the Malouf world: ancestors and interiors:

> An afternoon late summer, in a room
> shuttered against the bright envenomed leaves:
> an underwater world, where time like water
> was held in the wide arms of a gilded clock
> and my grandmother, turning in the still Sargasso
> of memory, wound out her griefs and held
> a small boy prisoner to weeds and corals
> while summer leaked its daylight through his head.
>
> I feared that room: the parrot screeching soundless
> in its dome of glass, the faded butterflies
> like jewels pinned against a sable cloak;
> and my grandmother winding out the skeins I held
> like trickling time between my outstretched arms.
>
> Feared most of all the stiff bejewelled fingers
> pinned at her throat or moving on grey wings
> from word to word; and feared her voice that called
> down from their gilded frames the ghosts of children
> who played at hoop and ball, whose spindrift faces
> (the drowned might wear such smiles) looked out across
> the wrack and debris of the years to where
> a small boy sat, as they once sat, and held
> in the wide ache of his arms all time like water,
> and watched the old grey hands wind out his blood.
> (*Poems 1959-89* 3)

This is one of the few Malouf poems which, while clearly being part of the Malouf poetic corpus, connect with Australian poetry of its recent past. An old person in a room where time is frozen makes one think of what is almost an Australian mini-genre of time-obsessed poems (it would include Judith Wright's "Brother and Sisters" and Tom Shapcott's "Elegy for a Bachelor Uncle"). It is a poem which, dealing with a frozen site, avoids any sense of process. And this is not in a celebratory way, as it is in Slessor's "Nuremberg", but in a sinister way. A reader at the time of its first publication might have focussed on these contextual elements or read it as a poem in which a boy's ancestry, his genetic history, constricts rather than enriches his life. The grandmother, instead of being a figure of familial comfort, appears as one of the Fates or one of the Norns, winding out the thread of her visitor's life as well as having the power, medium-like, to invoke and bring to life the previous children. At the same time, and as the section title, "Interiors", suggests, one might have read the poem as being concerned with what is inside the memory and suggesting, almost by an oppositional attraction, the idea of exteriors and, from that, the notion of crossing the boundary between interior and exterior. As the poem, "Sheer Edge", from the same collection suggests, that border is where poetry might blossom. But looking backwards, as it were, from the perspective of the full corpus of Malouf's poems, one might want to focus on the children in the photographs: they are not passive icons of genetic history but characters who look out towards the boy. They and the boy are, in the language of a later poem, "horizons / of each other's consciousness", creatures entering a present reality and thus crossing a border, as so many of the people, angels, objects and animals of Malouf's poetry do.

"Snow" and "Bicycle" from Malouf's first full-length collection published eight years later in 1970 speak to interiors which are breached by an outside agency. On the surface, and at the time, "Snow" seemed no more than a school teacher's anecdote about the way an impending change of the weather is sensed by a class of students who then become unable to concentrate. One might have aligned it with another school-teaching poem from the same book,

"At a School Athletics Day". But the crucial difference is that though this second poem remains self-contained enough to be a good anthology piece suited to study by students who know little of the complex web behind Malouf's poetry, the same cannot be said of "Snow":

> A stirring as among
> cattle that lift their heads
> through darkness to the scent
> of water, horses snuffing
>
> at thunder in the grass;
> and nothing today will keep them
> quiet or still
> in the pinewood desks, or summon
>
> their eyes to reflect
> figures and cold facts
> from the blackboard ...

This response to the arrival of something as miraculous as snow is generated at a level far below consciousness and the reference to horses and cattle suggests that Malouf sees it as an instinctive reaction, an 'animal' response, though later poems will have a lot to say about Malouf's idea of what the animal component of the human is. At any rate, the arrival has the capacity not only to arouse a dormant sense of wonder but to effect a kind of expansion of the schoolboys' consciousnesses as "something moves// towards them":

> an excitement whose crystals
> fall through their veins, the open
> spaces of the skull,
> wavering towards them

(animal eyes, the nostrils
flared) like the feathers
of angels, sky-flakes,
blessing the dull cobbles

and slant black roofs, bare playground,
pond. On their hands the taste
of stars, their foreign coldness,
colour of distances,

and all that is further off,
than flesh ... (*Poems 1959-89* 49-50)

"Snow" is placed near the end of *Bicycle* and the poem that follows it is called "Summer". Whereas "Snow" is set during Malouf's early teaching career in the north of England, "Summer" is set (surely) on Deception Bay north of Brisbane, a bay whose name is rich in possible interpretations. But "Summer", like "Snow", celebrates an expansion of consciousness, though this time the agency is erotic love. The impetus for the placing of these poems together looks, initially, like one of conscious contrast but I am inclined to think that the point is that there are many triggers that can lead to the widening of experience. As I'll show later, one of the most important features of Malouf's conceptual world is the understanding that the widening of consciousness is not simply a matter of accreting new experiences as though life was a long Grand Tour leading to greater intellectual, erotic and cultural sophistication. In the Maloufian world a door which is opened onto a new world of experience can be crossed in the other direction and "Bicycle" the book's title poem and second last is, at least partly, about finding that a door you have left open has been exploited by a creature from another world. As with "Snow" it is the imagery in which the visitation is cast that gives a sense of its complexity and significance. The poem's subject is one of the most homely of domestic objects, a bicycle, stored in the living room of a flat. The descriptive language, while couched in a deliberately bathetic, mock-heroic tone, still evokes the significance of the visitor:

> Since Thursday last, the bare living-room
> of my flat's been occupied
> by a stranger from the streets, a light-limbed traveller:
>
> pine-needle spokes, bright rims, the savage downward
> curve (like polished horns)
> of its handlebars, denote
>
> some forest deity, or deity of highway
> and sky, has incognito set up residence – the godhead
> invoked in a machine ...

Only the mirror, the poem says, remains unruffled by this visitor, presumably because a mirror in an interior is the opposite of a door: it shows the self as it is rather than leading to experiences which will make a new self. As the poem goes on to inflate the significance of the bicycle more and more, the comic tone drops away in favour of an ecstatic vision of the future sending its messages through all kinds of doors:

> Now time yawns and its messengers appear:
> like huge stick-insects, wingless, spoked with stars,
> they wheel through the dusk towards us,
>
> the shock-wave of collision still lifting
> their locks, who bear our future
> sealed at their lips like urgent telegrams (*Poems 1959-89* 59-60).

This sense of arrival from different realities, different times and different perspectives through doorways and walls that are more porous than is usually assumed is perhaps the keynote of Malouf's poetry which, according to the different poetic mode he uses, can be explored, exploited, assumed or, delicately, urged on the reader. But whatever the implications in the social, intellectual or artistic domains of experience, it requires an education of the poet's self. To my mind, one of Malouf's finest poetic achievements (also one of his most challenging) is a group of poems which appeared first in his *Selected Poems* of 1981. Titled "A Little Panopticon" it is prefaced by an explanation of the term as a name for a circular prison in which inmates could be observed all the time but also, figuratively, as "a place where everything is visible; a show room for novelties." Each of the eighteen poems takes its title from an important work of European or Levantine civilisation. I'll have more to say about this sequence later but, for the moment I want to look at one of the poems, "L'Education Sentimentale", which doesn't survive the culling of the two later Selected Poems, that of 1991 and *Revolving Days* of 2008.

All of the "Little Panopticon" poems have complex relations with their titles: some treat them as launching pads, others, like "The Interpretation of Dreams" or "A Critique of Pure Reason", seem to tag a title, usually with some kind of ironic significance, onto a self-contained poem and others, like "A Commentary on Galatians", are a kind of ironic rewriting. "L'Education Sentimentale" takes its title from Flaubert's novel and thus invokes the idea of a complete education involving amatory, spiritual, social and intellectual development: a kind of educational 'finishing.' The first half of the poem seems to me as good a summary as could be given of the essential interests that underlie the poetry of Malouf up to that point:

> Set off at any hour, from behind
> an inkwell, an open
> keyboard or from fingertips just touching, the electric
> phosphorescent sweat of two planets
> afloat among leaves. The embarkation
> sometimes for Kythera, at other times for Holy Russia,

a house of frozen saints, the Himalayas,
or anywhere away from
this heat, *les tristes tropiques*. Among night-fishers the octopus
climbs a flashlight beam. Waving its arms, dumb ecstatic,
it flops into our boat and the Pacific's
displaced a little, diminished towards Peru,
as the knifeblades get to work. Noble savages
also to be had
for pennies against a wall off Stanley Street. Embark
here for les Indes Galantes, wading out
off Broadbeach. Over the continental shelf another world
begins, not all's discovered or settled yet. An evangel
with eight arms brings news
of the underside of rocks, the further shore of consciousness
is fog in blacked-out winter capitals … (*Selected Poems* 97)

The opening lines, in my reading at least, categorise four agents of the expansion of consciousness: writing (probably poetry), music, meditation (in the intellectual sense, "fingertips just touching") and erotic love ("the electric / phosphorescent sweat of two planets / afloat among leaves"). Similarly it categorises the possible directions of expansion. The first is to Kythera, birthplace of Venus and, in Western art, an imagined world of gratification which, if not solely sexual, is at least sensual. The second is the frozen world of spiritual exploration – "Holy Russia, / a house of frozen saints" and a third, the Himalayas is, possibly, a site of expansion in the bodily sense of muscular mountain-climbing. The poem is 'set' at Broadbeach on the Gold Coast, though the very point of the poem is that this physical location can quickly dissolve as consciousness moves outwards or opens to allow the alien to enter and it is probably likely that Malouf wants us to rethink what is a bland name to all Australians – the 'Gold Coast' – in the light of the dozens of other coasts (blue coasts, ivory coasts, slave coasts) which the expansionary phase of European exploration foisted on the world. A captured octopus, not unlike the bicycle of the earlier poem, becomes an angelic messenger of another world in a way that looks forward to "The Crab Feast."

Of the agents of expansion, the erotic occupies a large space in Malouf's poems though he is rarely written about as a poet of what, in "Decade's End" from *Neighbours in a Thicket* is called the "love / that wrings us dry" (*Poems 1959-89*, 83). It is usually dealt with soberly, sensitively and discreetly: we are not in a world of poetic ecstasy. We could begin with a number of poems from *Bicycle* such as "Stars", "Easier", "Poem" and "Summer." If we omit the final poem of *Bicycle*, "Sheer Edge," which is a sort of envoi, then the opening and closing of the book have what looks like a deliberate mirror structure. The last poem, "Bicycle", which I have already looked at, balances the well-known "The Year of the Foxes" both dealing with equivocal and surprising intruders, and "Stars" parallels "Summer". In the former poem (which could be read as an answer to Slessor's poem about the existential terror of the emptiness of the universe) space is something that can be bridged by the simple act of reaching out and touching:

> a planet's dust, metallic,
>
> alive, is sifted down –
> hovers in a bright
> arc upon your cheek.
>
> Miraculous! I lean
> across the dark and touch it,
> you smile in your sleep ...
>
> How far, how far we've come
> together, tumbling like stars
> in harness or alone (*Poems 1959-89* 19.)

The latter poem, "Summer", is specific about the way love demolishes boundaries ("No walls: air moving free in open windows") and uses the metaphor of an exchange of absorbed and stored heat: "Our bodies hoard their summer – / at night, in each other's arms, we touch the sun ..." We could track such poems through, for example, "The Gift – Another Life" from *Neighbours in a Thicket* which includes the lines:

> I drowse between pencil-pines, the stars
> rise through me as in sleep I climb
> from the warmth of other arms to meet
>   myself – horizons stream
> away all fences down all frontiers
> open, I am free to cross
> five oceans even ... (*Poems 1959-89*, 123)

and "Inspirations" from *Poems 1975-76*, the first of Malouf's movements into poem sequences that foreshadow not only "A Little Panopticon" but also the poems of *First Things Last* and which is a rhapsodic celebration of love and introduces the important Maloufian theme of breath. And finally through to the rather more wry, short love poems that appear in *Typewriter Music* and *Earth Hour*. Again the positioning seems significant. *Typewriter Music* opens with "Revolving Days" which recalls an old love affair but speaks to the former partner as though the time of their separation had collapsed:

> We never write. But sometimes, knotting my tie
> at a mirror, one of those selves I had expected
> steps into the room. In the next room you
> are waiting (we have not yet taken back
> the life we promised to pour into each other's mouths
> forever and forever)
>
> ...

> I'm writing this for you, wherever
> you are, whoever is staring into your blue eyes. It is me,
> I'm still here. No, don't worry, I won't appear out of
> that old time to discomfort you. And no, at this
> distance, I'm not holding my breath for a reply. (1)

The final sentence is significant because, as "Inspirations" says, one of the many life-giving functions of breath is to summon up the loved one. *Typewriter Music* concludes with the punningly titled "Afterword" where, after a busy social day surrounded by "the loud/ lives, some of them those/ of loved ones or ones/ nearly loved" the poet finds a "you" who is "embodied silence". One of the first poems of *Earth Hour*, "Retrospect", collapses time in a way that recalls "Revolving Days" so that a fellow traveller outside Sèvres many years ago is met in a dream now looking like one "already gone/ too far into the forest" and gives not a message but warning "No, your glance// in the old conspiratorial way insisted,/ Don't speak, don't recognise me." And *Earth Hour* concludes with "Lerici" dedicated to Carlo Olivieri, which is, if not an overt love poem, a love poem nevertheless according to James Tulip (8) and which might well parallel "Afterword" as two people watch ships at anchor "after long/ journeying arrived at the high tide/ of silence, after talk."

But, as I have said, the erotic is only one of the agents of expansion when it comes to enriching the inner life. Another of them is music, the "holde Kunst". We can track the powers of music as far back as the fourth poem of *Bicycle*, "Keeping Time", where the author as a child is practising a Bach Prelude in a convent, a particularly unpleasant interior where "Heaven begins / with jagged bottle-glass". Although the poem ostensibly is about time and thus, like "At My Grandmother's", ties in with the themes of the poetry of an earlier generation, it also looks ahead to the way music appears in later Malouf poems as one of the gateways to experience. The mechanism involves the interaction of music with creative inattention, the kind of thing Malouf celebrates in "Inspirations" when he says:

"Not listening was a way of overhearing / smaller further voices". In "Keeping Time" the door opens only onto a greener and more fertile world left fairly vaguely defined. But in a later poem, "An Die Musik", from *First Things Last*, this green world is described as an Eden, a world we have always known and which we share with the plant world. The title of the poem is the title of Schubert's song and, in this sense, the poem seems to belong with the "Little Panopticon" sequence and this context helps a reader to deal with a poem whose tone is probably more comical and bathetic since that is the common relationship between title and body in those poems. In "An Die Musik" when we might have expected the slightly rhapsodic tone of Malouf's moments of entrance and expansion, we get a description of vegetables responding to musical works: beans growing to Vivaldi, pumpkins swelling to Strauss and zucchinis responding to Bruckner. But, despite this comical vision, the place of music is clearly defined in the poem as something we have always known, the:

> landscape we move through in our dreams, and in the Garden
> it was music we shared
> with the beasts. Even plants
> unbend, are enchanted. A voice wading
> *adagio* through air, high, clear, wordless, opens perspectives
> in the deepest silence; clovers
> hum; the jungle's layered
> sound-mix seeks horizons, arranging itself as avenues ...
> (*Poems 1959-1989*, 197)

But, as so often in Malouf, something that connects us to other, smaller lives can also connect us with the cosmos. The poem preceding "An Die Musik" is a longish prose piece (also with an ironically inappropriate title), "A Poor Man's Guide to Tuscany". Here a series of doors are imagined to open into other vistas and all involve art. A print of the Douanier Rousseau's "Joyeux Farceurs", for example, becomes an entrance not into the expected world of rain-forest but into another time and another place, a polar waste more like "The Sea of Ice" of Caspar David Friedrich. At the end the focus moves to music and the way in which the point of a gramophone needle can be an almost infinitely small entrance to "hours of unbroken sound." The chosen music is Joan Sutherland's singing of the mad scene from Donizetti's *Lucia di Lammermoor* or, rather, the famous E-flat with which it concludes:

> We are breathing, for as long as the note lasts, eternal E-flat weather, the atmosphere of another planet, whose note, as the planet spins, is always this one; so that we have to be grateful to Donizetti, to Lucia, to Sutherland, for so gracefully, so swiftly transporting us there, since it is not given to all of us to leap thus from planet to planet and that particular sphere is out of reach of all but the rarest of us – though to be able to reach it at all is, when one of our species makes the miraculous scoop and lands there, an achievement that brings glory to us all, even if we can only come to it, rather clumsily, via the ear, while our breath goes on being the air of our home planet, earth, this stretch of it, this August afternoon (*Poems 1959-89*, 195-6).

The previous poem, "Ode One", identifies opera as perhaps the central musical art:

> Our bodies meet in another kind of order
> than stroking knows or claws. Change is the dress
> we wear before the gods. How else should they
> perceive us as we are? who look smilingly
> on fingernail and city, rose, hawk, eyelid – opera
> (*First Things Last*, 43).

And the issue of this art is taken up in a prose-poem which is an imaginary letter from Mozart to his great librettist, da Ponte, in *Typewriter Music*, as well as in an important essay on opera included in his collection, *Being There*. It repeats the idea of music as being an edenic, prelapsarian language – "Music is the language of that state of grace we fell from and from which we never entirely fall" – and contrasts it with words which are an essentially sociable medium – "They form unions, found cities, make contracts in which responsibilities are established and dues paid, or they break them and start wars." But, as I have said, to touch one strand of Malouf's work is make others vibrate and in both the essay and "Mozart to da Ponte" there is a binary quite different from words and music and that is the opposition between the European North and its Mediterranean South. We are in the world of Auden's great poem, "Goodbye to the Mezzogiorno" which speaks of the inhabitants of the "potato, beer-or-whiskey / Guilt culture" who come, like their ancestors, "into a sunburnt otherwhere // of vineyards, baroque, *la bella figura*." Malouf has written of the added complexity of an Australian travelling north to enter the South and coming from a country where the values of the south are already familiar. Auden's distinction between those to whom to live is to be part of a continuing developing *bildungsroman* and those in the South for whom "living / Means to-be-visible-now" might be said to be dissolved in Malouf's work where presence is as important a component as development. When Auden says that Northerners such as himself travel to the South "hoping to twig from / What we are not what we might be next" you feel that this is a form of education of the self by the confrontation with opposites. Malouf, I think, would argue that the self develops by spinning out from within and that the opposites are always already contained within it. An earlier poem, "The Little Aeneid" (another title which connects to a classic text) details Malouf's journey north to Italy in mock-heroic style, casting himself as a minor Aeneas abandoning Troy/Brisbane for a new beginning:

> the apron
> strings of a suburban
> Dido snap, the new life

> beckons – a coast whose every promontory
> glitters with artefacts, plains
> all air, by moonlight ghostly
> with stick-white asphodel.
> In your loins the dragon seed
> howls for empire. Time
> like a new land awaits
> your entry. Give it
> a name. Three syllables: say, Italy (*Poems 1959-89*, 89-90).

This brief look at love and music in Malouf's poetry began as a gloss on the third line of a single poem, "L'Education Sentimentale" and might well expand out to the dimensions of a medieval sermon. I should say something about the end of that poem before abandoning it entirely:

> In the distance that is sleep your shadow falls there. Go out
> and seek it in piazzas, under bridges,
> in canals. Arriving late
> at a sad enlightenment, step ashore
> on the Cote d'Azur among flotsam café tables. A continent
> awaits its massacres,
> its fences, oil-rigs, prints of the invader,
> its laws. A century later, European trees will guide you
> back, their pale leaves falling
> in groves that teach the heart another sadness
> than the New World breathes. We raise, among evergreens, huge
>   sky-blocks listed
> already for destruction –
> nostalgic for moonlit futures and their ruins (*Selected Poems*, 97-8).

The dominant description here is of European expansion during the Enlightenment of the eighteenth century and during the nineteenth. But I think the real subject is the education of the self and that this imperial history is a metaphor for what will happen to the self. Its education, it seems to be saying, cannot be a process of continual acquisition of experience in the way an empire begins by acquiring overseas possessions. As with the history of empires – uprisings, massacres, and, eventually, a nostalgia for the collapse of the markers of the imperial project – so with the self. It isn't always an entirely safe and comfortable journey.

As the self expands so should the art. It is quite remarkable how different each of Malouf's books of poetry are. The fairly neat, self-contained poems of "Interiors" and *Bicycle*, which are familiar in form if not in content to anyone who was reading Australian poetry at the time of their publication give way in *Neighbours in a Thicket* to poems of very long lines and often intricate syntax. *First Things Last* seems like a deliberate assault on poetic convention or, perhaps more accurately, represents a desire to press against the possibilities of a poem in the same way in which the education of the self presses against limitations as it looks for doorways to other dimensions. There are two odes and a long prose poem all of which experiment with a long-breathed syntax. There are also a number of sequences which enable the poetry to increase the intensity of its meditation by looking at the topic from different angles and which also enable the poetry to begin to adopt narrative possibilities. This latter point is especially true of the difficult title poem which, according to James Tulip, presents:

> an operation in a hospital, tangentially. The patient loses awareness under anaesthesia, and then gradually regains consciousness. The process is observed or imagined as a metaphor of the mind's structure and of the mind's way of re-achieving knowledge and sense of values. (6)

The final poem is genuinely bizarre and challenging. In fact it sounds as though Malouf were writing in the style of Australia's premier surrealist poet, Philip Hammial:

Laying the small bones out
in rows for the moon
to suck. We call this *Living
from One Day to the Next.*

To lie tightly wrapped in butcher's
paper and bleed
events: you all know this one:
it's *Learning from History.*

You mount a bicycle
without wheels. What falls away
as you pedal uphill?
The Joys of the Flesh

The styles are as many as
the players. Strict rules
apply but can be broken.
Nobody wins (*Poems 1959-89* 179).

These stanzas, among other things, perhaps give a clue as to how the titles of "A Little Panopticon" should be read. A poem is written and then, with tongue in cheek, Malouf chooses a book title for it: call this "A Guide to the Perplexed" or "Theologia Germanica". Tulip goes on to say of these stanzas, surely with some authorial assistance:

> Malouf takes simple images from dreams or newspapers and juxtaposes them against giant clichés or proverbs. It is implied that this is the way society stumbles on its values ... The cryptic point made in the final verse (above) is for Malouf a serious statement. Styles, players and rules are for real, yet relative and provisional. (6)

The most celebrated of the *First Things Last* poems is probably "The Crab Feast", a ten part sequence which, according to Malouf, is "an attempt to deal with activities utterly of this world, like eating and sex, and see them as sacred" (Baker 235). The sequence form allows for multiple perspectives on the intimate relationship between crab and eater, and no single poem is required to be a totality. One can see the attraction of this for Malouf since it presents possibilities not really available to the kind of lyric poetry he has been writing and will go on to write. But, rather like Dr Johnson facing "Lycidas", I've never thought "The Crab Feast" to be a success: for me it remains an interesting experiment but its hectic dramatized mode does not, it seems to me, add greatly to the possibilities of the lyric.

In fact the same could be said for most of *First Things Last*. Although these pushings into new forms are important and a matter of virtuous risk-taking, I think it is Malouf's least successful book. As evidence for this is the fact that none of the experiments has lasted beyond that book. In the succeeding ones, *Typewriter Music* and *Earth Hour*, almost all of the poems are complexly structured and rather beautiful little lyrics. Though each may deal with only a small part of the complex conceptual web behind Malouf's poetry and be forced to avoid narrative development and multi-perspective viewing, they have enough intrinsic dynamics to be satisfying. "Mozart to da Ponte" is one exception though – it seems to belong to the world of *Poems 1975-76* and *First Things Last* – and so is "Seven Last Words of the Emperor Hadrian". This is made up of seven translations of the Hadrian's little poem, reputedly made just before his death, "Animula vagula blandula" and the title is a little joke in itself referring to Hayden's string quartet, "The Seven Last Words of Our Saviour on the Cross" but meaning here not the seven last words but seven versions of the emperor's last words. There is a progression in this sequence though it is not a narrative progression. Instead the versions get progressively freer: the first version begins "Dear soul mate, little guest / and companion ..." and the seventh with "So you're playing fast / and loose, are you? You've cut / the love knot..."

One can always find 'translations' in any collection of Malouf's shorter, more lyrical, poems. These begin with a set of five odes of Horace in *Bicycle* and continue through to versions of Rimbaud, Baudelaire and Heine. Poets translating poets is always theoretically complicated territory and this is increased when the translating poet is one obsessed with seeing the boundaries between selves and languages as being more porous than is conventionally thought. Malouf's translations are versions which find not only equivalents for the words of the original but also for the situation of the original so that the opening of "Horace I, xxxi" ("What is the poet's request to Apollo? What does he pray for as he pours out the wine from the bowl? Not for the rich harvests of fertile Sardinia nor the delightful herds of sunlit Calabria, not for India's gold or its ivory...") becomes:

> What gift should a poet ask for
> when the gods are in their giving
> vein? a million greenbacks
> droved in the Gulf country?
>
> oil gushers? a win on Tatts?
> a blonde dreamboat, or real
> estate in the heart of Surfers',
> our gilt-edged Paradise? (*Poems 1959-89* 53)

This is not a case of simply finding contemporary equivalents of situations, though, like an unimaginative updating of a classic play or opera. It is more about creating a version of the poet's voice – and the personality it expresses – which is different to the ever-so-slightly sober and serious (even when ecstatic) that we sense in Malouf's poetry. It doesn't copy the voice of Horace but, by imagining him dragged into the twentieth century, creates a figure which is neither Horace nor Malouf but which Malouf could possibly have been in another universe, or another part of this universe. In other words it allows Malouf to speak in a version of himself – breezier, more vulgar, more attune to contemporary trivia – than the one he habitually inhabits. As one might expect in a world where doors operate in both directions the translated poet is as free to enter our world as the translator is to enter the poet's.

The most recent of Malouf's books of poetry, *Typewriter Music* and *Earth Hour*, are, as I have said, a long way from the experiments of *First Things Last*. It may even be significant that there is a gap of twenty-seven years between *Typewriter Music* and its predecessor. In these books we meet a distinctly Maloufian lyricism that isn't really present in any of the earlier books. The temptation to see something of a waning of powers, an inability to sustain the long-breathed syntax of earlier poems, for example, because of encroaching old age, seems to me exactly wrong. These two books, it could be argued, contain Malouf's best poetry. He seems to have evolved a lyric style marked by a kind of playfulness that is not a result of the ironic detachment of the senior citizen but rather of a way of deploying surprises that both mimic what the verse is speaking of and, at the same time, animate the structure of the verse. It is true that there are examples, in these books, of sequences which approach a topic from many angles – "An Essay on Angels – the Short Version" is one of them – but other sequences, such as "Into the Blue" or "A Green Miscellany" seem to be aggregates of separate, self-contained poems in which each poem is required to sustain itself.

"Moonflowers", the third poem of *Typewriter Music*, is a good example of some of the features of the poems of these late books:

> Gone and not gone. Is this
> garden the one
> we walked in hand in hand
> watching the moon
> -flower at the gate
>
> climb back into our lives
> out of winter bones – decades

> of round crimped candescent
> origami satellite-dishes
> all cocked towards Venus?
>
> One garden opens
> to let another through, the green
> heart-shapes a new season holds
> our hearts to like the old.
> The moonflower lingers
>
> in its fat scent. We move
> in and in and out of
> each other's warmed spaces —
> there is
> no single narrative.
>
> And we like it that way,
> if we like it at all, this
> tender conceptual
> blue net that holds, and hold us
> so lightly against fall. (3-4)

As is often the case, a slight poem like this contains a lot of complexities. It also works by containing surprises which help to keep the poem energised. What seems to be a poem intent on 'capturing' the reality of a flower in words and which deploys the kind of formidable descriptive powers that metaphoric language can make possible — "crimped, candescent / origami satellite-dishes" — is really about a very complex conception of love, time and the erotic innocence of the Garden of Eden. Like "Revolving Days," which occurs just before it in *Typewriter Days*, it wants to compress and interleave time. The final word "fall" deliberately recalls the Garden of Eden (there is a third meaning of "fall", of course, which would chime with the seasonal references in this poem, but it is only available in American English). There are other surprises: where we might expect a solemn tone, there is, as so often in Malouf, the slightly grotesque comedy of puns so that here the moonflowers are all "cocked towards Venus". It is a reminder that Malouf's universe of porous borders exists at all levels from the most trivial to the most powerful. His is not a poetry where epiphanies are used to provide climaxes in the high style. There are also syntactic surprises. It is only the hyphen before "flower" at the end of the first stanza which prevents that word being a verb and many of the later poems have examples of these sort of disorienting enjambments, again, not done solemnly but, you feel, with a smile. And the syntax of the third stanza is so fluid and complex that it takes several readings to find a structure that will make it all cohere grammatically.

There is another important issue which might be dealt with in looking at the poems of these two most recent books: that of perspective. Contraction and expansion have always been a feature of Malouf's poetry and dovetail with the obsession with crossing borders and through doors: things look different if you stand at a different point to look or if you have entered a creature with a different perspective. "Stars" from *Bicycle* is precisely about how love can alter perspectives. The stars which are so mind-bendingly far away and apart can be seen framed in the pane of a window or in a glass of water by a bedside. In "Asphodel" from *Neighbours in a Thicket* the experience of falling into a subterranean pond suddenly compresses all geological time into a few moments.

A poem from *Earth Hour*, "Good Friday, Flying West", is an example of Malouf's interest in contraction: in this case of historical time:

> This knot the breeze unpicks. Our jet-stream flaps
> and ripples, lays a trail
> of thunder over the earth. Stars
> dissolve, the pluck and flow of the planet takes us

> back, half a day
> or centuries; driftways
>
> descend from Mt Ararat. Unrisen
> ahead the dazzling dinning bee-hive cities.
> Museums not yet open. Artefacts
>
> in the minds of town-dwellers
> waiting to take shape
> at dawn: the pitcher swelling
>
> in shadow on a shelf, the bowl
> of wheatgrains on its altar still unbroken
> Eocene clay, undreamed of in the earth (52).

Again, the last word, "earth", is deliberate, used here in its double meanings of "the planet" and "clay, soil" which, themselves, contain a radical change in dimension. In the poem the experience of travelling towards Europe – a version of the journey discussed in the essay "The South" in *Being There* – involves an inevitable change of time zone and thus, metonymically, is a journey towards the past. But the twelve hour movement becomes drawn out into the entire length of historical consciousness. The view of Mt Ararat recalls the biblical story of the flood (written down in the early first millennium BC) but before that there are the cities of ancient Mesopotamia, first concentration of human lives "the dazzling dinning bee-hive cities." The fact that museums are not yet open refers simultaneously to the current plane journey (it will be night in Europe and hence too early for museums to open) and to historical time: the inventors of the tools of early man and the early civilisations will not have imagined them as something to be kept for public display. The fact that the poem uses the same sort of trick enjambments as "Moonflowers" – "flaps" is read initially as an aeronautical noun and "unbroken" is read initially as an adjective modifying "bowl" but really modifies "Eocene clay" – will offer some evidence, though admittedly scanty, for the importance of this device as controlling both tone and structure of these lyrics. "Good Friday, Flying West" also makes a subtle allusion to Auden: "the pluck and flow of the planet" recalls "the pluck and knock of the tide". It reminds readers that, despite the claim Wallace Stevens might have as an early influence on Malouf, it is really Auden, the Auden of "Goodbye to the Mezzogiorno", and "In Praise of Limestone" who is an abiding and generally valuable presence. A poem from *Typewriter Music* which is about how a blank page can conjure up an entire arctic landscape, animals included, takes its title from Auden's best known assertion and sets out to rebut it.

A separate issue – though it can be subsumed under the general rubric of perspective – is Malouf's use of the pronoun "we". In poems of love, it always refers to the couple but in many other poems, especially the later ones, it expresses a desire to speak for all rather than for an individual with a distinctive and exotic view of reality. "We take these givings // as ours and meant for us…" he says in "Shy Gifts" – an example chosen more or less at random and a very typical one. I think this is a technique derived from Auden who pioneered this kind of reader-and-writer intimacy of tone, especially in "In Praise of Limestone". At any rate it shows how Malouf's poetry, while extending the self by the kinds of processes of expansion and reception of visitors that I have written of – and thus concentrating intently on the self – wants, simultaneously, to expand outwards into a larger community, imagined or otherwise.

What can be said of Malouf's poetry by way of conclusion? He is, to an extent, a poet of his place and his time though he is a poet of such scope that it makes one realise how little value these literary-historical labels have. But he is, perhaps, a provincial poet in that Brisbane, unlike Sydney or Melbourne was clearly, after the war, an inadequate cultural home for figures like Peter Porter, Rodney Hall, Judith Rodriguez or Malouf. Malouf, typically, avoids the simple condemnation of the provincial, pointing out that every starting point in the education of the self is somewhere and that the places on the edge have exotic revelations that the great centres do not. It could be said that place is an obsession in his work, and that it might not have been had he not grown up in Brisbane before and after the war. And the time does matter as well. Sceptical as I am of such generalisations, there is some truth in the idea that the post-war world is one rejecting large cultural statements in favour of a focus on the self. Malouf is, profoundly, a humanist poet and will thus irritate those who feel that poetry should derive from something different to the experiences of the self-expressed in lyric terms. But he never takes the great humanist dictum, "Man is the measure of all things," to be an excuse to reduce the vast dimensions of reality (cultural, geographical and cosmological) to something smaller that can be comfortably dealt with by Everyman. The imperative in Malouf's poetry is that the self must expand rather than that the universe must contract.

Works Cited

Baker, Candida. "Malouf." *Yacker: Australian Writers Talk About Their Work*, Picador, 1989, pp. 234 – 263.
Jose, Nicholas. "Metamorphic Malouf." *Malouf*, special issue of *JASAL: Journal of the Association for the Study of Australian Literature*, vol. 14, no. 2, 2014, pp. 1-8.
Malouf, David. *Being There*, Random House, 2015.
---. *Bicycle and Other Poems*, University of Queensland Press, 1970.
---. *Earth Hour*, University of Queensland Press, 2014.
---. *First Things Last*, University of Queensland Press, 1980.
---. 'Interiors' in *Four Poets*, Cheshire, 1962.
---. *Neighbours in a Thicket*, University of Queensland Press, 1974.
---. *Poems 1959 – 1989*, University of Queensland Press, 1992.
---. *Poems 1975 – 76*, Prism, 1976.
---. *Revolving Days*, University of Queensland Press, 2008.
---. *Selected Poems*, Angus and Robertson, 1981.

---. *Typewriter Music*, University of Queensland Press, 2007.

Tulip, James. "Appreciating David Malouf As Poet" *Malouf*, special issue of *JASAL: Journal of the Association for the Study of Australian Literature*, vol. 14, no. 2, 2014, pp. 1-8.

Chapter 6

"Singing in my careless hand": Dorothy Porter's verse novels

ANDY KISSANE

Dorothy Porter wanted to make poetry popular again, to bring it back into the mainstream and attract the readers that had abandoned it in the twentieth century, as the novel became the dominant literary form. She expressed that desire when discussing the mood and melancholia of T.S. Eliot's *The Waste Land*. She said, "I want to break away from that modernist fatigue. I want some green leaves to grow. I want poetry to get people intoxicated and drunk again. I want poetry to be seen as something festive, fun and dangerous" (Digby 39). One way to capture some new ground for poetry was to challenge the relative domination of the lyric, which eventually resulted in Porter writing five verse novels. This chapter examines the successes and the limitations of these novels as narratives and as poetry.

Porter's first verse novel, *Akhenaten,* was published in 1992. It is a verse biography of the Egyptian pharaoh of the eighteenth dynasty, Akhenaten, beginning with his childhood and ending with his death and the desecration of his name and city. The first section, "Malkata" reads like a *bildungsroman* or "coming of age" novel. In "Cat-Nap" the young Akhenaten lies on the mosaic fish floor of his father's harem, with his cat, Nofret:

> We sleep together
>   through the prattle
>   through the sticky afternoon.

> My father's stupid.
>
> I will collect cats
> not princesses. (7)

Later when his cat dies, it is his cousin, Nefertiti who comforts him. Porter's poetic building block is the dramatic monologue in the voice of Akhenaten, in which she adroitly combines a blend of the regal and the domestic to dramatise a privileged childhood. Part of the charm of this book is the imagining of figures from ancient history about whom we know very little, if we confine ourselves to the archeological record. One of Porter's strengths is her ability to suggest a lot in a few lines, a few words. In "My Mother", Akhenaten says of his parents:

> my father plays
> in his inoffensive way
> with his health
> or his harem.
>
> Mummy plays
> with gods
> Mummy frightens
> iron. (10)

The contrast between the two parents is vivid. Like many Porter poems, this poem ends strongly with the epigrammatic "Mummy frightens / iron." The punchy ending, the telling image, the memorable line are repeated strengths in Porter's poetry. Her lines are relatively short, typically between one and four words, drawing particularly on the free verse lines of William Carlos Williams. There is energy in her lines, but also constraint and they are a fair distance from the pentameter, hexameter and longer line lengths that have traditionally been found in narrative poetry. If you are setting out to tell a story in verse, would you choose such a minimalist line? Most poets wouldn't. It is a credit to Porter's skill that she manages to tell stories with such a minimalist line, but this self-imposed constraint can also have a negative effect on the telling of the story, as we shall see.

That Akhenaten initially reads like a *bildungsroman* is made even clearer by the penultimate poem of the first section. In "Our First Time", Akhenaten celebrates his first sexual experience with Nefertiti:

> I can't stop kissing her
>
> when her tongue
>   filled my mouth
>   for the first time
> my cock went berserk
> it wouldn't listen
>
> now it flops sticky
> and happy
>   in her hand
>
> and I'm not embarrassed
>
> she's still
>   my best friend. (20)

There is nothing in the language or the atmosphere to locate it in the fourteenth century B.C. It reads like a contemporary adolescent love poem, except perhaps that many contemporary voices are not necessarily as innocent or endearing. This poem also reveals a number of tropes that are characteristic of Porter's narrative poems. Firstly, the poem is located in the moment: Akhenaten is still kissing Nefertiti and "can't stop shaking / or laughing". It's an euphoric moment conveyed in a direct, straightforward manner. The adverb "berserk" is particularly effective; it has a colloquial force that feels both right and fresh. The character of Akhenaten is compelling because he is both modern and ancient, easy to relate to and exotically different. The other trope that appears again and again in Porter's verse novels is the reference to hands. Hands are most often suggestive of desire or intimacy and frequently Porter portrays a lover through the mention of his or her hands. The motif has always been a kind of shorthand in characterisation, and James Wood has commented on how Tolstoy repeatedly describes Anna Karenina by referring to her "light step" (70, 81). In Porter's novels, hands become a symbol for all that is longed for and loved. Given her minimalism, it is not surprising that Porter relies on the repeated suggestiveness of a range of motifs.

After a strong start, there's a sense in which the forward movement of *Akhenaten* flags. Akhenaten becomes a pharaoh, builds a new city, takes a wife. But there's little urgency in the narration of these events. Rather *Akhenaten* depends on the individual poems keeping the reader engaged. This is the only verse novel of Porter's in which the titles of the poems are printed in the contents page. In her other books, individual poems, although titled, seem secondary to the progression of the narrative.

Much is made of Akhenaten's sex life, which involves not only sex with his queen, Nefertiti, but also involves sex with his daughters and his younger brother, Smenkhkare. Jennifer Maiden argues that the

> earlier Nefertiti poems are much more rounded and radiant — and much sexier than the Smenkhkare poems. Porter constantly but subtly reinforces that affectionate, habitual sex is more exciting than irritable, addicted sex. She has always been a very moral poet (43).

This interesting claim is not really borne out by a close reading of the poems. If anything, it seems to be a construction of Maiden's as a reader and reviewer rather than anything that is inherent in the poems. "Nefertiti Rides Me" uses an explicit, everyday language that is common in Porter's verse, but much rarer in contemporary poetry:

> Nefertiti rides me.
>
> Her cunt
>   slippery on
>   the hot skin
>   of my belly. (35)

The direct explicitness of the opening is designed to hook a reader and carry them into the poem, which is an impassioned lyric to heterosexual intercourse. Akhenaten's voice is exultant, urgent and not wholly centered on himself:

> I want to hold her
> I want to lie still
> but she's not finished
>   her eyes are shut
>   her breath
>   a stammering breeze
> now, now
>   oh, yes
>
> she growls like the desert
>   melts like sleep
>   and anoints me
>   exquisitely. (35)

This rendering of female sexuality and agency feels particularly modern, though Porter skillfully uses the metaphor of a warhorse and the verb "anoints" to also link it to Akhenaten's time. The poem ends with perhaps the strongest praise that the character of Akhenaten could give, "I love her more than Aten." Compare this with "My Sleeping Brother" which reads in full:

> Asleep
> Smenkhkare is cool.
> And more fragrant
> than melting scented wax.
>
> I lean over him
> and trail my hands
> in his ripples.
>
> But perhaps
> I should stick to the safer lakes
>   of Maru-Aten;
> nothing is more dangerous
>   for me
> than swimming
>   in the breath
> of my sleeping brother. (112)

Both poems utlilise the sense of smell, both make references to breath, both present Akhenaten as not being fully in control. The Smenkhkare poems that follow dramatise the process of falling in love with a similarly sensuous emphasis on touch and smell. At times, the words and phrases are almost identical. In "Ebony Cats" Akhenaten says of talking to Smenkhkare: "I play / like one of my kids / with the ebony cats on the table / my fingers / silly" (118). Earlier he says of Nefertiti in "Our First Time": "I can't stop shaking / or laughing // she's as silly as me" (20). All of Porter's love poems celebrate the moment and the intensity of love at that instant. "In My Own Time" self-reflexively addresses the love poem itself, as well as proclaiming of Smenkhkare:

> It wasn't the same
> with Nefertiti.
>
> There are no poems
> to describe
> holding your own brother
> in your arms. (126)

Porter also makes much of Akhenaten having sex with his daughters, playing up the taboo of incest and highlighting the opposition of Nefertiti and his daughters to it. Christopher Pollnitz stresses that it is "Akhenaten's polymorphous sexuality, not his religious iconoclasm" that leads to his downfall. According to Pollnitz "pharaonic incest was a ritual expectation" of Akhenaten and his subsequent self-loathing "reduces the verse novel to a historical romance" (243). I'm not sure I agree with "reduces" here, which implies some unarticulated hierarchy of genres, but the romance genre is certainly central to Dorothy Porter's verse narratives. It is my contention that the process of falling in and out of love is one of the main drivers of Porter's narratives and her poetry. The centrality of love is not limited to the verse novels, but is anticipated by earlier sequences such as "The Night Parrot" from the book of the same title and "Carmen" from *Driving Too Fast*.

Porter's verse biography of an Egyptian Pharaoh is a strikingly original work. The depiction of Akhenaten's regal court is intriguing, but it is in the love poems where this verse novel really soars. This trend, as we will see, continues in the remaining verse novels.

The publication of *The Monkey's Mask* was a much hyped event and critics such as Lyn McCredden have commented on the uniformity of the media response at the time (48-50). The book, and the campaign associated with it, did much to sell poetry as accessible and sexy, and much of the appeal was linked to its promotion as a crime thriller. I doubt that the same scrutiny would have been applied to any well-marketed prose novel. Poetry that sold as well as fiction became a cultural phenomenon that was worth analysing.

Again Porter utilizes the dramatic monologue and uses a single monologist, the private detective, Jill Fitzpatrick, who is hired to find a missing university student, Mickey Norris. Jill proclaims in the opening poem "Trouble": "I want you, trouble, / on the rocks" (3). But as the poem suggests, it's not just work she's after, but "private trouble/oh, pretty trouble//to tidal-wave my bed". In the second chapter, Jill is sidetracked when she meets Mickey's poetry tutor, Diana. We learn in "Cafeteria" that Jill is thirty-eight and that "her heart breaks // like surf" (17). The poem "Diana" gives us Jill's first impression:

> The door reads
> Dr Diana Maitland
>
> I knock twice
>
> she's thirtysomething
> maybe forty
>
> her hair honey-blonde
> streaks
>
> falls in her eyes
> she pushes it back
>
> with a fidgety
> nail-bitten hand
>
> she's got eyes
> that flirt or fight

she's gritty
she's bright

oh christ help me
she's a bit of alright! (26)

This is a quick portrait and like the monologue at its best says more about the speaker than the subject. The word order of "her hair honey-blonde / streaks" suggests Jill's emotional confusion, while the "nail-bitten hand" introduces the customary motif of the hand and also succinctly suggests Diana's potential guilt. The poem ends with a chant-like rhythm and the uses of the triple rhyme "fight-bright-alright" which is reminiscent of the endings of some of Sylvia Plath's poems. It's not long before Jill Fitzpatrick has the trouble she craves. Diana asks her how many women she has slept with, while Jill admits that, "We keep meeting for coffee / we don't talk about Mickey" (29). And with characteristic Porter succinctness, in "Spring", Fitzpatrick ponders:

am I in love again?

my hands and heart
aching

for blossom
   or wild wild risk. (30)

The affair with Diana, who also has a husband, Nick, completely takes over the narrative until Mrs Norris rings with the news that they've found Mickey and she's dead. Jill thinks as she takes the call: "I did fuck all / apart from / fuck her teacher" ("Fuck all" 47). Admittedly romance is a standard feature of the detective genre, but I'd be surprised if there was a fictional private eye who was as reluctant to work as Jill Fitzpatrick. She's not reluctant in love, it's the trouble she longs for from the start: "because her voice / her breasts her mouth her smell / make me stupid" ("I'll ring you" 58). When Jill is hired again by Mickey's mother, the poem "Work" ends with the lines "Today / I'm not working // I'm seeing Diana" (65). For the first five chapters, the love story has dominated the novel. At this stage, Jill's job as a private investigator appears to provide little more than character detail, while the whole murder story appears to function as a frame in which the central romance narrative can develop. "Her clever hand" brings together three of Porter's favourite tropes—the car as the place where life is lived; music; and the hand as a talisman of sexuality, desire and intimacy:

> I drive and perve
>
> her calves do a silky stretch
> her hand taut with blue veins
>
> as she slots in k.d.lang (68)

There's a friendly argument about how Jill doesn't listen to boys, echoing the parallelism of one voice answering another that Porter first developed in her poetic reworking of the opera, Carmen. The poem ends with an emphasis on the pleasure of touch: "she slips her clever hand / between my thighs // to make me quiet" (68).

The love poems are interrupted for a while by a number of poems about the poetry scene as Fitzpatrick returns to her detective work. This is also a familiar move of the romance genre — bring the lovers together and then find a way of splitting them apart. Porter's satire of the Sydney poetry scene does that. There's a couple of book launches and a joke about how someone reading for fifteen minutes can stretch to an hour. For anyone who has been to a poetry reading that felt like bad karaoke, there's the cutting curse in "Hippy poets" of:

whales and rainforests
line after blubbering line

get me a harpoon
get me a bulldozer

better still
fetch my wicked woman

darling, don't make me sit
through this shit

on my own. (89)

Two poets appear as possible suspects, the Christian, Bill McDonald, who has had some correspondence with Mickey and the influential Tony Knight, who runs a casting couch for young female hopefuls. For anyone familiar with Australian poetry, it's hard not to read this without thinking of the poetry wars of the 1970s and the poets grouped around the conservative Les Murray and the avant-garde John Tranter. *The Monkey's Mask*, Porter's project to make poetry popular stands in opposition to these established poetries. In one sense the book dramatises a dream for a different sort of poetry, as suggested by "Sex and poetry":

> I never knew poetry
>   was about
> opening your legs
>   one minute
>
> opening your grave
>   the next

I never knew poetry
could be
as sticky as sex. (139)

This dream for a different sort of poetry surely draws on Frederico García Lorca's concept of the duende, developed in his speech, "Play and Theory of the Duende". In popular Spanish culture, the duende is a "playful hobgoblin, a household spirit fond of ruling things, breaking plates, causing noise and making a general nuisance of himself" (Maurer ix). But Lorca was drawing more on the Andalusian usage of duende, where people sensed that certain bullfighters and flamenco artists had duende, because of their ability to provoke emotion in the viewer. There is a nebulous aspect to Lorca's discussion of duende. Quoting Goethe, he refers to it as "A mysterious power which everyone senses and no philosopher explains" (57). Maurer, one of Lorca's translators, identifies four elements in Lorca's vision of duende: "irrationality, earthiness, a heightened awareness of death and a dash of the diabolical" (ix). This heightened awareness of death is the aspect of duende that most informs Porter's work. It is suggested in "Sex and poetry" by the reference to poetry "opening your grave" and is especially noticeable in her crime novels with their series of deaths. It's not just a death-defying spirit that Porter wanted for poetry; she also wanted to write the sort of poetry that had a profound effect on its audience, a spine-chilling effect that is both unmistakable and difficult to explain.

Does Porter's poetry have duende? This is a difficult question to answer. Lorca argues that the "duende's arrival always means a radical change of forms" (62). Certainly at the time of publication, Porter's verse novels seemed new, although there were other poets, both locally and internationally writing in the same form, such as Alan Wearne and Vikram Seth. As a critical concept, duende seems allusive. At times Lorca focuses on it as a creative process in which every artist "climbs each step in the tower of his perfection by fighting his duende" (58). Later he suggests that "All arts are capable of duende, but where it finds greatest range, naturally, is in music, dance and spoken poetry, for these arts require a living body to interpret them" (63). Porter was famous for the power of her performances and having witnessed a number of them, I think she did have duende in performance. If duende also exists on the page, then it's my gut reaction that you're more likely to find it in the love poems than the poems that strive for the "black sounds" that Lorca praised (57).

Deaths are a generic requirement of Porter's crime novels, yet I don't think the deaths themselves have duende. Despite Porter's interest in darkness, the crime story is the weakest part of *The Monkey's Mask*. The problems exist largely at the levels of characterisation and plot. These difficulties can also be explained by the constraints of the minimalist line that is both Dorothy Porter's strength and her weakness. The Porter line evokes and suggests a lot, but it is not really suited to the sort of complex characterisation that is the staple of the prose novelist. The generic demands of the crime novels might have also acted as a limitation, for the characterisation is stronger in *Akhenaten* and particularly in *Wild Surmise.*

In chapter six, "Mickey's Poems", Diana emerges as a possible suspect through the way she actively attempts to divert attention, as if her analysis of the poems as clues can throw Jill off the scent. In "The death smell" Jill says to her, "'You don't give a flying fuck, do you?'" (129). Should we read this as a lover's tiff or as Jill intuitively realising that Diana was involved in Mickey's murder? And then there's Diana's taunt: "'You're a great fuck'"... but "'you're a very ordinary / detective'" ("Terrific day" 135). Jill's friend, Lou is suspicious of Diana and warns, "'That woman's trouble. / I'm telling you / big bloody trouble'" ("Advice" 143). We're not told what Jill really thinks at this stage, perhaps because as Roland Barthes put it, for the story to go on, it cannot be told (135-6). We have to assume that either Jill is blinded by her lust for Diana or that Jill is not a very good detective.

The next two chapters, "Verse and Jesus" and "Brisbane" dramatise

Jill's pursuit of the two poet suspects, Bill McDonald and Tony Knight. In a meeting in a park, Bill McDonald pulls a knife on Jill. In "Fear me" Jill prepares for this threat by uttering the feminist chant:

> at my crust
> I'm violent
>
> right down deep
> I'm violent
>
> at my finger tips
> I'm violent
>
> in the glands of my breasts
> I'm violent
>
> in the shield of my cervix
> I'm violent
>
> in my feral womb
> I'm violent
>
> fear me fear me fear me
>
> I'm female. (167)

Finola Moorhead reads this poem as representing "hatred for women" (186), while Kathleen Mary Fallon objects that by ignoring its place in the narrative, Moorhead has engaged "in a willful misreading and misrepresentation in its decontextualizing" (195). I agree with Fallon that the poem is not anti-women, but I find it hard to believe in Jill's need for it at this point. Fallon suggests that the novel is not social realist, but a "Gothic tale of spiritual sadomasochism and Evil" (192). Even Gothic tales require a certain amount of verisimilitude—a reader wants to be convinced by the materiality and plausibility of the threat. From what the narrative suggests about Bill as a conservative Christian poet and from his subsequent foiled attempt to reveal what he knows to Jill, it's hard to imagine him pulling a knife. Bill has his reputation to protect and is in a state of panic, but the fight with the knife seems designed to emphasise the courage and fearlessness of Jill. It is difficult to believe that Bill would actually do this and the event fractures the credibility of his character.

Bill's subsequent murder, by Nick and Diana, is another plot event that stretches credibility. Are Nick and Diana, a left-wing lawyer and a successful feminist academic, likely to follow-up the allegedly accidental strangling of Mickey during sex, with the murder of Bill McDonald? It's clear that the detective genre requires these sorts of complications, but the genre at its best carries its reader into crime scenes that are convincing and credible. I just don't believe that the characters of *The Monkey's Mask* are capable of this sort of violence. Nick, as Moorhead points out, is a name for the devil, while Diana is a Latin version of Artemis, the huntress, the archetypal strong female (186). Fallon reads them both as representations of evil, something that, quoting Bataille, she argues "has a sovereign value for us" (192). Porter is certainly interested in evil, which becomes the focus of her next verse novel, *What a Piece of Work*. Although the plot of *The Monkey's Mask* dramatises evil, the characterisation lacks the sort of psychological complexity that is the staple of prose fiction, that convinces in the way that Dostoevsky's Raskolnikov is a convincing portrait of a murderer.

For example, Nick is little more than a cardboard cutout. He flirts with Jill, he tries to have sex with her and when he is rejected he still acts as if he has won. We don't know enough about him, from the inside or the outside, to be able to comprehend his strangling of Mickey and his fatal tampering with Bill's car. Diana is a more convincing portrait of evil, though she seems to be primarily motivated by a desire to protect her husband, as "Wives and root rats" argues:

> Barbara and Diana
> have something in common
> besides hating each other
>
> they're loyal wives.
>
> Mrs Bill McDonald
> ran in the same maze
>
> you love the bastard
> you cover his shit. (227)

If Nick and Diana are genuinely evil and responsible for the death of two people, then why does Jill let them off the hook? Mrs Norris is defined by being an upper class North shore wife and there's a class antagonism in the way that Jill dismisses her likely reactions to how Mickey died: "Mrs Norris' missionary position / face // gagging on the broken hyoid bone / of her daughter's sex life" ("Heading north" 246). Essentially from Jill's perspective, Mickey's parents are not cool, although their wealth and morality are not valid reasons for not revealing the truth about their daughter's death. This is what really infuriates Moorhead, that Jill says nothing of what she knows to Mr and Mrs Norris, yet still collects a fat cheque. Fallon accuses Moorhead of wanting her ethical and moral dilemmas simple, but there's a huge dose of cowardice at the heart of Jill doing nothing that seems to run against the conventions of the detective novel. Conventions can certainly be broken, but in finishing the novel in this way Porter foregrounds the romance genre over the detective genre. The only explanation we have for Jill's inaction is that she still loves or desires Diana enough to let her off the hook. If Diana is truly evil, then Jill's apathy makes Jill complicit with that evil. If as Diana says, there's no way of making the mud stick, then surely Jill could still try, she could tell the parents the truth, she could go to the police.

It is instructive that in Samantha Lang's film of the novel, this is exactly what Jill does. The encounter with Nick is moved from the car to the beach and Jill secretly records Nick agreeing to Jill's assertion, "You killed Mickey." Nick responds, "Yeah. And my wife came as she watched." In the film, Jill solves the case and then provides the police with filmic evidence that Diana and Nick knew Mickey, as well as the taped evidence that Nick killed her. Why doesn't Porter do something like this in *The Monkey's Mask*? One possibility is that she wanted to resist the demands of genre, resist closure and let the reader do the work. But the reader is told exactly what Jill thinks, that "reckless, careless / sex killed Mickey" ("Reckless, careless and sexy" 245), and that "Nick takes big risks / with his big hands" ("Heading north" 247). The reader is also told enough to know that Diana and Nick are responsible for the murder of Bill McDonald. The case is solved for the reader, but the killers go free, they are even spared the ignominy of a scandal.

Ultimately it comes down to a question of how you read. Mary Jane Fallon argues for one way of reading—that this is merely a story. She has this urge to "write in bold capital letters—FINOLA! THEY ARE FICTIONAL CHARACTERS. PORTER MADE THEM UP. DON'T GO TO THE COPS. NO ONE WAS REALLY KILLED" (195). But there's something about this argument that ignores how most people read and how fiction works. The reader reads as if these characters exist, as if the events occurred, as if the writer has something to say, as if the story has a message and brings news of the world. I suspect that the ending of *The Monkey's Mask* was a mistake, that Jill's cowardice, although human, was not the best way for Porter to end her innovative exploration of crime and romance.

The escape of the murderers makes the romance the pulsing heart of the book. The novel poses the question, "Can you love someone who is actually evil?" In the final poem, "The monkey's mask", Jill Fitzpatrick summons Medusa's power to turn anyone who looked at her to stone. Jill is scathing on the false poets that the novel satirizes: "turn those fraud poets / to marble / a staircase leading nowhere / in a Stalinist museum" (256). She does not spare Nick: "turn Nick / to sandstone / and let him crumble" (256). But for Diana, all Jill can manage is "turn Diana ... / loose" (256). Diana might not have been worthy of Jill's desire, of Jill's love, but Jill wants to set her free and spare her any form of justice.

The Monkey's Mask is a portrait of obsessional and all-consuming love, much more than it is a credible crime novel. It ends with the assertion that "Mickey's ghost walks / in this tropical rain" and "she's wearing a monkey's mask" (256). It's hard to know how to read the epigraph from Basho that gives the novel its title. Does Mickey really wear the monkey's mask? Surely it is Diana, who is masked, who is an illusion, a fake. And surely the contemporary cultural obsession with love, which is both celebrated and critiqued by Porter, is the real heart of this flawed, but intriguing book.

Robert Browning is generally acknowledged as one of the masters of the dramatic monologue and "My Last Duchess" is his most famous monologue. This chilling portrait of the Duke of Ferrara is a model of how a thoroughly unlikeable character can command our attention as he gradually suggests the terrible fate of his past wife and alludes to the danger to be faced by the next Duchess. By the time we realise the depth of his depravity, the poem is practically over, a poem which runs for fifty-six lines in its entirety.

I don't know if "My Last Duchess" was a model for *What a Piece of Work,* but the two poems have one element in common: the monologist of each poem is a monstrous human being. In "My Last Duchess", Browning works hard to hide the monstrosity of the speaker through his urbane politeness: "Will't please you sit and look at her?" (772). There's a tension that plays out in the poem between the civility of polite conversation and the uncivil, completely unprovoked violence of the speaker. What is the Duchess's crime?

To smile at everyone, it seems, or to not realise soon enough the murderous intent that lurked beneath her husband's jealousy and his "nine-hundred-years-old name" (772). It is a poem that critiques patriarchal marriage and the treatment of women as property to be sold, and the power of the poem comes from the way this critique is embedded in the voice of the monologist. As soon as we realise how despicable this Duke is, we leave him, hoping that the new Duchess doesn't end up as a painting on the wall or a bronze statue.

It is clear from very early on in Porter's verse novel that Doctor Peter Cyren is not a nice piece of work. From the suggestion in the third poem, "Lunatic Art" that Peter collects photos of his psychiatric patients, the reader starts to doubt the reliability of his intentions, and indeed, anything he says. In "Black sun" his attitude to patients is aloof and condescending:

> they rock
> they drool and dribble
> they talk to their frayed sleeves
>
> their scufflings carry
>   on the hot wind
>
> they're the living end. (19)

Cyren is an egotist and a pain, which has a curious effect on the love poems that begin the second section, "Red". Cyren falls in love with Fay, who he meets at a bar, but rather than being carried along with the emotion, these poems come across to the reader as sleazy. In "Cakes and toast" the Duke's violence is echoed in Cyren's obsessive lust:

> My mind is already
> hoarding Fay.

It likes
to take her away
and break her
into small delicious bits. (38)

Cyren berates the staff for their lack of care when treating the patients, but care is what he clearly lacks. He doesn't seem to care for anyone—not his patient, Tamara, whom he sexually exploits, not Penny-Jenny who is very likeable, not Frank, who writes poems just as Francis Webb did.

Unfortunately, *What a Piece of Work* is principally a portrait of Peter Cryren, of a man who doesn't grow in complexity as a fictional character should, but who is as one-dimensional at the end as he is at the beginning. Cyren is an archetypal representation of evil, but it is not a representation that engages and intrigues. Porter's critique of mental institutions is historically justified and Peter Cyren appears to be completely convinced that he is doing the right thing and acting for the best. Peter has no doubts about his methods; there's no struggle to understand his motivations or the practice of intervention and treatment. Neither is there a portrait of a profoundly misguided doctor who is genuinely trying to help people. Peter Cyren doesn't care for anyone, is simply driven by his own power, his own megalomania. In "Clean hands" Cyren protests his innocence to a doubting Fay: "You tell me / you can smell the stuff / on my hands" (144). It's "not poison / just a gel" he explains, as he discusses the use of shock therapy without anaesthetic. His justification of the treatment that "can drag them back / from cliff edges" (146) lacks any compassion for patients' rights, because after all, they're merely mental patients. The poem ends with Cyren telling Fay, "don't sniff / round me / like I'm Doctor Mengele // these hands are clean" (146). But the reader can only conclude the opposite—that Cyren is a version of Doctor Mengele and that he is culpable. One problem with *What a Piece of Work* is that the central character is a simplistic and unchanging bad man. As a character,

Cyren is static rather than dynamic, fixed rather than open.

I'm tempted to blame this on the limits of Porter's brief lines, but the problem is deeper than this and is surely related to the conception of the work. Porter takes her title from Hamlet's speech to Rosencrantz and Guildenstern: "What a piece of work is a man! how noble in reason! how infinite in faculty! in form and moving how express and admirable! in action how like an angel! in apprehension how like a God!" (*Hamlet* 2.2, 317–20) The epigraph is ironic, for Cyren lacks a sense of nobility and infinity and is only God-like in his arrogant assumption of power. This representation of consciousness is as far removed as possible from Leopold Bloom in James Joyce's *Ulysses*. The sense of struggle in Cyren is minimal; his compassion for others is non-existent. He is "a piece of work", but not in the sense that Hamlet suggested.

The other related problem is that it is through Peter Cyren's voice that we meet the other characters of *What a Piece of Work*. This is the last time that Porter uses a single monologist and the limitations of one voice are acute here. One senses that many of the other characters—Penny-Jenny, Tamara, Fay and Frank—would be more compelling and interesting if they could speak for themselves. The great Australian poet, Francis Webb, and his tragic incarceration in Callan Park seems to be the model for Frank, but we really only get the bare facts and some hints at Frank's deprivation, rather than a portrait from within. Frank is just one cog in the plot, among others, and the plot dwindles to an ending rather than builds to a climax, as Cyren's credibility is soured by the fire inquest and Tamara's suicide. As in *The Monkey's Mask* there is no sense of justice as Cyren escapes into private practice. Overall, the acclaim that this book has received—including its shortlisting for the Miles Franklin in 2000—is quite puzzling. It feels much more like an epic poem than a novel, for it lacks the element that made the novel the premier literary form— the presentation of human experience and consciousness in all its richness.

Wild Surmise marks both a shift in approach and a return to form. The reliance on a single monologist is replaced by a shifting narrative schema that utilizes second person narration, third person narration and two distinct first person narrators—Alex Leefson, the astronomer, and her husband, the English academic, Daniel Morgan. In prose fiction there is always a jolt if a novel switches from third person to first, as Charles Dickens does in *Bleak House*. In *Wild Surmise* the jolt doesn't occur, perhaps because you never become assimilated to one way of telling the story. There's a tendency for some of the third person poems to fall a little poetically flat, as if their function is to fill in necessary detail, while the first person poems are the ones in which Porter is really going to sing. But the flexibility of this approach allows for more polyphony in this novel, especially coming after the monological *What a Piece of Work*.

Wild Surmise is also much more removed from genre fiction than Porter's other novels, except for the innovative biographical portrait, *Akhenaten*. It begins slowly with a set-up that is rooted in daily life. Initially Alex's quest is dramatised as the search for knowledge about one of Jupiter's moons, Europa. But the quest quickly shifts into romantic territory when Alex's old flame, Phoebe, tells her she is coming to Melbourne for a "black holes gig". In "America—The Adjective," Alex responds to Phoebe at the podium:

> Spruiking her quasars, her black holes
> and galaxies
> like Big Mac specials. (57)

This poem is partly a portrait of desire and the desired one, but its reach is expansive. After the first stanza which establishes that the setting is a lecture, Porter begins the next six stanzas with adjectives that detail negative American traits: articulate, territorial, vulgar, puritanical, narcissistic and insular. These one-word lines lead into a variety of descriptions about Phoebe and her lecture, such as:

> Territorial.
> Her mind not only knows
> but owns
> the cosmos. (57)

It is not a flattering portrait of Phoebe, but it builds to an important critique of cultural hegemony:

> Everywhere, everyone
> is just waiting
> to become America. (58)

It is a critique that arises convincingly out of the story, yet its impact transcends the relationship of Alex and Phoebe. Here, Porter has something to say and her analysis is insightful, convincing and confronting. It is "so American" to be insular and narcissistic, to be confident and yet vulgar and to position yourself and your country at the centre of the cosmos. Admittedly it is a caricature and a generalisation, yet it is mud that sticks, just the same. It is common to find Australian writers who are knowledgeable and well-read in American literature, but the converse seems much rarer. As a political poem, as social criticism, "America—The Adjective" works. Porter's customary and suggestive economy serves the thesis of the poem, which stands on its own, but also enhances the development of the narrative, establishing the power dynamic that exists between Alex and Phoebe, with Phoebe as the more powerful.

Given that Phoebe and Alex are both astronomers, it is not surprising that the book is littered with references to quasars, black holes and microbiological life that might populate the seas of Europa. But the scientific jargon exists less as verisimilitude and more as a source of new and striking metaphors that Porter can use to reinvigorate the tired love poem. For example in "Adultery", Alex notes:

> And my old desire wakes up
> like a desiccated Martian
> flood plain
> sniffing a huge fresh flood. (59)

Or as Alex suggests in "When Venus erupted," when drinking with Phoebe:

> When Venus erupted
> she was smothered in lava
> when Venus erupted
> all her oceans boiled away
>
> did she harbour life?
> did she turn fierily sterile
> to spite herself?
>
> All affairs are like this. (107)

In "The Wonder", the rapture of Phoebe's voice is juxtaposed with the rapture of looking up at the stars. It's a common technique of Porter's to get this double focus, so the poem is about both the wonder of being in love and the wonder of astronomy. In Porter's verse novels, the metaphorical field often seems more important than the story. Once the field is established, Porter has the skill to be able to adapt and modify her metaphors so that quasars, volcanoes and oceans appear in a variety of poems, with a different tone and effect each time they are used. The power of these metaphors increases by association, resonating backwards and forwards in the verse novel, accruing implications and associations that become increasingly complex. Often it seems as if Porter's chosen metaphorical web is what is really driving the novel, rather than the traditional elements of character, plot and story. This is particularly noticeable in *Wild Surmise*.

Although the metaphors in poems such as "Radiation" are fresh, such as "feeling her mouth open / like an anemone" (80) or "I feel my skin / flake away / in a leprous snowfall // as if I've strayed / and played / in Jupiter's radiation belt" (80-81), the Alex-Phoebe love story cannot avoid formulaic manoeuvers. The "Volcanoes" section of *Wild Surmise* is dominated by Alex's unrequited love for Phoebe, by Alex's sense that the weight she gives to the relationship is not shared by Phoebe. "All affairs are like this", Alex thinks, "You die / of excitement" ("When Venus erupted" 107-8). Phoebe seems to largely exist as an obstacle and quest for Alex to grapple with, as someone who is ultimately unobtainable.

But Phoebe's characterisation doesn't significantly detract from the novel, because Daniel is, in my view, Porter's finest creation as a character. As a creative writing academic with an obsession with poetry, he is Porter's alter-ego. Daniel's reading list is very close to the reading list Porter set when I studied Advanced Poetry Writing with her at UTS in 1992, an inspiring course that had a profound influence on both my understanding of poetry and my own writing. Many of her favourite poets, such as Plath, Akhmatova, Cavafy, Blake, Dickinson, Dante and Shakespeare are prominent. In writing Daniel, it's this poetic heritage that provides Porter with her metaphorical net. When Daniel first sees Alex and Phoebe together, in "Greasy Joe's", he summons Dante:

> Am I in Hell?
>   or the most noxious terrace
>   of Purgatory
>   where you grin and sing and bear
>   it (127)

Later "Diagnosis" ends with these two succinct stanzas:

> The diagnosis is clear.
> My marriage is cactus.

This is my Gallipoli.
Just hit the beach shooting. (131)

Unlike many of Porter's other metaphors in *Wild Surmise*, Daniel's reference to his wife's affair as "my Gallipoli" comes from nowhere and is surprising and powerful. It's a bold use of the association of Australian male identity with the ANZAC myth and effectively suggests that Daniel's sense of worth is tied up with his relationship with his wife. The tendency of males to resort to violence when things go wrong is suggested in the final line with its suicidal overtone, "Just hit the beach shooting." This novel is built around a love triangle, but what sustains it is Porter's ability to dramatise the three sides of the triangle. Daniel's pain and bewilderment is effectively and convincingly portrayed in poem after poem.

In "Charged Particles," Alex enthuses about the prospect of Jupiter making Europa pregnant. This contrasts poignantly with Daniel's post-chemo state, when he can't remember the last time they had sex. He waits for her:

> to get to her bloody feet
> come over
>   and for the first time in a very long while
> touch him. (193)

In *Wild Surmise* Porter dramatises the intensity of Daniel's pain and longing, a pain that is endured rather than resolved. In "Mediocrity", Daniel says to Alex, in his mind perhaps more than in person:

> I am your boring satellite
> your minor planet
> your unnamed moon
> your black asteroid (196-197)

This is an affecting and moving poem where the metaphors Porter has used to suggest love—moon and black asteroid—are now reconfigured as metaphors that signify the human, the mediocre and the ordinary. If Porter's love poetry is her finest achievement, then her exploration of the relationship between Alex and Daniel is her most complex and adult rendering of love.

Wild Surmise, to use Mikhail Bakhtin's term, is dialogical, not monological (18). Rather than being a dramatisation of a love affair, the love affair functions as a way of interrogating the nature of love. In "Love", a complex understanding of this quality is foregrounded. Reflecting about Alex, Daniel says that, "I've forgiven nothing." But in "Love" he still goes on to compare his love to Pushkin duelling to avenge his wife's honour:

> Love, like Pushkin,
> that gets shot horribly in the guts
> and still takes forever to die. (237)

The romantic and heroic stereotypes of love, ushered in by the reference to Pushkin, are undercut by the pain of Daniel's death. It is as if this novel has worked to construct a different language for love, a language that is dominantly human and grows out of tough experience. Porter is equally adept in using Alex's voice to construct this re-examination of love. In "You once asked me" Alex reflects on her love for Phoebe and Daniel, claiming that "I never loved Phoebe / as I loved you" (282). The poem ends with a striking and beautiful image:

> You were the champagne
> glass
> desperate to be heard—
>
> right there singing
> in my careless hand. (283)

The use of "hand" here has a cumulative power for those familiar with Porter's other work, but it is the adjective "careless" that really gives the line and the ending its punch. It is an adjective that suggests regret, longing and self-reproach on Alex's part. It is also appropriate that Daniel, a devotee of poetry, is a champagne glass "singing". This book sings in its exploration of mundane, married love. In comparison, the lesbian love affair merely keeps the wheels of the romantic comedy turning. The themes of *The Monkey's Mask* have come full circle. Now poetry, rather than providing the clues in a murder mystery, is celebrated and honoured through Daniel, the most interesting and complex character that Porter created.

In *El Dorado*, Porter returns to the crime genre she so successfully plundered in *The Monkey's Mask*. This time the detective is a single father, Bill Buchanan, who speaks in an ocker drawl that befits someone from the "Homicide Department / of Hard Fucking Unfair Knocks ("Thin ice" 9). The first poem "The hand" begins with a characteristic Porter motif, with the image of a child's hand poking out of a shallow grave:

> The little girl's
> dead hand
> is sticking stiffly
> up
> as if reaching
> to grab an angel's
> foot. (3)

It is quickly established that Bill's quest is to catch a serial killer, one who doesn't sexually molest the children, but who ritually buries them, with the mark of a "gold" thumbprint on the forehead. In "Making them gold", the child killer identifies himself with a jingle published in *The Age*:

> *My hands make them gold.*
> *My hands make them neverold.*
> *I am where they want to go.*
> *I am El Dorado.* (5; author's italics)

With four dead kids in twelve months, Bill is desperate and turns to his childhood friend, Cath, a Hollywood bigshot whose occupation is to design imaginary worlds for big budget fantasy films and *"has always seen things / no one else can see"* ("The albino guinea pig" 30). She functions as an amateur clairvoyant and as Bill's confidant. Bill is struggling with the demands of raising his feisty teenage daughter and with the loneliness of loveless middle age. In "The pocket", Cath's "annoyingly youthful looking" and "smooth-skinned / animated face" contrasts with Bill's:

> ... lined pitted exhausted
> middle-aged male face
> that grimaces back
> from his shaving mirror
> every morning. (49)

The appearance of Cath, who Bill was in love with as a teenager, only makes matters worse. Bill's unrequited love for Cath, which he still harbors forty years later, is contrasted with Cath's immediate affair with an "absurdly young herpetologist" who tells Cath "about the sex lives / of real snakes" ("Research" 75). The beginning of the novel is dominated by poem after poem whose function is mainly expository. This is compounded by the bleakness of the child murders and the angst-ridden life of Bill Buchanan who is saddled with a difficult daughter, a lonely, sexless life, the reappearance of his childhood crush, and the responsibility for finding a rampant child killer. It's as if Porter set out to place her protagonist in the worst hell imaginable. Reading this, it is hard not to be weighed down by the mass of exposition and the bleak and depressing material. The demands of the narrative set-up have been foregrounded and one consequence of this is that the poetry rarely gets close to anything that has a lyrical impact; it never gets close to singing. This is one of the inherent difficulties of the verse novel form. By writing a narrative in verse, the author creates an unwritten expectation that the poetry will not just tell a story but will also excel as poetry. It's a hard act to pull off, perhaps an impossible one, and it is not one that Porter entirely manages at the start of *El Dorado*.

Happily, the momentum picks up in the second section "Atlantis", beginning with a startling and beautiful lyric, "I touch":

> I touch her lovely wild
> face.
>
> I've been here before.
>
> The white beach.
> The glistening trees.
> The staring savages
> on the shore. (85)

This poem has a wonderful economy and power. The positioning of "wild" at the end of the first line gives it a resonance and emphasis that conjures up both the risk of exploration and the strictures of a civilizing society. "I've been here before" is a very matter-of-fact line, yet it also manages to suggest that the experience is simultaneously like other experiences and unlike them. The conceit of the poem is to compare the moment of colonial invasion with the moment of love, recalling both Keats's "wild surmise" (699) and Porter's previous verse novel, as well as suggesting that this relationship has its own subtle power dynamic. The "staring savages" puts the lover and the loved one squarely at the centre of the frame, which is how people tend to see themselves when they are caught up in romantic love. The suggestion that the savages are "on the shore" implies that the lovers are at sea which is another resonant metaphor. That the trees are "glistening" is surprising. Surely Australian trees don't glisten in the light? The association strengthens the sexual undertones of this word. This poem moves from physical touch to the beauty of nature within the context of invasion and possession. It's a sophisticated, memorable and powerful lyric that is typical of Porter at her best.

The age gap between Cath and Lily is used by Porter to heighten the contrast between innocent youth and the grown-up world. Is falling in love merely childish, a desire to live in some version of fantasyland, the sort of place that Cath spends her life creating? The lure of being forever young is symbolised by the serial killer presenting one of his victims with the novel, *Peter Pan*. Is this fetishisation of youth one of the problems of contemporary western culture? At the heart of *El Dorado* is this contrast between fantasy and reality, the tendency of people to desire the comforts of a fantasy when confronted with the on-going mundanity of daily life. It's not completely clear where Porter's allegiances lie, but she certainly wants the reader to consider the question.

The crime genre is never just about solving the crime. The detective's love life, his work struggles, his home life, issues with alcohol and past failures are common tropes. Just as the romance genre almost always brings the lovers together, then splits them apart, so the crime genre tends to throw up a number of red herrings and false leads, otherwise the crime is solved too quickly. Porter keeps the wheels turning in *El Dorado*, but it's the love story that has the greater urgency and impact. In contrast, the crime story struggles to establish the verisimilitude that is an essential building block of fiction. As *El Dorado* builds to a climax, there are a number of plot points that are unconvincing. For example, the serial killer entraps Cath by pretending to be her lover, Lily, then manages to drug and kidnap her from a daytime café. How this difficult feat is achieved is not really explained. Then the killer releases Cath by leaving her in a vault at a Melbourne cemetery. For some puzzling reason—the effect of the drugs seems the only possibility—Cath can remember very little about this encounter, though she is still able to make the link with a boy Bill and Cath had tormented and locked up in their childhood.

Now close to discovering the identity of El Dorado, Bill sets off alone, driven by the mistaken belief that the killer has his daughter. He finds the killer, who is the child psychologist Axel Pine, the assumed identity of his childhood enemy, Raymond Putney. But incredibly, for an experienced detective, Buchanan is also drugged and taken prisoner by Pine. How Pine does this is very shadowy and seems as inconsistent with Pine's experience and abilities as it is with Buchanan's. At the level of both plot and character, this is implausible and unconvincing. And as if to mirror what has already happened with Cath, Bill is released from an imminent death in a burning house by a "blazing El Dorado" who hurls Bill through "the exploding window" ("The Fire Snake" 364) and provides a suicide note to explain that *"my mercy is my revenge"* ("Suicide note" 365). It all seems very "unreal". There are a number of echoes of T.S. Eliot's great modernist poem "The Waste Land" in these developments. For example, Bill's potential last thoughts in the poem "Where the drowned go" echo Eliot's invocation to "fear death by water", as does the end of III. The Fire Sermon:

> Burning burning burning burning
> O Lord Thou pluckest me out
> O Lord Thou pluckest
>
> burning (62)

Bill Buchanan is also plucked out of imminent death through the actions of a suddenly benevolent serial killer. This is the same idea used twice in the conclusion of the story. It's all too easy, lacks verisimilitude and never develops the nail-biting tension of a good page turner. Porter doesn't really meet the demands of crime fiction in this verse novel, which delivers a plot outline without the flesh and bones or the tension of a convincing thriller. Writing crime is not one of Porter's strengths, and judging by *El Dorado*, it's not where her real interests lie.

This question of what is real and what is imagined and fantasised underpins both the romance and the crime strands in the narrative. When Mark Kelso's child photographs (a reference to the controversy surrounding Bill Henson's work) are condemned by El Dorado, Cath responds that "'It's not real, Bill. / It's just a shoot'" ("The dark dripping wall" 174). Alternatively, in "Ordinary" Cath watches Lily as she is about to milk her tiger snake, and her mind wanders from a fantasy to the reality of Lily's actuality:

> Cath's head is popping
> with gorgeous-breasted
>   Minoan priestesses
> wreathed in writhing
>   purple pythons.
>
> But this snake
>   is real
>
> Real –
>   like Lily herself –
> her olive-skinned face
> her red-checked
>   shapeless
> flannelette shirt. (114)

Later, after Cath has been estranged from Lily and is on the verge of begging forgiveness, comes the strong poem, "Reasons to back out now". It begins with arresting lines:

> One.
> I have always opened my arms

when love
smashes through my front door. (294)

It ends with extended metaphor of a high stakes card game:

Ten.
Smother me with swollen red hearts.
Club my grinning skull to diamond bits.
Then bury me with pitch-black spades.
Love, oh high stakes love,
deal me in. (295)

It's when Porter writes about the high stakes of love that her writing burns, that it convinces, that it soars. The love poems seem "real" perhaps because Porter is careful to build in an awareness of the illusions and madness of love. Her poems of longing and desire provide some of the strongest moments in her verse novels. She interrogates love, from first glance and touch, through a multiplicity of situations, to the loss and death of the beloved. Her achievement is particularly impressive in *Wild Surmise*, where her exploration of the novel's central relationship constructs a language for love that is tough, complex and capable of singing. She excels as a love poet, one who is capable of laying out the narrative of love and inhabiting the mind and body of the lover with an intensity that is moving, arresting and lyrical.

Works Cited

Bakhtin, Mikhail. *Problems of Dostoevsky's Poetics*, translated by Carly Emerson, University of Minnesota, 1984.
Barthes, Roland. *S/Z*, translated by Richard Miller, Hill and Wang, 1986.
Bataille, Georges. *Literature and Evil*, translated by Alastair Hamilton, Marion Boyars, 1995.

Browning, Robert. "My Last Duchess." *The Norton Anthology of Poetry*, edited by Alexander W. Allison et al., W.W. Norton, 1975, pp. 772-3.

Dickens, Charles. *Bleak House*, Penguin, 1971.

Digby, Sue. "Festive, Fun and Dangerous." *Island*, vol. 57, 1993, pp. 34-9.

Dostoevsky, Fyodor. *Crime and Punishment*, translated by Richard Pevear and Larissa Volokhonsky, Vintage, 1993.

Eliot, T.S. *Selected Poems*, Faber and Faber, 1954.

Fallon, Kathleen Mary. "Ham-Fists In Those 'Male Size Golf Gloves'." *Southerly*, vol. 55, no.3, 1995, pp. 191-7.

Joyce, James. *Ulysses*, Penguin, 1969.

Keats, John. "On First Looking into Chapman's Homer." *The Norton Anthology of Poetry*, edited by Alexander W. Allison et al., W.W. Norton, 1975, p. 699.

Lorca, Frederico García. "Play and Theory of the Duende." *In Search of Duende*, edited and translated by Christopher Maurer, New Directions, 2010.

Maiden, Jennifer. "Sex and Power by the Nile." *Australian Book Review*, vol. 140, 1992, pp. 42-3.

Maurer, Christopher. Preface. *In Search of Duende* by Lorca, Frederico García, New Directions, 2010.

McCredden, Lyn. "The Mask Slips." *Arena Magazine*, vol.48, 1995, pp. 48-50.

Moorhead, Finola. "She Doesn't Prove Who Did It, Anyway." *Southerly*, vol. 55, no.1, 1995, pp.177-92.

Pollnitz, Christopher. "Australian Verse Novels."*Heat*, vol. 7, 2004, pp. 229-52.

Porter, Dorothy. *Akhenaten*, University of Queensland Press, 1992.

---. *Driving Too Fast*, University of Queensland Press, 1989.

---. *El Dorado*, Picador, 2007.

---. *The Monkey's Mask*, Picador, 2000.

---. *The Night Parrot*, Black Lightning, 1984.

---. *What a Piece of Work*, Picador, 1999.

---. *Wild Surmise*, Picador, 2002.
Seth, Vikram. *The Golden Gate*, Faber and Faber, 1986.
Shakespeare, William. *The Kingsway Shakespeare*, George G. Harrap, 1927.
The Monkey's Mask. Directed by Samantha Lang. Arena, 2002.
Wearne, Alan. *The Nightmarkets: a Novel*, Penguin, 1986.
Wood, James. *The Irresponsible Self: On Laughter and the Novel*, Pimlico, 2005.

Chapter 7

John Watson and the Comedy of Landscape

Martin Langford

Few things have puzzled us more, in recent times, than our relationships with our environments: not just rural and "natural" environments but built ones as well. Increasingly, it all seems like the one bewilderment: perplexity about how to see the green world is inseparable from anxiety over how to imagine the constructed one. As recently as 1978, Les Murray was able to write, "our culture is still in its Bœotian phase, and any distinctiveness we possess is still firmly anchored in the bush" (179). The fact that poets like Peter Porter, engaged in a dialogue with Murray about this that stressed alternative – "Attic" – sources of authority: "the permanently upright city where speech is nature" (23), felt that they had to pursue such things overseas, only confirmed the weight of Murray's argument. The key thing, however, was that we inhabited a polarity, and that what one saw when one looked at either country or city depended on which viewpoint one looked from.

For the Bœotian, land was a source of the numinous and a ground for narrative, as in David Campbell's "Cocky's Calendar" (77), in which the permanence of the land is the means by which the transience of the human becomes visible:

> On frosty days, when I was young,
> I rode out early with the men
> And mustered cattle till their long
> Blue shadows covered half the plain;

And when we turned our horses round,
Only the homestead's point of light,
Men's voices, and the bridles' sound,
Were left in the enormous night.

And now again the sun has set
All yellow and a greening sky
Sucks up colour from the wheat –
And here's my horse, my dog and I.

Antithetically, we imagined cities as either the apotheoses of achievement Porter sought, places where civilisation was at its peak ("Jerusalem Athens Alexandria / Vienna London" Eliot 72) or, since such a description could hardly apply to the majority of towns, as variations of the inadequate place: from Blake's industrial nightmares and Dickens's slums to the deserts of ennui and alienation of the twentieth century. Gradually, however, this polarity broke down. This was a world-wide phenomenon. Perhaps an increasing number of people came to see things through the prism of the city, or perhaps the polarities themselves were no longer sustainable: as our knowledge of ecology became greater, all land became at least potentially visible, and not just the useful and picturesque bits. It is a change too big to explore in a brief chapter: all that can be offered here is a comment on a sampling of its effects in Australian verse, and a note on one poet who has explored them.

For the generation after Murray and Porter – irrespective of how they characterised their verse, or of which side of the "poetry wars" they thought of themselves as being on – poets no longer wrote out of a simple polarity between country and city. They still saw differences there, but they were becoming less and less central to their perspectives. If neither the Bœotian nor Attic perspective was as compelling as it had been, it was also true that neither was replaced by a comprehensive alternative. This, for instance, is Laurie Duggan:

> Vaguely curved
horizon, white caps (some of these turn out to be seagulls), breakers, surfers between the flags – one just fell off his board – and a dirty textured sand beach. Apple-green dustbin with two sharp ridges, a faint ridge and rounded lip–partly rusted; and behind this, Norfolk pines, a white railed path, slope of interconnected grass root systems, rock inscribed FOSSIL SUCKS, power lines hung down to two-toned green lavatory/changing shed (half obscured), and the rock ledge with rectangular swimming pool. In front of all this about 30-40 people move with varying degrees of grace towards and away from the water (22).

And this is Robert Gray, in 1993:

> Makeshift as chicken coops, houses are strewn
> along
> the muddy strip
> of coastline, under
> the escarpment's great, black
> uplifted wave,
> where sun goes early
> off the narrow land and
> the heckling pit
> of the sea. This from a lofty railway
> among weeds. The sun as though
> an eraser is at work
> in the tufted heights, reducing them
> to a smear. Below,
> garbage among dry stalks; newspaper, greaseproof wrap
> on wire fences. A hawk balances
> above a toilet block. (72)

There are a few differences in style or emphasis: Gray is more willing to explore the scene with metaphor; he paces his phrases using line-breaks. But the similarities are pronounced: both display an unhierarchical agglomeration of details, and are unwilling either to draw conclusions or otherwise explain what they see. Neither perspective could remotely be described as either Bœotian or Attic. These representations are much more circumspect. The scenes are unpretentious, familiar and resistant to interpretation – schematized in terms neither of the sacred nor of cultural achievement. They are examples of the amorphous, ad hoc environments that humans so absent-mindedly project everywhere, it seems, they have needs to fulfil: mostly of a practical nature, but sometimes with a few, barely-conscious, aesthetic gestures thrown in. In the Duggan excerpt, there are apple-green dustbins, Norfolk pines, graffiti, toilet and change sheds, and a pool; in the Gray: houses "strewn / along / the muddy strip / of coastline" (l 1-4), a railway among weeds, garbage, wire fences – and another toilet block. In rejecting, or ignoring, the earlier schematizations, this later generation was also rejecting the versions of the numinous that underpinned them: in Porter's city the divine might become available through talent and effort; Bœotia was underwritten – though with local variations – by belief. But it is hard to see traces of divinity in these scenes – and with the retreat of the divine comes a problematisation of all ground. Neither country nor city, neither culturally ambitious nor resonant with pieties, these are little more than environments with physical attributes: verbal sketches from a generation which had become reluctant to project where it could not substantiate.

In recent years, the problematised environment has become a pervasive subject matter for poetry. One might cite, for instance, Martin Harrison's "Incident at Galore Hill"

> Right then, I was struck by the space, the shadow,
> perhaps by neither ... It was the ground's bareness
> which stayed with me" (*Music*),

Jill Jones's "Where we live"

A canvas of anxiety
inscribes walls
and metal
where birds
and people go over
paving and crossings (63)

or Louis Armand's sequence, "tendances morbides" ("'we knew nothing of thresholds & distance'" 69). There has been some exploration of the possibility of investing the environment with alternative spiritualities: John Anderson (passim) and Louise Crisp (*uplands*) have meditated on whether it might be possible to write a poetry which sees the landscape through Indigenous eyes. On the whole, however, poets who did not have an Indigenous heritage themselves have been wary of that leap, and most have felt no alternative but to explore the environment in the difficult light of a culture which has grown cautious about its conclusions.

One poet who has explored this territory, and who deserves to be much better known, is John Watson. Watson studied literature with William Maidment at Sydney University in the sixties, but spent his working life as a mathematics teacher. In 2003, he published *A First Reader*, and has since published *Montale: A Biographical Anthology*, e*rasure traces*, *Views from Mt Brogden and A Dictionary of Minor Poets*, *Occam's Aftershave* and *Three Painters* (*Collected Works* 1 to 4), together with a large number of chapbooks, versifications of other texts, and other volumes of light or occasional verse. Maidment argued for the ludic as an essential element in good writing, and it is an important vein in Watson's practice:

On An Edict of William Carlos Williams

If it ain't a pleasure
You're probably using
Seminar-earnest

Unplayful language.

You know the kind:
Where language has been pulped,
Compressed to a mud brick
And hurled at the head.

Contrariwise there's the playful
Such as, "What famous admiral
Said, 'Kiss me hard-on'? Answer:
Fellatio Nelson."
Lacking this element
Like scientists still looking
For a suitable retort,
It ain't a poem. (*Reader* 64)

As statements of aesthetic preference tend to be, this is a little more full frontal than Watson's normal note, but it does, very broadly, define his attitude. No matter how 'philosophically' he writes, he cannot help but inflect his ideas not just with humour, but with the pleasure of the text. When one insists on poetry as delight, one's practice can overlap with light verse. While some of his work might be accurately described as such, overall, the term does not give a sufficient idea either of its thoughtfulness or philosophical scope. Moreover, "light verse" has so many pejorative connotations, one must qualify the term to say that whereas he does frequently practise what has traditionally been called light verse, the lightness is more a matter of lightness of touch, as of a pleasing inconsequence: an expression of a desire to explore the text in such a way as to invite the reader into a communion of surprise, delight and absurdity.

Even when he is writing light verse, he works in a tradition which hasn't been explored much in this country. Australian light verse has largely been grounded in the colloquial, and to some extent in the anti-intellectual. We have had much less of a history of poets being immersed in the tradition and writing light verse as a way of taking pleasure in it, but this is the very different position from which Watson works. Thomas Peacock is a distant literary cousin: a friend of the Romantics, steeped in their verse, whose practice was nevertheless a satirical play on their absurdities. Watson does, in fact, cite Peacock's *Gryll Grange* as a key text, alongside Oulipo and the work of Queneau. Unlike those writers of light verse, however, such as Peacock or C.S. Calverley, whose work was tensioned against traditional metrical models, Watson's imagination was captured by the Modernists – by French film, and by the music and literature of twentieth-century Europe. Although he does write light verse using traditional forms, much of his work plays with and against the tropes and discoveries of the modernists – exhibiting layers of parenthetical self-consciousness, for instance, or unexpected authorial interventions. Unlike, however, some of his contemporaries, whose renderings of pre-existing works, even when cast in humorous terms, were written with specific literary arguments in mind: Louis Armand's "Patrick White as a Headland" (Plunkett 17), for instance, or John Tranter's versions of "Dover Beach" (24, 71), Watson does not wish to replace or, in many cases, even critique the past. For him, the play is enough: it is a way of engaging with favourite texts – of paying them homage, and of engendering his own.

He will, however, undermine less credible texts at the same time as taking delight in them. The prose work, *Views from Mount Brogden*, for instance, is prompted by those nineteenth century conversations in which settlers tried to decide which traditions should be transplanted to the new land. It purports to be the diary of a nineteenth-century minister whose intention to write an ecclesiastical history of West Wyalong mutates, upon familiarisation with the district, into The Possibilities of Adaptation in the Bland, in which he explores whether the "ancient festivals" of Europe might be suitable for this "new and fertile soil":

> *Shrovetide skipping, for example, when ropes are set across the street requiring the passers-by to skip through them. In the rough and sparse and tree-stump littered tracks winding in and out of mallee clumps, what could I devise to institute such a skipping procession and have it accepted?* (*Views* 12).

He continues:

> *how my mind dwells on the Olympian Games Upon the Cotswold Hills and on the curious Election of the Mayor of Oak Street. Then when I observed some black swans and iridescent ducks amongst the reeds, inevitably memory drifted to the question of Upping the Swans* (13).

Later, he tries his hand at writing a Christmas Mummers play for the locals, with a cast including Father Christmas, John Oxley, Old Betty, Captain Bluster, The Doctor, Governor Bligh, Fletcher Christian and The Digger of Bottles (100). He takes too much pleasure in pursuing the absurdities of cultural transplantation for the satire to become pointed: this is writing which resolves to delight rather than anger. Gentle, however, as it is, the absurdities speak for themselves: the demolition of the Reverend's ambitions is as comprehensive as it needs to be.

But he also has an overtly thoughtful side. He never loses his desire to play, but in other poems, he is engaged by more serious matters – such as time, or the way we experience the environment:

Manifesto

As *the object* was to Francis Ponge
    So to me *the incident*, fraught
        And fretted with grooves, nodes,
Branches, digressions, reconciliations.

FEEDING THE GHOST 1

Had I not been for a moment delayed
    By a mountain of ash in the main street,
    The Water-Board offices might not
Have shut their doors and drawn the blinds

For a night of condensation inside
    Just as I arrived, nor the sun
    Wanting to be part of the action gestured
As it sank into the palms' coiffure.

A laburnum bent over the bus-shelter
    And swallows diverging from the river bank
    Flew in flat curves beset with cusps
Then in shadow the beautiful pastry-cook

Waved from her window calling to me something
    About our all too human feeling
    Of expulsion from Paradise when we see
Nesting creatures in trees in a crowded field.

I waved agreement but was already distracted
    By a woman driving away with her dress shut
    In the car door. Then, returning
To my own car I found my camera

Unaccountably stopped down to an f-setting
    Requiring film of almost legendary speed
    When in fact it was now getting dark.
A horse looked up from its trough

Water pouring back from its mouth; and pigeons
    Partitioned the sky so that dusk had the street
    In the several available mirrors looking
Like a lake painted by Seurat.
                Ponge's pebble,

His cake of soap, even his sun,
        Are relatively immobile and thus
        Encourage their own contemplation.
This is the provenance and charm of the object.

Contrariwise, the incident is wayward,
        By its nature intransitive and unrepeatable,
        Beginning here and ending somewhere else,
Often losing itself on the way.

For instance, as I was driving then
        Into the sunset, over the railway bridge
        Below which at the time a goods train
Slowly passed, covered in wattle pollen,

Workmen blocked the road, draped
        With power lines being raised slowly,
        Stanchions tilted and swaying, eventually
Made perpendicular. There in the car

I thought about Preston Sturges,
        At sixteen installed as manager
        Of the Deauville branch of his much
Married mother's face-cream business

Where he invented for her a kiss-proof lipstick
        (Pre-dating by several years his invention
        Of a vertical take-off aeroplane),
A business based on a recipe

Acquired from her Turkish husband. One night
        She had left in haste, all in black,
        For a party given by Isadora Duncan
To whom she lent the fateful scarf.

> After the road-block the traffic
> > Seemed to move more easily. The sun
> > Lingered above the palisade
> Of the railway embankment bordering the lake
>
> And for an interval seemed even
> > To confer on this incident — or chain
> > Of interfluent incidents —
> The stasis of an apple or cliff-face. (*erasure traces* 39)

Much of this is the product of an imagination populated by comic impulses: the earnest persona, with its *manifesto* about *incidents* (l 2); the formal touches ("Had I not been for a moment delayed / by a mountain of ash in the main street" ll 5-6), suggesting so much more control than is ever actually displayed; the disregard for the compulsion of narrative – the failed attempt to get to the Water Board is simply overwhelmed by the "interfluent" (l 67) flurry of the inconsequential and the distracting, and not mentioned again. Watson, moreover, takes a comedian's pleasure in this anarchy of the mundane – not least because he has the skills to articulate it: to theatricalise the inanimate (the offices drawing the blinds "for a night of condensation" (ll 8-9), or the sun, "wanting to be part of the action" (ll 9-10), gesturing as it sinks into the palms) or to calm it – with the "stasis of an apple or a cliff-face" (l 68) in a universe in which nothing stays still.

Like the Gray and Duggan excerpts, Watson's poem is set in a decontextualised environment with no attempt to isolate clusters of significance that might characterise it as Bœotian, Attic – or anything else. Some of his encounters are with artefacts (the mountain of ash, the camera, the Preston Sturges narrative) and some are with aspects of the natural world (the swallows, the pigeons, the sunset) but neither takes precedence in any hierarchy of meanings. He has, however, taken the decontextualisation further than they have: he has withdrawn his speaker from coherent sequence, by changing the relationship of viewer and scene from one of static objectification, to one of participation in a "chain / Of interfluent events" (ll 66-67), because he has recognised that the experience of the environment cannot be isolated from the presence of the viewer – that interior and exterior are the one Moebius strip. The seamless way the speaker switches from watching the installation of the power lines to thinking about Preston Sturges (so well-suited to being the presiding spirit for all this inconsequentiality), as if the unpredictability of the daydream were on an experiential par with the unexpectedness of occurrences in the street, has the effect of inviting the whole crazy "sequence" inside: reality is what the viewer – or participant – notices.

The work displays a confidence with spatialities which may stem, one might guess, from a mind habituated to mathematical representations. The incident is "fretted with grooves, nodes, / Branches, digressions, reconciliations" (ll 3-4). The swallows "Flew in flat curves beset with cusps" (l 15). The pigeons "Partitioned the sky so that the dusk had the street / In the several available mirrors looking / Like a lake painted by Seurat" (ll 30-32). And of course, there is the way the drive to the Water Board is envisaged as a "chain / Of interfluent incidents" (ll 66-67). It is as if, prompted by the increasing capacity of mathematics to describe complex physical events, Watson thought he would see what language could do with them. This facility with the visual and spatial pervades his work. In "A Scientific Prospect", from the sequence, *Nine Views of Mt Hay* (*Reader* 11), he imagines that the mountain, evidently because of its curious, desolate features, might be a suitable place on which to spread out some deck chairs, and watch the origin of the earth, if only a suitable mirror might be found, at exactly the right distance – half-way, in light-years, between the origin and the present.

Neither mathematics nor light verse would, until recently, have been regarded as likely sources for serious poetry. But in the endlessly changing crossweave that is literary possibility, both offer ways of thinking about important contemporary concerns. On the one hand, there is an increasing convergence between what writers

– particularly poets – will accept, in terms of substantiation, and what the sciences and maths-based subjects have always required. The latter, of course, haven't changed. But the poets are becoming wary of extrapolation, and cautious about the epistemological status of claims. Gods, sources and essences are becoming increasingly difficult to use in a poem. It is not, however, simply a matter of an increasing strictness of argument: our imaginations are becoming accepting of maths – if other forces are difficult to justify, at least maths is a way of describing the world in a way one can trust.

As for the lightness of the touch: it wasn't long ago that one had to maintain a certain gravitas if one wanted one's verse to be taken seriously. It is still a tone which is available to the poet – one thinks, say, of the work of Alison Croggon or Peter Boyle. But this is a period which permits great variation, and there are many poets who work with less intense tones, closer to those of conversation: Ken Bolton, say, or joanne burns. It could, in fact, be argued, given their widespread use, that these are the default tones of contemporary verse – continuous with the tones of colloquial speech and casual interaction (and closer, in many ways, to the tones of eighteenth century poetry than to those of the nineteenth). If that is the case, then Watson's ludic and indirect manner is, in fact, closer to that of the mainstream than it might look at first glance. It is just that he arrived there by an unusual route – through light verse and the play of absurdity, rather than through colloquialised verse and the play of literary or linguistic ideas.

It has become a commonplace that landscapes are functions not only of the needs that are projected onto them, but of the ways in which they are seen. A recurring theme for Watson is the way the landscape can barely be said to exist without the consciousness that makes it available. In "Empiricism" (*Reader* 69), Watson ponders the paradox that the empirical world – which he doesn't doubt exists – cannot be accessed without human perception:

Empiricism

For which the discovery by Patrick Heron of a Matisse subject becomes a double emblem

The sparrow camel (or ostrich), in which appellation
Sir Thomas Browne reaches out and touches Miss Moore,
Stands glaring across a fence, resists language
And asserts only that it is not an emu.

Touching Miss Moore, we are daily reminded
Of her limpid example as we uncover appearance,
Of how waterfall-like everything can be;
We part tussocks of bracken and find the stream

About to fall through its whole length, like an upended plank,
On to some splash rocks' springboard far below.
Merrily it makes its way towards the brink
As if sharing a secret with the rapids downstream.

It or they, or this gawking pincushion of feathers
Staring in a field near the sudden chasm,
These, or almost anything in the honeyed particularity
Elsewhere, could be taken to represent the empirical.

For most touching in Miss Moore's steadfast
Advocacy of the real world as manifest
At its most curious extremities, its bell curve's
Flattening, such as are found in, for instance,

The underwater air-breathing mammal, flying fish,
Swimming birds, the flightless foraging land-bird
So shy that hibernation is forced upon it merely
By the snapping of a forest-floor fern,

FEEDING THE GHOST 1

Equatorial snow, the place of maximum rainfall
In the whole world, where a ten minute walk
In blazingly brief sunlight affords great pleasure,
Oddities elected to represent silent majorities —

These return us to the theme of the empirical.
Francis Bacon steps from his coach, curious
To feel the snow and its refrigerative effect on a duck
Thereby succumbing to a highly empirical pneumonia.

Everywhere the sharp edges of flint-like
Observables, like a paddock of plovers,
Confer their primacy. The early sun
Making the mountain a mile away like mica

Lit from behind, an X-ray photograph
Held up to a fierce light, joins the melee
As it clears the hill behind us. The sparrow camel
Moves away from the electrified fence.

That the empirical is lovelier and sustains us
More than all the empyrean empires
As Locke (and Hume revelling in pineapple) saw
Makes all the more engaging as its emblem

The following: "In 1948
Walking on the tip of the Cap d'Antibes
I saw that we had arrived at the subject
Of a Matisse painting complete with pine branches

And branching road. Moving sideways until
The viewpoint was precise I found my arm
Striking the stone wall. Moss fell.
I found there old palette scrapings of scarlet,

Ultramarine, violet, lemon and emerald, all
Oxidising between stones." Thus we have
The persistence both of physical substance
And physical means, all remaining

In the absence of the artefact made from them.
But even so, that landscape lacks true grit.
There should be sparrow camels pecking the ground
And bringing to that glaring flux a measure of indignation. (69)

Patrick Heron's "double emblem" refers both to the way the existence of the scene still requires human verification (supplied, in this case, by the absent painting), and to the way we regard the empirical as being congenitally lacking – as somehow also requiring verification – as if we were forever indignant that there is not more to it than it barefacedly and untranscendentally supplies: the "sparrow camel" should be "pecking the ground" and "bringing to that glaring flux a measure of indignation" (ll 58-59) in response to this – an indignation which is, after all, only a version of the fascination, celebration and resentment that prompted Matisse to paint. If "Manifesto" is both about a particular landscape, and a meditation on landscape in general, "Empiricism" is specifically the latter. With a controlled indirection that Miss Moore might have been proud of, Watson leads us by "this gawking pincushion of feathers / Staring in a field near the sudden chasm" (ll13-14), past Francis Bacon's "highly empirical pneumonia" (l 32), to the spot on the Cap d'Antibes which contains such a serendipitous cluster of verifications: the smears of paint which are evidence for Matisse's original act; the scene itself, the original for the painting; and, most enigmatically, the complex homage of the absent painting – yet another attempt to engage sensually with a world which does not exist without the senses.

Watson's sense of the strangeness of things drives this poem: he knows the empirical is not a straightforward issue: that everything resolves to the irresolvable act of perception. He notes how "waterfall-like everything can be" (l 7). He refers to the "sharp edges of flint-like / observables" (l 33) – with all the conditionality and interdependence that "observables" implies. But the way he apprehends strangeness is to delight in it. This represents an important difference between Watson's attitude, and that of many of his peers who otherwise work in similar territory. Another difference, at least with some of his contemporaries, lies in the tightness with which he manages the arc of the text. It is a long way from a gawking sparrow camel to an anecdote about a place at which Matisse once painted, but Watson covers that ground without missing a beat. That he is able to do so is partly a result of the way the wayward incidentals of the poem are governed by the taut play of the ideas they exemplify, and partly to the lightness of touch with which he unreels his surprises: starting with Sir Thomas Browne's crazy name for the ostrich (quite possibly the starting point for the whole poem), with its glaring resistance to language, generalising into Miss Moore's world of "Oddities elected to represent silent majorities" (l 28), past the arguments of Locke and Hume, and the anecdote about the painting of the Cap d'Antibes, and then back to the sparrow-camel and its indignation.

The tension between the puzzling nature of things, and the playful nature of language, underpins a great deal of his work. An awareness of that tension – or a desire to explore it – may in fact be the place at which Watson begins to write. "erasure traces" (*erasure*) is a longish (27 pages) riff on the way the selective choices of the creative act are both clumsy and comic, in comparison to the way a river is a "model of erasure, revision, recision" (12). Later, he suggests "The river might also be representing / The world history of art ..." (27) – so ruthless and efficient is it in its deletions. This is a quieter, more overtly thoughtful poem, but even here, one feels that his creative alertness wasn't aroused until he found a vein of word-play to exploit: "Thus let Riparian / Become Parian" (24). In his "Biographical Anthology" of Montale, prompted by the "mistaken" nature of Montale's metaphors – moonlight, for instance, for snow

– Watson, as MTC Cronin notes, "magically mistakes himself for Montale" (*Montale* – cover).

It may, at first, seem surprising that a voice grounded in wordplay should be a vehicle by which to explore the decreasing number of things one can say with confidence about the physical world. But the less one can assume, the greater the number of things that are strange and unpredictable. And play allows access to that strangeness: the comic voice offers a solution to perhaps the key technical problem faced by poets who write about non-human aspects of the world. To the extent that poetry is an energised articulation of alternative perspectives, a fundamental issue with all philosophically-based verse arises from the fact that ideas and environments are inarticulate: they may be the object of meditation, but they themselves cannot participate in any dialogue. And so the poet has no mechanism by which the voice of the poem – the means by which the poem either lifts off the page or dies – can move beyond commentary or explication. It must remain, literally, one dimensional – stuck in the monotone of the poet's knowingness. The reader may be invited to witness the poet's thoughts, but not to participate in them. Watson's personæ, however, by becoming the site at which expectation and actuality interact, allow the voice to flex two-dimensionally, and thus for the reader to enter the poem. The principal tension in "Manifesto" is between the speaker's verbal sophistication with physical behaviours – he is, after all, defining and meditating on the nature of incidents – and his somewhat hapless misreadings and responses despite this, exemplified by his many moments of surprise – at the camera's f-stop being changed, or at the water pouring from the horse's mouth. It is as if no mere display of cleverness could ever manage the irrepressible unexpectedness of events. But because of the openness and availability of the speaker's voice – schoolmasterly, jokey, modest, attentive – the reader also commits to his disjunctive and confident anticipations, and therefore shares in the discomfort as reality runs interference on expectation.

By limiting the capacity of the speaker to interpret what he sees, the landscape becomes a participant in the comedy. As a function of perception, this unpredictable world – "a theatre of events / Decisive, unsyllogistic, / Pure, quite uncontingent" ("Tableaux" *Reader* 6) – becomes available to the reader through the act of sharing the personae's misapprehensions and astonishments: rather than merely looking on, the reader participates in the comedy. It is always difficult to find ways of making the inanimate and the non-human available to poetry. That Watson has found a way to do so is no small achievement.

Works Cited

Anderson, John. *The Forest Set Out Like the Night*, Black Pepper, 1995.
Armand, Louis. "Tendances Morbides." *Strange Attractors*, Salt, 2003, pp. 69-78.
Campbell, David. "Cocky's Calendar." *Collected Poems*, Angus and Robertson, 1989, pp.74-79.
Crisp, Louise. *uplands*, Five Islands Press, 2007.
Duggan, Laurie. "Blue Hills 11." *The Collected Blue Hills*, Puncher and Wattmann, 2012.
Eliot, T.S. "The Waste Land (V: What the Thunder Said)." *Collected Poems*, Faber and Faber, 1969, pp. 59-80.
Gray, Robert. "The South Coast, While Looking for a House." *Certain Things*, Heinemann, 1993, pp. 72-73.
Harrison, Martin. *Music*, Vagabond Press, 2005.
Jones, Jill. *Ash is Here, So are Stars*, Wakefield Press, 2012.
Murray, Les. "On Sitting Back and Thinking About Porter's Boeotia." *The Peasant Mandarin*, University of Queensland Press, 1978, pp. 172-184.
Peacock, Thomas Love. *Headlong Hall and Gryll Grange*, edited by M.Baron and M. Slater, Oxford University Press, 1987.
Plunkett, Felicity, editors. "Patrick White as a Headland." *Thirty Australian Poets*, University of Queensland Press, 2011, p. 17.

Porter, Peter. "On First Looking into Chapman's Hesiod." *Living in a Calm Country*, Oxford University Press, 1975.

Queneau, Raymond. *Exercises in Style*, translated by Barbara Wright, New Directions, 1981.

Tranter, John. "Grover Leach." and "See Rover Reach." *Studio Moon*, Salt, 2003, p. 24,71.

Watson, John. *A First Reader*, Five Islands Press, 2003.

---. *Erasure Traces*, Puncher and Wattmann, 2008.

---. *Montale: A Biographical Anthology*, Puncher and Wattmann, 2004.

---. *Occam's Aftershave*, Puncher and Wattmann, 2012.

---. *Views from Mt Brogden* and *A Dictionary of Minor Poets*, Puncher and Wattmann, 2008.

Chapter 8

Pam Brown's Ghostly Signature: "Half here/Half gone"

Lyn McCredden

Already, in her 1974 volume *Automatic Sad*, poet Pam Brown's melancholy protagonist is seriously dissatisfied. S/he sees "... dark corners / and black holes here" ("The Collapse" 17), losing her head "midframe in the city again / with a bag of banal images" (17). S/he is "desperate / in similar sad thoughts / think(s) maybe some angel ... might roll into the house and unwrap the mystery I've been solving for thousands of years" (17). Poet, social critic and existential being are close here, but distinct; each ghosts the other, playing hard to get and hard to pin down, with each other let alone with the reader. Is "The Collapse" an indicative poem of tentative hope and poetic generation, or of melancholy/ruefulness/ irony/ self-disappearance, or both? Between irony, social critique and tongue-in-cheek, Brown's poems are little disappearing acts. Or at least putative attempts at self-deconstruction, being both within language, and pressing to be somewhere beyond it: "Half here / Half gone" (106)

Brown is good at disappearing. A great number of her verse forms court slenderness, create restlessly invisible protagonists. But in her characteristically brief, precise, step down lines, many poems wrestle with the opposite of disappearance: a longing for connection, recognition, substance, a readership. In 2005 I published a critical article on Brown's poetry, entitled "'untranscended / life itself'" (McCredden 2005), in which I argued that the ghostly and the public, worldly personas of "Pam Brown" were intimately related despite their differences, and were jointly engaged in a persistent theological or spiritual quest, even as all poetic signs pointed to the Now, and the Here. Brown's characteristically spare, understated poetry, which nevertheless sometimes bursts into almost fulsome prose, is chock-a-bloc with earthy, earthed, witty and ironic gestures, immersed in the concrete laneways and apartment blocks of her urban settings, but always also maintaining a curious distance from the worlds it frequents.

Two decades after *Automatic Sad*, the protagonist (an inner urban poet and librarian) munches on her "thought burger, ("Funk Descending" 46) still enmeshed in "this whacky genre, / this poetry" ("Seven Days" 47) She is both at home in the seedy vigour of her world, and apart: flâneur, observer, reality checker and unsatisfied outsider. A little bit Rimbaud, a little bit Rambo in her political diatribes; but prototypically Australian too, a tourist wherever she finds herself (or doesn't) waiting to arrive somewhere else. Australian because? One kind of Australian anyway: self-disparaging, witty, an intellectual and artist unsatisfied in a post-religious world experienced as all there is; surviving in her familiar digs, but just as often wanting to be somewhere else. This posture can be both flip, and deeply melancholic, ontologically unstable, in rapid succession:

> We
> whoever **we** are
> can't be anything
> other than children
> surrounded,
> as we are,
> by all these
> freedoms –
> little howling babies
> rattling at the bars
> of the playpen.
> I'm sitting on
> an air-conditioner
> under this window
> framed by the silvery arc

of the bridge
beyond the city's valley
on this
dusty purple evening.
I've just turned
46
in my stupid
Eiffel Tower t-shirt.
("Seven Days" 51)

Australian, poet, middle-aged, a lover of foreign places and trends, a self-disparager, Brown's protagonists are usually self-critics, as well as social commentators disconcerted by fellow humans who are nothing but "howling babies / rattling at the bars / of the playpen." They are outsiders mostly, musing momentarily as they gaze into the "dusty purple evening", residually Romantic, registering their own stupid lack of growth or understanding. The "we" in "Seven Days" approach (always slantwise) the national (the bridge, like O'Hara's "On Seeing Larry Rivers' *Washington Crossing the Delaware*"), but "ours," excoriate the social, Western, capitalist world ("surrounded / as we are, / by all these / freedoms – / like howling babies,") and reveal the personally existential ("just turned / 46"). Readers are asked to listen to these multiple registers of dissatisfaction – aesthetic, humorous, political and ontological – as they twist around each other. Are readers, pushed hard in this poem and across Brown's oeuvre, to grasp the impact of such restless poetics, being asked for empathy? Political solidarity? Any kind of solution to the cultural and personal pain represented? Or are we mere bystanders, like the protagonist, unable to imagine any kind of haven?

One clue to our positioning as readers might be to listen, as Brown does, to an earlier poetic fellow-traveller, Mina Loy, who also created poetry of restless loneliness. In *The Last Lunar Baedeker* (1923) we read Loy's poem "Human Cylinders":

> The human cylinders
> Revolving in the enervating dusk
> That wraps each closer in the mystery
> Of Singularity
> Among the litter of a sunless afternoon
> Having eaten without tasting
> Talked without communion…"
> (Loy online, "Human Cylinders" Poetry Foundation)

It's not difficult to hear the kinds of influence Loy had on Brown: the spare, modernist lines; the mixture of Romanticism in retreat, and modernist concerns shared by Eliot's Prufrock, which introduce us to a post-war world of loss and disconnection (in Loy), of singularity that might be heroic or ridiculous. Brown found a poetic mirror in Loy for her ongoing restlessness, a poetic baedecker, sympathetic to her own refusals or failures to find a haven. In the same Loy poem we read:

> The impartiality of the absolute
> Routs   the polemic
> Or which of us
> Would not
> Receiving the holy-ghost
> Catch it   and caging
> Lose it
> Or in the problematic
> Destroy the Universe
> With a solution. (Loy online)

Loy was not simply after a "solution" to her travelling self, and nor is Brown. But equally, each keeps seeking, in the world of art preeminently, for places to rest between bouts in the cage – those babies in their play-pen, working for survival, engulfed in, but needing to travel beyond what is habitual, mundane, banal. Brown, like Loy, writes without belief in a solution, but also *with* a poetic sense of the impossible "absolute," the need not to catch and cage "the holy ghost". In Brown's terms, what is needed now are "new maps for Mina" ("Not Myrna, Mina" 20), a new aesthetic beyond the "wasm" (19) of modernism, wherever that might be. But while Brown, and her poetic heroine, Mina Loy, are both restless travellers (literally and poetically), both recognize the potency of connection to a wider, mobile, potentially liberating artistic community.

Poetic community

The first poem in *50-50*, "Twitching," is a set of wry, twisted platitudes reflecting on where the protagonist "comes from," her pedigree delivered in flip comments which mount up as you read: "what's the name of the crematorium / which keeps / *my* parents' / little plaques? *Something Gardens* / probably" (11). This speaker, coming from the forties and, *still* alive in 2000, reports, in a distancing third person, that:

>   your geographic friends
>   confirm
>
>   you are the you
>   putting in
>   an appearance
>
>   & the olden days
>   of fuck and vanish
>   are finished. ("Twitching" 12)

In *50-50* the recurring protagonist is still hardly satisfied. Stranded between the mid-century and the millennium, the "you" being reported on by friends, the one slipping in and out of focus, wants something or someone more; but the chances of coming across more tangible signs of the self turn into "a silver paperclip / your only trace" (15), and the retrospective, ironized search for self leads to the poem's summation: "everything's / a particle" (16). Communion, with the self, let alone with others, seems impossible. "Hypnotic," the poem following "Twitching," probes in negative terms a lack of faith in the power of poetry and poetry's (perhaps necessarily) dissolving communities; the protagonist declaring, in the aftermath of her modernist ancestors, "my true / environment / is a dust bin" ("Not Myrna, Mina" 20).

However, behind these wry declarations of solitariness and lack of connection, an opposite impulse hovers, a desire for relationship, an imagined community which once existed and might again. Perhaps this kind of desire is related to the larger yearning of age, or more directly to the change in the times, from the communal movements of the 1970s to the turn of the millennium. Hope for connection is, however, met largely by negativity as *50-50* progresses. The protagonist certainly doesn't imagine finding satisfaction in "a world / of shrunken / bandwidths / where / everyone's called / 'andrew'/ & you have to / bring a plate" ("little delirium the second" 22); nor in "the skyline's monotonies" of her urban world; ("Lament" 24), nor with "phagophobic ravers / [who] stagger off at dawn, / drug-whacked/& whooping" ("Leaning" 27). While temporary havens are imagined, their efficacy is doubted even as they are established: off on retreat to write and think, the protagonist finds only a "here – / the obscene whiteness / of the sand   & beauty / I can't live up to" ("First Things First" 74).

Yet momentarily emerging from this dissatisfaction and alienation, the fugitive self in *50-50* does construct a palpable if unsteady hope in poetic community, an imagined place, a loose connection of poetic friends, that can be reached for, from which postcards can be written:

> dear K   I'm reading
> dense U.S, poetry
> *still*   beside
> the sea which has
> no influence. ("First Things First" 75)

There is K, friend and fellow poet, who will understand the history and jokes tucked away in throwaway lines; and there is "dense U.S, poetry" which has been a home for quite a while. The past can be recalled as community, even if it means flirting with the dangers of nostalgia. Past poetic communities are a preoccupation in the volume *Text Thing* (2002). "At the Ian Burns Show MCA 1997" looks back wryly but longingly at the solidarity of "anti-authoritarian art spiels," the "'Art and Language' days,' the mid-seventies," communal houses, karaoke, and the long-ago communities of:

> direct-action practicing populist artists
>   (anti-institutionalist-intellectual-academy)
> vs
> theoretical conceptual post-object artists
>   (yet not always nor certainly pro-academic) (*Text Thing* 53)

This was somewhere to belong, to find meaning and purpose. These are achievements that are not merely relegated to oblivion by the poet in the present, even as their pastness is registered in the humorous earnestness of those early positions/collectives. There, communities of artists lived together, "… for a decade / all under the same / tin roof" (53).

Even as Brown offers us the lonely protagonist unable to solve her need for connection, there is a deep desire for community evident in another way in Brown's poetry. Critic Brian Henry writes of the 2003 volume *Dear Deliria: (New and Selected Poems)*:

... the names of contemporary poets — usually in epigraphs and dedications — are the community. The writings and company of Australian poets Adam Aitken, Ken Bolton, Laurie Duggan, Cassie Lewis, and Jennifer Maiden and American poets Charles Bernstein, Tom Clark, Eileen Myles, Alice Notley, Jack Spicer, and Susan Schultz appear throughout *Dear Deliria*. (Brian Henry, review online)

And there are many other poet friends that Brown turns to across the decades, as fellow travellers, and for their poetic influence – Mina Loy, Gertrude Stein, Frank O'Hara, James Schuyler, John Forbes, Lyn Hejinian, Jo Burns. Some (poets and readers) outside such imagined community may find this cliquey or exclusionary, especially when placed together with Brown's signature dismissiveness of the banal, suburban and (often Australian) anti-poetic, as well as of academics and critics. In her canny review of Brown's *True Thoughts* (2014), Astrid Lorange writes of Brown's own preference for the poetry coterie, rather than anything like a sustained community:

> Brown's insistence on coteries as the organising unit of poets is interesting, and no doubt objectionable to some. My point here is not to discuss her claim, but to begin by saying, by way of a disclaimer, that the very act of reviewing might support such a claim: a review is a critical attempt to locate and relocate the logics of a poet and their work according to associations, resemblances, equivalents and opposites. (Lorange, review online)

Arguably, what emerges slowly and most significantly across Brown's oeuvre is not poetic snobbery or coterie-dwelling, but the constant oscillation in her work between the poetic and the non- or anti-poetic, often resulting in a rush back into the arms of poetry and poetic buddies, possibly coterie, but just as often leading to an existential querying of poetry's and poets' impact and meaning. So many poems reach out for friendship, cordiality, acknowledgement of poetic contexts, but also constantly and painfully they measure the sense of loss invading the poet protagonist's poetic accomplishments, questioning the efficacy of poetic language and any poet's vocation. In "Seven Days," from *50-50*, the post-poetic hovers close:

> today,   as
> the union rep says,
> is p.o.e.t.s. day –
> "piss off early,
> tomorrow's Saturday." ("Seven Days" 54)

And what hope for the artist and poet, when the protagonist declares, somewhat disingenuously:

> Art is mostly
>   showing off
>   the cleverest decoration ("Twitching" 15-16)

and, if not this, then the poet outs herself as self-obsessed and self-citing, fetishizing the dirty little realities of language:

> Resting like a relic
>   In a field of meaning –
> Push[ing] the rocks around
>   for transformation –
> gravel rash, scab, scar,
>   all
>   factors that
> fall squarely.
>   (like that)
> ("This & That: (I cite myself)" 63)

There would be little hope of poetic community or connection, much less transformation, if these portraits of the poet – at times vain, or self-obsessed, lonely and unregarded, unsatisfied and leaning on a few dispersed poetic friends – were all that was possible. But there is another strain of Pam Brown's poetry that seeks to have an impact publicly (if not communally), to reach out beyond the potentially imprisoning solipsism of many of the poems. These political poems do not offer "solutions," whether from 'the absolute' or 'the polemical' in Loy's sense, but seek to maintain freedoms envisioned, freedoms of the artist who can see the idiocies and injustices of society, but who equally does not desire simply to preach or teach, to cage the holy-ghost, to "destroy the Universe / with a solution" (Loy, "Human Cylinders", online).

Beyond Solipsism: out of the play-pen

Those howling babies in "Seven Days," Brown's very own creation story (after the scriptures, after Leonard French), are grasping and unsatisfied, merely playing at being alive. "We / whoever **we** are" ("Seven Days") share a human condition, connected to each other by a common lack, and by greed. The poet registers her protagonist too, as belonging within the play-pen (part of the "we"), along with "'a conjuration / of imbeciles'" – the parliamentary candidates, the "bloated ill-temperament" of the times, the Cash Converters and "the premature ejaculators" ("Not the Town"). All are needing transformation, though the poem's portrayal of poetic power is unpromising; can poetry do more than "push the rocks around," picking at scabs? For critic Ann Vickery, reviewing the 2010 volume *Authentic Local*, there is a larger, public critique created by Brown:

> Pam Brown's poetry attends to the soundbites and transitoriness of contemporary Australian life. Her dazzling wordplay gives us glistening souvenirs of overblown politik-speak, uncontrolled Western consumption, and the daze of the habitual and housetrained. (Vickery, review online)

But do "glistening souvenirs" add up to social critique or impact? Brown's excoriating social criticism often includes as target the poet/ protagonist along with the random populace which is often depicted as unthinking, consumerist, habitual, sometimes as aridly academic and theorist. In the 1994 volume *This World, This Place*, poems about social degeneration and "bloated ill-temperament" abound. It is the world known and experienced by the protagonist, the "Here", where

> ...artists paint backwards brilliantly redesigning
> ways to approach images, buildings, things, nature.
> pellucid gothically dressed art-theorists taxi across
> the city rimmed by developers' craters   to suck on
> plastic cups as the buoyant-as-in-jolly literary agent
> tells how   when shickered she vomits over the balcony
> on to the tops of banana trees which flourish
> on regurgitation   not so the actual readers
> nor the actual writers of the actual books ("Here" 74).

This poem certainly offers one distinctive form of literary community, where "a celebrity resides on every inner-suburb street", "dancing in dogshit mingled with jasmine" (74). The protagonist is a part of this world, as well as repulsed by its hierarchies of wealth, education, greed and pretension. Artists can thrive here, learning to "flourish / on regurgitation," to paint "backwards" for contemporary tastes, listening (attentively, one would imagine) to the supposedly amusing narrative of the vomiting agent, but at a great distance from actual readers and writers and books.

This kind of "social awareness" will not get the poet onto the VCE reading lists – no solution, no simple victims or perpetrators – nor recommend her to the literati. It is, nevertheless, poetry of searing vision – of class and power pretentiousness at personal and social levels – in a "city of brutal solution", of "indolent glut / of wondrous scent   and a festival of cockroaches" (74). But what does such poetry "achieve", beyond derision, or provision of ironic fodder for the solipsistic protagonist? Despite the poet depicting "herself":

> dreaming away.
> my loftiest dream
> would be to become
> the kind of poet
> who is an ant
> in society's armpit.
> the big problem
> is that halfway
> or maybe three quarters
> of the way   into
> my poetic "career"
> I go unread
> ("Mellowly Existential" 36)

we are left asking whether such self-ironizing amounts to a transformatory poetics? This is, first of all, the question the poet is asking herself; and then she is asking it of her vocation, her peers, her invisible readers. Is being "the kind of poet/who is an ant/in society's armpit" enough? This comic self-deprecation sits beside a powerful social critique which mounts in *This World, This Place* (1994) as well as the later *Text Thing* (2002), undermining any stable place to stand. The "Holy ghost," let alone any "solution," has long ago left the building; the poet doesn't advocate solutions but generates anger and ridicule. The "here and now," patently, is not enough; it's a place of shopping, unthinking citizens; and the poetic vision in response is one of mock-apocalypse at best, where "the ground trembles / as traffic exits the shopping / complex parking station" ("Not the Town" 61). The ant finds its (hardly noticed) sting.

Brown's recurrent targets, here, in this world, are multiple and suggest the need for more fire-power than an ant's sting. In *This World / This Place* they are Australian (and global) capitalism, "paradise propped up," "blinding, glinting" ("The Money times" 72). Literary critics too are targeted, "serious / like adolescents / reading Sartre / on a railway station / big sooks / of oz lit…" ("Lit Crit" 68). Then there are the money-grubbing developers and compromised fellow poets, consumerism, affluence and privilege, affectation, political correctness in a mid-career manifesto of sorts:

> …But they have *everything* here. Look at all these *things* in this overstuffed city…This
> dumb belief in immortality. On this side, everyone lives as if there is time to become someone else…
> I could weep, pathetic, turn it down, I could weep.
> This world, this world, this world is shit.
> Weep away, say the angels, gold comes from shit. ("This World" 13-14).

The final line of this diatribe is whimsical as well as empirical. There has been abundant research on the amount of gold and other precious metals washed down the sewers of the Western world. And this is the political point, really, as well as an existential and aesthetic one, the poet learning how to turn shit into gold, metaphorically. Whether it amounts to an *ontology*, a mode of being let alone a flourishing in this world, is another question (see below).

Ontology: where to stand?

Writing poetry, reading the great poets, ironic self-disparagement, attempting to connect with other poets (community, coterie or individuals), travelling away and coming back, critiquing the world of the here and now; all of these strategies have been employed by Pam Brown as she creates (or extemporizes on) her poetic selves and worlds, seeking an imagined place from which to write and be. These strategies, we learn, will never be more than temporary, as restlessness and self-questioning set in again. But how far can irony (of self and world) take a poet? Brown's oeuvre is punctuated by a playfully serious melancholy, acerbic and ironic by turns, but also revealing vulnerability, a relentless on-guardism. Her observing poetic selves seek "singularity," but also suffer from its limits, as the poet attempts to see beyond the banal, to create what? The possibility of critical and poetic communion? To "set your own curriculum" ("Seven Days")? Lorange (via Dworkin and Roudiez) represents these procedures positively, as paragrammatics: "a tactic for both reading and writing poetry that forms networks of signification otherwise unachievable by conventional habits of grammar-use and interpretation." But there is also a vertiginous sense of loss, of not quite getting there, of constantly fending off sentimentalism and nostalgia on the one side, and the ironic, dystopian, and sometimes abyssal on the other. This constant being on guard often leads Brown's protagonists to exhaustion (those tiny fragments of breath and meaning), even as the poet writes on.

So, in her own creation story:

> Life drifts on
> between
> palpitations
> and
> good advice –
> you need
> **activities**
> as if activity,
> in the sense of
> **becoming**
> **more active**,
> is a worthwhile
> aspiration
> & morally sound
> as well (more
> howling-baby
> homilies). ("Seven Days")

"Becoming" is the subject here, though "becoming active," receiving advice, registering the body's struggles, being more moral – all are suggested fill-ins offered to the protagonist. Instead, "Life drifts on / between ...", but nevertheless demands a guardedness, an alertness against the crush of expected outcomes for a life. The speaker knows that s/he does not desire any of these possible modes of being; but it is reasonable to suggest that there is still a dissatisfaction which hovers, in the drifting, a longing for something or somewhere else. Deciding how to be by reacting against what might be egregiously or unwittingly suggested by others, is also not necessarily satisfying. Irony, producing either personal torpor or social ridicule, is subversive possibly, but does not necessarily offer transformation for individual or culture. So can another mode of being – even happiness – be discerned in Brown's onrush of paragrammatic poetics? Or is *that* the mode of being?

50-50's "Abstract Happiness", beginning with its ironic, self-deconstructing title, bolsters the image of an oppositional protagonist powerfully digging her heels in:

> Recondite
>   & difficult
>   you supplicate
>   via failure –
>   it's only a tiny part
>   of the plan –
> refusing to be shoved
>   into virtue
>   by ambitious hooligans
> waving their dividends
>   like paper flags. (61)

The testy, juddering lines are blurted, extemporizing (seemingly), a thinking (or reacting) as you go. What you know is that you will not bow, will not be "shoved" into others' ideas of virtue, into dividend-driven systems. Those who push their values in your face are "hooligans", but you still feel yourself a failure and all you have is a tiny plan, to continue reacting (including writing poetry, if you're a poet). "This week's agenda – / an interest / in distant places" (66). It seems that, despite the most stinging effects of tetchy, distancing irony, and flights to "distant places," what is being considered is understood as triage, a temporary solution.

Lorange puts it differently, and persuasively, citing Brown's own claim to being an anarchist:

> "[I]n my idealised world, I would prefer classical anarchism," Brown says to Kinsella. Anarchism emphasises the fact of incommensurable things co-existing. In the same interview with Kinsella, Brown offers a name for the mode of thought that shapes partial attentions into poems: *on the qui vive*. Not just 'on the look out,' but also 'who's side are you on?' Brown's poetry works to elaborate these partials into high-stake claims. If Brown's into anarchism, it is of the methodological variety, like Feyerabend's anarchistic science in *Against Method*. It calls for a specific kind of approach (to the construction of propositions, in Brown's case, making a poem) that is properly prepared for any kind of unexpected outcome, by product, breakthrough or breakdown. (Lorange, review online)

There are a number of wonderful caveats hovering here, caveats to seeing Brown as the classical anarchist (after all, there is, according to the poet, no caveat-less place to rest, finally): it is in an "idealised world" that such "classical anarchism" might be possible. And as Lorange points out, there are distinctions to be made: Brown may be an anarchist of the *methodological* kind, but always being "properly prepared for any kind of unexpected outcome, by product, breakthrough or breakdown" also sounds exhausting, poetically perhaps, but certainly existentially. What is produced by such a stance, and what are its tropes and poetic techniques? Irony is certainly one strategy. Going elsewhere is another recurrent trope.

Other places present themselves, drawing you away from the known and familiar, the mundane of "Ultimo", "…the view / – from the balcony – / grey and darker grey" (94); the mundane of "Pique":

>   silent,
>   not spiritual,
>   the city is empty
>
>   antispectacular
>   & as
>   deodorized
>   as heaven. (67)

There is here, at the core of this poem, a kind of beauty, a non-heaven, the here and now momentarily emptied of its spectacle, trash and smell; almost a peace. But even this momentary, potential purity is built on negatives, the *absence* of so much that troubles or pollutes, the absence of a hell produced by an empty, deodorized heaven. And it *is* only momentary, as the pique returns, targeted at the tedium of those better off, developers, the strutting denizens of the city, fake poets, poetry itself. And, at this poem's climax, a resentment of self:

>   …here am I
>   nibbling
>   my jejune nourishment
>   with the laxity of
>   of a cultivated
>   & singular minority
>   languidly
>   erasing
>   all legend
>
>   flick flick flick. (70)

The poet protagonist is folded back (folds herself back) into ordinariness and insubstantiality, lax and languid, undernourished and bored. The very sustenance sought for in poetry is erased, a "jejune nourishment". However, what nibbles at the edges of this poem is an awareness (in the protagonist, in the thrust of the poem, in the reader) that the very vehicle being used to ironize, disparage and belittle poetry and the poet – "flick flick flick" – is a poem. The self would disappear, engulfed and dismissed as nothing more than a member of "a cultivated/ & singular minority", yet simultaneously announces itself in the act of disappearing: "& here am I". Perhaps this is the minimalist redemption offered by poetry, that every poetic act, including those which would declare the emptiness and mundanity of existence, of the here and now, of the unnourished, restless self, is necessarily transformed in its materiality (human breath and voice, persistence of desire, the ironizing of all that needs repudiation, constant vigilance and renegotiation – all those Brown poems) into an act of communication, a seeking for community or meaning where there is none. Behind all the strategies and barriers, the postures and mock postures, and the irony, is there a voice which is vulnerable, shared and needy, reaching out beyond those barricades?

Perhaps this is unBrownian, attempting to identify "a voice". The barricades might be endless, which sounds promising for the poet, who seeks a place in which to keep on writing. But poets, protagonists and existential beings cross paths, are often soulmates. If:

> there is no
>   destination –
> just a place
>   no site
> not olympic
>   village site
> nor harbourside
>   casino site

> nor section
>   of expressway
>   just east
> of where
>   coincidence
>   has determined
>   your residence
> in a city
>   you returned to
>   to remember
>   why you left
> ("City" 71)

then paragrammatics, irony, social ridicule, personal ridicule, going elsewhere, grasping at poetic community (or coterie), seeking meaning as it disappears, are all cogent responses. Anarchism, with its attendant ontological vertigo is congruent with this poem's sense of coincidence and displacement. But what can be said of this poem – and many in Brown's oeuvre – that employ the material, languaged strategies of poetry to deny given realities, even as such denials build the very realities being denied? All the no, nor, not of "City" instantiates the very reality – Olympic village, harbourside, Casino, the place where you live – it is seeking to escape from or disempower. This is another way of saying that language deconstructs (is bigger than, out guns) the individual user of language every time. And if that proposition is agreed to, momentarily, is it a hopeful or an abysmal condition?

Kevin Hart's 1989 theoretical volume *The Trespass of the Sign: Deconstruction, Theology and Philosophy* offers a framework in which to think about this question, and Brown's language work. In the opening chapter of his book, Hart, very much in Derridean mode, writes:

> ...philosophical essays or literary texts, all discourse, appears to be structured by a distinction between presence and a fall

from presence. And one common instance of this distinction is between presence and sign. (Hart 11)

The argument of *Trespass of the Sign*, complex as it is, is by now well disseminated. In relation to Brown's work it is rewarding to think about her poetry's recurrent desire to move beyond the here and now of language – beyond realist representation, the trope of elsewhere, never finding a resting place in language. This restlessness, being "half here, half gone," permeates the poem "The Long Years," which is about remembering (and willing, perhaps impossibly, the other to remember with us); and it is a poem about poetry and language as bound on a wheel which promises presence, takes it away, brings it back, like memory, like idealism, like travelling away and coming back, like reaching for community, like living in the palpable world and attempting, over and over, to move beyond it:

> remember the present   or yesterday
> as I remember   the idea of our lives
>   and our actual lives.
> and your use of that term,   again
>   and again. "re-invention"
> as a cure for loneliness –
> like watching a woman
>   with a string of pearls   slowly
>   testing each one
>   in the wine.

> here we are waiting   for the natural end
>   for some future winter   as I remember it,
> and in these long years
> we may eventually locate   the places
>   beyond memory   in imagined countries
> where English is the last language. ("The Long Years" 18)

Between the ideas of our lives, and our actual lives, falls the shadow. In this poem memory, ideas, imagining, re-invention, retellings, writing poems are all modes or strategies of survival, aspects of ontology that are both honored and finally, poignantly (not sentimentally!) seen as part of what must be set aside. There is another place, possibly, which will be the place "beyond memory   in imagined countries / where English is the last language". The most foreign, post-human, post-temporal, post-global, post-poetic of places. It's a place, seemingly, where there is no need for social rage; no loneliness ("remember…as I remember"; no sad / suspicious woman dipping her pearls); no use for irony or sentimentality. This is the haven, the place of being that is pointed to – angrily, solipsistically, idealistically, humorously, ironically – in so many Brown poems. It's a place of presence and being, beyond the sign.

Works Cited

Brown, Pam. *Dear Deliria: New and Selected Poems*, Salt Publishing, 2002.
---. *50-50*, Little Esther Books, 1997.
---. *Little Text*, http://linkeddeletions.blogspot.com.au/2014/03/reviews-of-pam-browns-books-please.html.
---. "Not the Town." *Text Thing*, Little Esther Books, 2002, pp. 60-61.
---. *Text Thing*, Little Esther Books, 2002.
---. "The Collapse." *Automatic Sad*, Tomato Press, 1974, p.17.
---. *This World, This Place*, University of Queensland Press, 1994.
Hart, Kevin. *The Trespass of the Sign: Deconstruction, Theology, Philosophy*, Fordham University Press, 1989/2000.
Henry, Brian. Review of *Dear Deliria: New and Selected Poems*, by Pam Brown. *Jacket* 23, August 2003. http://jacketmagazine.com/23/henry-brown.html
Lorange, Astrid. Review of Pam Brown, *True Thoughts*. March 21, 2014. http://linkeddeletions.blogspot.com/2014/03/astrid-

lorange-reviews-pam-brown-true_21.html
Loy, Mina. *The Last Lunar Baedeker,* Jargon Press, 1982/1923.
"Human Cylinders" cited at poetryfoundation.org
---. "Human Cylinders", Mina Loy, Cited at Poetry Foundation website,: https://www.poetryfoundation.org/poems/51872/human-cylinders
McCredden, Lyn. "Untranscended / life itself." *Australian Literary Studies,* Vol. 22, No. 2, 2005, pp. 217-228.
Vickery, Ann. Review of *Authentic Local,* 2010. http://www.sydneypoetry.com/profiles/blogs/pam-browns-authentic-local

Chapter 9

Randolph Stow's "Hungry Waiting Country"

Caitlin Maling

Many decades after he had left Western Australia and settled in Suffolk, Randolph Stow would continue to be asked if he considered himself an Australian writer. In interviews, Stow would attempt to distance himself from ideas of roots, denying the label "Australian" for his preferred "Anglo-Australian" ("A Conversation" 71). Similarly, Stow frames his interest in Western Australia as purely related to childhood, the town of Geraldton being the place where he just happened to grow up ("Mostly Private Letters" 354). Since Stow's death in 2010 interest in locating him on a cultural map of Australia has continued. With the re-release of his major fiction works through the Text Publishing Classics series in 2015 and the publication of Suzanne Falkiner's 2016 biography *Mick: A Life of Randolph Stow*, Stow is enjoying a resurgence, one that continues to try to locate him as an Australian or Western Australian writer. Yet as in his lifetime, Stow's poetry remains relatively critically neglected despite the most comprehensive selection of his poetry appearing in 2013 accompanied by an extensive introductory essay by John Kinsella. The Kinsella essay demonstrates how consideration of Australianness in Stow's poetry and prose almost always relates to consideration of landscape. Part of the confusion around assigning Stow a definitive designation as a Western Australian place writer must be that Stow does not write about place in any one way. He writes great traditional satirical pastoral poems such as "The Utopia of Lord Mayor Howard" (*Outrider* 14), in addition to what some might term anti-pastoral or early post-colonial poems such as his sequence

"Stations" (*A Counterfeit Silence* 57), but he also writes poems that fuse the inner landscapes of the mind with the outer landscapes of Western Australia. These are the most complicated of his poems, existing in the mid-state between a social voice and the private, lyric voice of Stow's *Counterfeit Silence*. The very human element of Stow's work has often been overlooked in favour of ideas of landscape. As a first step towards overcoming this neglect, this essay thinks through the ways Stow approaches landscape but moves beyond existing analysis to link this to Stow's own broader conceptualisation of environment. I will consider the intersection of the private poetic voice of Stow's love poetry with his knowledge of and use of details of the Western Australian landscape. The poetics that Stow develops in these poems are not reducible to a singular genre or theme, instead as Kinsella puts it "what Stow performs is a *synthesising* poetics" (50). Stow blends his own peculiar texts of land and literature into a new poetry, one uniquely his own, an objective correlative for what Stow terms the "mindscape" of the artist ("Raw Material" 407).

Critical oversight of Stow's poetry was originally ascribed to the poetry being less accessible than his prose and more private (Hassal *Strange Country* 75). To this Dorothy Hewett provides the notable rejoinder that it is no more difficult than any other modernist poetry (59). Now in an age of proliferating poetic postmodernisms, ideas of difficulty and inaccessibility must no longer be considered impediments to the detailed critical study Stow's work deserves. This is especially the case as Stow considered his poetry, and his love poetry especially, among his best work ("Mostly Private Letters" 352). Discussion of his love poems has primarily been limited to the series of mythic poems he notoriously described as:

> private letters written to people with whom I have a relationship, about which, for one reason or another, I want to say something to them, directly; but I say it through the circumstances of the myth-figure who gives each poem its title ("Breaking the Silence" 400).

Stow proposes that these figures, including Endymion, Enkidu and Persephone among others, serve as objective correlatives for their real-world counterparts ("Breaking the Silence" 400). While there has been some crossover in discussion of how land features in these love poems, the interaction between land and the love lyric has not been considered in any great depth. For example, Beston's essay "The Love Poetry of Randolph Stow", while briefly noting that Stow's landscape is always Western Australian, assesses landscape for only one paragraph and then only for how it performs as a metaphorical vehicle for the poet's emotions.

The exception to this type of metaphorical consideration of landscape is Fay Zwicky's (1986) treatment of Stow in two articles, "Speeches and Silences" and "The Price of Silence: Further Thoughts on the Poetry of Randolph Stow". Zwicky makes an intriguing, if not entirely convincing, proposal that writers such as Stow are "transfixed by the impersonal force of place—its anonymity and inhumanity taking the place once occupied by the attainable, desirable She in love poetry" ("Speeches and Silences" 29). For Zwicky this is a function of the anti-lingual masculine nature of settler Australian society coupled with the post-Romantic period's constant scrutiny and challenge of the ideas of audience and communication ("Speeches and Silences" 26-27). The existential interpersonal angst of modernism in Australian poetry is transferred onto the landscape "as if to compensate for the detachment from his fellow man, the writer reveals a deep and sometimes ambiguous involvement with place" ("Speeches and Silences" 29). Zwicky argues that "in the fruitful loss of individuality ... man merges with his environment, progressing from the particular to the general, and thence to the universal" with Stow demonstrating "an understanding of man in his environmental features themselves" where "the inhuman forces of nature impinge more powerfully than the presence of any human agent" ("Speeches and Silences" 29). There is resonance in these statements, especially her idea of Stow's man being recognisable by "his environmental features" ("Speeches and Silences" 29). Yet as

Zwicky develops her argument this resonance gets lost. She frames this type of relationship to land as necessarily negative in which any human interest is subsumed or replaced by the inevitable emptiness of landscape. Stow's work extends beyond this, deepening and complicating ideas of human interrelationships through his portrayal of an ambiguous relationship to place. Despite the landscapes in his poetry often being of the desert, this desert is not necessarily one vacant of either life or human emotion.

"Strange Fruit" from *Outrider* is one of Stow's more elusive and cryptic poems:

> Suicide of the night—ah, flotsam: (the great
> poised thunderous breaker of darkness rearing above you,
> and your bones awash, in the shallows, glimmering, stony,
> like gods of forgotten tribes, in forgotten deserts)
>
> take care. Take care. For your campfire falters, and firelight
> folds, and will clamp around you its charcoal calyx,
> and already for many hours your eyes (my terror)
> have drowned in deep waters of dream, till I grow fearless.
>
> (Embers of crocodiles love you from the mangroves.
> Dingo ears yearn, yearn towards your tranquil breathing.)
>
> Day and the firelight guard you from harm so darkly
> rehearsed, removing me far; for by day I dread you,
> fearing your quester's ear, that might interpret
> what sings in my blood; your eye, that might guess my fever.
>
> But so long as the harsh light lasts I stalk your horses'
> desolate spoor: a stature among the anthills
> should you look back; and prowling—and yearning, yearning,
> howl out my grief and grievance, and burn in fever.

(Embers of crocodiles love you from the mangroves.
Dingo ears suck the wind for your tranquil breathing.)

I am the country's station; all else is fever.
Did we ride knee to knee down the canyons, or did I dream it?
They were lilies of dream we swam in, parrots of myth
we named for each other, 'since no one has ever named them...'

Alone for an hour, in a thicket, I reached for strange fruit.

Now you sleep by the fire. And these are my true eyes
that glare from the swamps. And the rattling howl in the gullies
is my true voice. That cries: *You shall try strange fruit.* (22)

At first reading, this poem seems to add credence to Zwicky's argument of dissolution of human interest in favour of the environment. It could also be positioned in the troublesome rubric of the Australian desert as a metaphysical site of existential despair. As Kinsella notes, this trend in Australian literature simplifies the actuality of the desert and I would add that it is similarly reductive of emotion (36). The opening of "Strange Fruit" with "bones" and "forgotten deserts" invites these comparisons. As the poem progresses it leaves the clichés of desert for the lushness of mangroves. Probably written out of Stow's experiences living in the Kimberley, this is not so much a desert poem as a poem of the tropics. Perhaps one of the hard parts about placing Stow and this poem specifically is the relative lack of other literature and criticism emerging from the remote north west of Australia where Stow spent time living on missions. This part of the country is defined by both extreme desert and extreme water, by wet and dry seasons not common to the urban centres of most of Australia. It is thus easy to ignore the tropics in this poem in favour of the desert. When we examine the poem however, we find more tropic than desert. Emotion is not circumscribed but overflowing in images of blood, "deep waters of dream" and uncontrollable fever.

The use of repetition, alliteration, assonance, and heavy enjambment all contribute to a sense of overflow, not one of stagnation. The poem is in effect a dark serenade, the speaker wearing the land as a mask to sing their "rattling howl" to an unidentifiable other as day sets. Where in European serenades there is often a sweet wind and the soft fall of starlight, here we have a landscape lit by "[e]mbers of crocodiles" and "[d]ingo ears" that "suck the wind". The natural features of the Australian landscape are ill-fitted to the restrained passion of the traditional serenade.

Similarly, Stow adopts the idea of a serenade as a poem of separated lovers at nightfall, but what is being separated in "Strange Fruit" is not entirely clear. There is obvious distance between the speaker and the other figure, but there are also the more complicated partings of the speaker and the land and the speaker and himself. Lyric poetry is defined by a straining against impossibility (Keller 80). "Strange Fruit", with its biblical connotations of a fall from Eden, presents the consummation of love, not as impossible, but as perilous because of its inevitability. What is threatened and imperilled is the speaker's sense of self. This occurs not as a result of confronting the nothing of a desert but out of confronting a tropical overgrowth of emotion. In the first instance of the love being spoken, the speaker wears a cloak of "embers of crocodiles" and "dingo ears" that "yearn, yearn". Just as Stow uses mythic figures in other poems as masks to allow him to share private desires, here the features of the landscape also cloak the speaker and allow him to voice desire. These moments are placed in parentheses outside the conscious action of the poem and almost unwillingly acknowledged. These are strange images, dream images. It is not a coincidence that in the closest stanza to the consummation of love, and the only stanza the two figures appear together in, is of a dream: "Did we ride knee to knee down the canyons, or did I dream it?" and "They were lilies of dream we swam in".

Stow cites as influences "in English, the older poetry, Romantic and Renaissance" ("Mostly Private Letters" 352). The formal artfulness of the opening twenty lines of "Strange Fruit" speak to this tradition in the use of the refrain. As with Stow's unsettling of the tradition of the serenade, his artifice in these opening lines is opposed to the wildness of the contents. The quartets are overflowing, heavily enjambed even across stanzas. In contrast the refrain couplets are contained, literally by parentheses, and endstopped. The sense is one of approach and retreat, a prosodic courtship that is out of step with the eeriness of the contents of the poem. People have discussed Stow's early work, of which this poem is a part, as being obsessed with time (Hewett 62). The two steps forward and one step back of the opening lines effects a stasis in keeping with the idea of this being a dreamscape or interior scape. The speaker uses the refrain to try to keep separate the aspects of self they are denying. This sense of time is not simply a function of the interiority of the speaker, it also reflects Stow's two primary impressions of the environment of Australia: vastness and timelessness ("Raw Material" 407). Stow writes:

> The sense of the past is linked with this vastness. It is a country in which one can be aware of a tremendous range of time. It is very easy to feel – even to 'remember' – the period when there was no animal life on earth. And on the hottest days, in the most desolate places, it is possible to know, almost kinetically, the endurance of *things* ("Raw Material" 407).

The speaker in wearing the mask of the landscape begins to reflect not just the physical features of the land but these intransient qualities as well.

The poem breaks form, shifts registers and stops the use of parentheses on what is by far the shortest line of the poem and its most declarative statement, "I am the country's station; all else is fever." There is bravado in this line that reads not as an epiphanic moment for the speaker but as a cry of desperation. In saying so emphatically I am "the country's station", the speaker denies being anything else. The identity the speaker claims is one of land. The "country's station" is a peculiar cry, an image of what is abstract, general and contained. The station is an outpost of civilisation in the wilderness, a house, where previously the speaker has sought himself in the mangroves. The Latin stem of station, *statio*, is a standing-still, in seeking "station" the speaker cries for fixity. While there is a very real lyric other in this poem in the form of the companion, in the image of the station the speaker seeks to wall himself off from the other of the landscape. In this very brief moment, we see Stow wrestle with his familiar key themes of settlement and belonging. For Stow the idea of colonial Australia as existing in a binary between Eden and prison was very resonant ("The Southland" 410). "Strange Fruit" presents an interesting inversion of this binary. The natural, lush, edenic sounding land is the tempter luring the speaker from the more contained, more akin to prison, of the station. Station also carries overtones of the Stations of the Cross, an archetype of the western religious tradition Stow implies is in some way ill-suited, or dangerous, in an Australian context.

While not a poem necessarily about the ghosts of settlement, it is haunted by unrequited or requited yearning. Most confusing is the actual dream of naming the "parrots of myth" "since no one has ever named them …". There are multiple resonances of the Adam and Eve myth present in this tercet that illustrate the ways in which Stow binds this love lyric to his greater concerns. Firstly, there is the idea of Australia as Eden, as a land empty and free to be named. The quotation marks around "since no one has ever named them …" highlight this statement as an insertion or extra-textual dialogue, implicitly questioning it. Knowledge of Stow's interest in the anthropology of Indigenous cultures and his particular fascination for languages are sufficient to raise questions regarding his intention in this statement. In her biography Falkiner highlights how from a young age Stow's bond to Western Australia was "increasingly complicated by an uneasy awareness of the colonial usurpation that enabled it" (18). Whether or not Stow was familiar with the

Abel Meeropool (Lewis Alan) 1937 poem "Bitter Fruit" or its most famous incarnation in the 1939 Billie Holiday song "Strange Fruit" is unknown, but the song haunts any contemporary reading of the poem. It places the bodies destroyed by colonisation front and centre in the poem. On some level the Eden yearned for is one of a true terra nullius. A dangerous yearning.

It is not just a matter of the poem being a comment on colonisation, this is first and foremost a love lyric. With the fall came an awareness of carnal knowledge as sin. This carnal knowledge is "what sings" in the feverish blood of the speaker. It is possible that Stow's use of masks in his love poetry is a function of his having an unacceptable sexuality for his time and place. It was only well after he had left Australia and was living in England in the mid-1970s that he would admit in correspondence that some of his love poems were about men (Falkiner 375). The pairing in "Strange Fruit" could speak to this unease. The other being a "quester" riding "knee to knee" with the speaker is more masculine than feminine. There is also inversion in the male speaker occupying the Eve figure in the poem, who, when left "alone for an hour" "reached for strange fruit". Whether the fruit is acknowledgement of romantic desire or a desire for country the outcome is the same. The speaker stops approaching the land through the distance of parentheses, it is no longer the "crocodile" and the "dingo" yearning but the speakers "true eyes" and "true voice". The question is whether the fever has broken and the speaker has reached a true epiphanic moment in relationship to themselves, the other and the land, or whether this is the climax of fever, the speaker being overtaken by desire or the land.

Judith Wright says of Stow that he seems to write towards a "post-human wholeness" ("Australian Poetry" 25), and this idea of what exists beyond the human filters through "Strange Fruit" and Stow's wider catalogue especially as regards his interest in the Tao. In his approach to the Tao, Stow sought the universal, stating that "the implied model of Taoism does conform with the randomness and mysteriousness of the world of sub-atomic particles" ("Home and

Away" 374). Zwicky's insights into Stow's poetics also draw off an idea of a universal, in Zwicky's case the idea of a post-human love. What the ending of "Strange Fruit" does is not so simple. The land subsumes the speaker almost involuntarily. The post-human state is one of terror. The question must be asked as to what motivates the speaker, or the writer, to search for this "post-human wholeness". A level of "Strange Fruit" which has yet to be discussed thoroughly is Stow's often stated sense of distance or separation from the rural Western Australian society from which he wrote ("A Colonist" 359). In at least one interview Stow speaks of writing out of landscape because of his inability or disinterest with the society of settler Western Australians ("A Colonist" 359). Similarly, in his other poems such as his famous "The Land's Meaning" the speaker receives wisdom from other members of society but remains separated from them (*Outrider* 20). Writing on "The Land's Meaning", Kinsella says that "[t]here is a sense of loss of subjectivity to forces greater than the self ... But there is a quest (always a thwarted quest) for awareness, for empowerment of the individual through epiphany, at work" (37). The ending of "Strange Fruit" definitely has a sense of this thwarted epiphany, in this case deriving from a failure to find solace in the post-human and recognition of his ongoing separation from his society. The ill fit of the various imported myths and poetic forms with the contents of the poem also reflects separation and longing for connection. In Stow's novel *To the Islands*, the young narrator Rob living in Geraldton speaks of being doubly isolated from both the literature of Europe and the wider literature of Australia (Hassal *Strange Country* 9). In "Strange Fruit" the speaker is isolated from himself, from his loved other, from the land and from any myths which might help him understand his situation.

While obviously a powerful poem of human emotion, as a poem of landscape or nature the risk that "Strange Fruit" and many other Stow poems runs is one of pathetic fallacy or, from our current ecocritical zeitgeist, anthropocentrism. The best sense of how Stow considered the union of place, person and emotion comes from his own writings. In most of his interviews Stow stresses a realism in his approach to place which is almost scientific. In an interview with Anthony Hassal he states, "I always was a quite fanatical realist, always attempting to be more exact about things, birds, beasts, and flowers, and so on, and about people. What I *was* rejecting was social or socialist realism, which was rather a tyranny" before continuing, "I go on still trying to be as exact as possible about what things look and sound and smell like, and how people actually talk, and what they look like when they talk, and so on…I could call myself a hyper-realist" ("Breaking the Silence" 399). Much work remains to be done assessing Stow from an ecocritical perspective. For current purposes it is enough to note how the precision of natural detail in Stow's poetry speaks to a concerted direction of gaze outside the human that is counter to anthropocentrism. As discussed in the Hassal interview, Stow's emphasis on accuracy allows him to balance the emotionally charged tone of his poems. It is thus in "Strange Fruit" that the natural images are not imported from Europe but are distinctly Australian.

It is interesting that Stow's first collection *Act One* displays a much greater separation between poems focussing on landscape, lyric poems of personal subjectivity and poems in a variety of received forms. Of what he called his "juvenilia" that he chose to reproduce in his 1989 selected works, *A Counterfeit Silence,* the majority of the early heavily Romantic poetry is occluded and what most remember are the Australian Geraldton poems. These poems display less of the psychic components that characterise those of *Outrider* almost as if the poet is learning first the landscape. "Seashells and Sandalwood" (*Act One* 20) is a litany of place objects: "sunflowers and ant-orchids, surfboards and wheels, /gulls and green parakeets, sandhills and haystacks". The following poem "Sea Children" shares the same level of detailed description "beyond the arm of the harbour, on the banks / of teased and surf-washed seaweed, there would be / frail sea-eggs, and sponges, and shells with curious marks" (*Act One* 21). These are poems where the human gaze is placed secondary to the natural detail in the poem, where we see Stow develop the intuitive language of Western Australia he deploys in later work such as "Strange Fruit".

It is fitting that Stow often invites comparisons to Eliot, for while Stow emphasises realism it cannot be denied that his poetry is rooted in personal emotions. In "Tradition and the Individual Talent" Eliot introduces the analogy of the "filament of platinum" in a "chamber containing oxygen and sulphur dioxide" to describe the mind of the poet in the creation of poetry. Eliot's essential modernist argument put very simply and without getting into the peculiarities of his separation between emotion and feeling, that poetry is produced through the mind of the poet interacting with the wider poetic tradition. He writes "[t]he poet's mind is in fact a receptacle for seizing and storing up numberless feelings, phrases, images, which remain there until all the particles which can unite to form a new compound are present together." Eliot downplayed or attempted to deny the deeply personal emotional content of his own poetry in favour of readings placing his poetry in a lineage of tradition. The contradiction between Stow's statements on a universal realism and his cryptic definition of his poems as "mostly private letters" speak to this binary. The highly inter-textual nature of Stow's poetry also is akin to Eliot's own poetics; however, what is more pertinent is the way in which Stow's deep and intimate study of the land and its people functions in his own personal poetry chamber. What makes an argument for Stow as an Australian, or Western Australian, poet is how the land and its features appear as inter-texts in their own rights, forming reference points and relationships to his literary and mythic texts, such as the fall in "Strange Fruit". This is what Hassal overlooks in his otherwise perceptive statement that for Stow "landscape...is an all-purpose image, reflecting the self, the other than self, and the lover with multifaceted indifference" (*Strange Country* 79). Writing at a time when there existed no other recognised settler Western Australian poetry, Stow became one of the first to write out of that specific place in a way which examined what it meant to live there in the here and now (Hassal *Strange Country* 8). Largely written before his departure from Australia, Stow's poetry reveals a writer not exiled from a European consciousness but one that finds in the interaction with landscape a different consciousness, one that allows the natural interaction with the literary.

When asked to contribute to *Westerly* on his understanding of Western Australian writing, Stow diverges into questions of what actually constitutes the environment. He states that:

> 'environment'as the artist meets it is almost too complex a thing to be written about at all. The boundary between an individual and his environment is not his skin. It is the point where mind verges on the pure essence of him, that unchanging observer that for want of a better term we must call the soul. The external factors, geographical and sociological, are so mingled with his ways of seeing and states of mind that he may find it impossible to say what he means by his environment, except in the most personal and introspective terms. ("Raw Material" 405)

This again seems to run counter to Stow's own self-definition as a realist and definitely seems more akin to the metaphysical than Eliot's modernism. Landscape cannot be other than the personal in Stow's definition of the environment. Dennis Haskell, commenting on Kinsella's extensive introduction to Stow's selected works cautions against a reading that emphasises the post-colonial aspects of Stow over psyche (43). In an insightful reading of Stow's "The Singing Bones", Haskell writes that:

> '[o]ut there, beyond the boundary fence' becomes a mental and psychological space, 'unmapped, and mainly in the mind'. Crow-laden desert landscape in Stow's work is both literal and an objective correlative for the torments of the mind.' (43)

Here again we encounter Eliot in the idea of the objective correlative which he famously defined in "Hamlet and His Problems" as:

> a set of objects, a situation, a chain of events which shall be the formula of that particular emotion; such that when the external facts, which must terminate in sensory experience, are given, the emotion is immediately evoked.

It is important to note that in Haskell's reading the land is also treated literally not simply as a formula for the transmission of emotion. In "Strange Fruit" the very real lushness of the Kimberley landscape is transmitted, but with it comes the personal torments of a mind. Landscape was what Stow took it upon himself to learn in Western Australia and this involved a knowledge or unease with how occupation of the landscape by settler Australians altered it and impacted upon the First Nations People of Australia. While not always successful, Stow is sometimes able to comment deftly on aspects of colonialism because, as we see in his description of environment, it is something that has been personally processed. It is, as Stow writes, that "the world out there is raw material. But only part of it—all the rest is mind" ("Raw Material" 407).

While Stow limited the poems he considered working as "objective correlatives" to his mythic or masked poems, Haskell rightly expands out the label of objective correlative to considerations of Stow's overall oeuvre ("Breaking the Silence" 400). Just as the land on some level functions as a mask in "Strange Fruit", in many of these poems the identity of the masked figure, and their complicated love, is bound up in landscape. Examining one of these mask poems from Stow's *A Counterfeit Silence*, "Ishmael", it becomes clearer how inextricable psyche and landscape are in Stow's work:

> Oasis. Discovered homeland. My eyes drink at your eyes.
> Noon by noon, under leaves, my dry lips seek you.

The red earth arches away to gibber and dune.
I shall not return to this uncharted spring.

Antarctic seas work statuary of ice,
and sand-toothed wind, in the hungry waiting country,

raises unseen its pale memorials
to lioness, sphinx and man. These blinding images
I call to mind to mould the mind, inviting
desert and sky to take me, wind to shape me,

strip me likewise of softness, strip me of love,
leaving a calm regard, a remembering care.

Whoever loves you, whoever is loved by you,
speaks from my heart. That said, enough of speaking,

a clean break now. My ghost will not come creeping.
One night for words, and then my tenure ends.

The hawks wheel in the dawnlight, the dawn breeze blows
from the heart of drought, from the hungry waiting country

—and what have I to leave, but this encumbering
tenderness, like gear for ever unclaimed. (55)

Even more so than in "Strange Fruit" the identity of the lover in "Ishmael" is ambiguous. Stow has said of his masked love poems that they are "private letters" written to real people ("Breaking the Silence" 400). Again, though, if we ask the question what or who is being parted with here, there is no singular answer. We see the speaker attempt to alter themselves through interaction with the landscape "inviting / desert and sky to take me, wind to shape me". The natural forces in the land acting to "strip me ... of softness", "strip me of love" remove the burden of human emotions from the speaker. Except far from removing love, this stripping results in a further statement of emotion that addresses a human other: "whoever loves you, whoever is loved by you, / speaks from my heart." The speaker then again denies the human in the form of denying speech "that said, enough of speaking". Still the poem continues, even past the point where the speaker's "tenure ends" to finish – or remain unfinished – on the question of emotion, "what have I to leave, but.../ tenderness."

Kinsella writes that love is:

> where Stow's version of Blake's "contraries" dwells. Love is simple and complex, of an excruciating othering but also de-othering. It is private, so very private, but also looking to announce itself and remain safe, secured, damaged as little as possible (56).

This contrary is embodied in "Ishmael" in the back-and-forth between silence and speech, the retreat into nature and the propulsion back into emotion. Stow says that the speaker in his work is "not the Romantic 'I.' Just a man talking" ("Mostly Private Letters" 352). This seems strange considering the deeply lyrical nature of his poetry; however, it is in keeping with the tension or unrealised contradiction between Stow as a poet seeking the universal in the Tao and one so precisely located in Western Australia. It is also embodied in his prosody. As in most of his love poems, in "Ishmael" the composition takes the form of long-lined not quite metrical couplets, uneven pairings of lines that stretch out beyond the normal boundaries of Romantic couplets. There is a sense of both containedness and what cannot be contained, the ability of poetry to speak but not necessarily to be heard. When Zwicky writes of Stow's modernism and retreat into landscape as being in part motivated by the modernist questioning of the idea of an other poetry can speak to, she only describes half of Stow ("Speeches and Silences" 27). The other half is a very real reaching out into speech, the speech of "just a man talking" to a loved other. Stow himself acknowledged how this push-pull operated in his life, writing in a 1959 letter that he:

> didn't *need* friends. I walk by my wild lone in the cold wet woods. Nor do I *need* love; nor am I likely to get it. But love and friendship would make so many things easier – especially overcoming melancholy, inertia, ennui.
> On second thoughts, love is precisely what I don't want. It is too binding, too demanding, too observant. (Falkiner 239)

To leave "Ishmael" as purely a lyric love poem is also to do it a disservice. Stow's choice of "Ishmael" as this particular objective correlative is a peculiar and telling one that leads to a consideration of landscape. As in "Strange Fruit", "Ishmael" represents testing out imported myths onto the land of Australia. Zwicky writes of Stow's "Ishmael" that it is:

> not functioning in any newly-created vacuum of nihilism. The heritage of *Ecclesiastes* lies at the very roots of European civilisation. Only the metaphors have changed. Instead of rose-gardens and footfalls in memory's passages, we have harsher scenery of stone and waterless wastes. The impulse towards self-annihilation has not changed. The land itself seems to be the instigator of pain and desolation; its pitiless insouciance and its power to manipulate human life through the agencies of morally insensible forces like fire, flood, and drought render the human figure negligible, a victim programmed for loss ("The Price of Silence" 107).

Here again Zwicky assigns considerable agency to the land and sees its primary function in Stow's poetry as an expression of existential angst. This is certainly true, but as we will see there are further layers to Stow's "Ishmael" that are specifically about inter-human relationships. There are also considerations peculiar to his identity as an Australian writer. Firstly, there is no one Ishmael in the poem. As Melville imported Ishmael from the *Ecclesiastes* into the New World in *Moby Dick*, Stow brings both the American New World and the biblical Ishmael of the Old World into Australia. It is a fulsome union. Western Australia, and Stow's Geraldton in particular, exists as Kinsella puts it as:

> a town of the seaworld and the landworld. Not just a coastal town, but a place of congress and conflict between different modes of living and making a living. His writing of that area speaks the language of the sea *and* the land. (13)

The biblical Ishmael wanders the desert and Melville's wanders the ocean, while in Stow's poem Ishmael exists in a liminal space of "red earth" but also "antarctic seas" and "desert and sky". Both Ishmaels are searchers for homeland, but Stow's is a strange inversion. The speaker starts in "Oasis. Discovered homeland" before leaving it. This reflects the ill-fit between the figure of Ishmael and the "hungry waiting country," this land that is neither desert nor ocean but between them, outside the myths of new and old world. There is a sense of regret or loss at the parting, at not being the person to take in this "gear for ever unclaimed" to be a true "Ishmael" who survives and who finds a home.

It is thus tempting to accept Gabrielle Carey's assertion that:

> Stow had a deeply personal relationship with Australia. By that I mean that the nation and the idea of Australianness wasn't an abstract notion. I believe that, for Stow, it was almost personified. And it was a person with whom he had a tumultuous, love-hate affair. Like a lover he had tried to please, or a parent from whom he sought approval, Australia couldn't return his affections, couldn't match his emotional pitch, couldn't embrace his artistic intensity. (29)

It is an interesting question as to what burden is placed on a writer when they are granted the status of being the voice for a particular place; this was a question which was put to Stow more than once ("A Colonist" 357). If we assess the "you" in the poem as being the land of Western Australia, or Australia more generally, we see the speaker absolving themselves of the responsibility of speech, of speaking for: "[o]ne night for words, and then my tenure ends. Attachment is a burden an "encumbering / tenderness." It is possible to read the poem as being one of many poetic farewells to Australia. Yet the central image of "the hungry waiting country" does not sit well with a purely Australian landscape reading of the poem. The images of desert and the "dawn breeze blow[ing] / from the heart of drought" seem aligned with the Western Australian landscape, but it is not without complications. In a poem of "Ishmael" and therefore of biblical homelands, an "unclaimed" "waiting country" is an uneasy fit for Australia. It aligns too closely with the image of Australia as terra nullius. It is possible, as in "Strange Fruit", to read the speaker's leaving or refusal to occupy the tenderness as a refutation of there being a homeland to be claimed. It is more likely, though, that the "hungry waiting country" is an instance of Stow's inner geography.

In an interesting reading of the *Outrider* sequence in terms of their relation to the French voyager poetry of Stow's great influences Rimbaud and Baudelaire, Carl Whitehouse positions all geographic and landscape references to be points of psyche (116). Frustrated with the dominance of nationalistic readings of Stow's work, he instead proposes that the division or partings in *Outrider* and the images of desolate country are representative of a divided self that can never be united. The two, or three, Ishmaels in this poem could be read in this way, as could the journey to/from speech. The "hungry waiting country" and "gear for ever unclaimed" become aspects of the self that are being left as the speaker sets forth. Similarly, "Strange Fruit" from this perspective features what Whitehouse terms two selves: "nomadic Cain" and "pastoral Abel". These selves cannot be reconciled, resulting in ideas of suicide, the "strange fruit", which are left unresolved (Whitehouse 126). Whitehouse's is a persuasive reading uncovering aspects of the poems which had been neglected; however, in both poems there is something more specific at work than a generalised divided self. Both instances, as in other poems throughout *Outrider* and Stow's work more generally, display the speaker being specifically divided from love or the loved other. "Strange Fruit" reads more as a poem of refutation of carnal desire, while in "Ishmael" the speaker seeks "tenderness" and "love". It is interesting that Whitehouse identifies separation as having "arisen because conventional society has suppressed the senses, thereby banishing that unity between conscious and sensate life that had characterised childhood" (122). Stow's framing of the environment as of conscious and unconscious mind follows a pattern of neglecting ideas of the body in favour of the mind. It is worth noting that this concurs with readings of these poems as not necessarily arising out of a generalised existential despair but from a localised body. The speaker desires something which their conscious mind does not want them to desire. This results in a cry of separation of body from mind. Similarly the prominent binary of speech and silence can be read as questioning what good poetry or speech can do in a modern world, but it can be also be a question of allowing the body to speak, to voice its desire.

It is also a common critical mistake to read the features of the landscape purely as real Australia. Melanie Duckworth isolates the image of "that planet (ah, Christ) of black ice" from Stow's "Outrider" as being of some other continent to Australia, a psychic space of "alienation suffered" (109). Similarly, ice reappears in "Ishmael" as nether-space, neither Australian nor European as does the purely mythic space of "lioness, sphinx and man". In contrast there is also a distinctly Australian local presence in the work, "the hawks circling" in "Ishmael" the dingos and crocodiles of "Strange Fruit". Dorothy Hewett states:

Stow is the inheritor of both the Romantic and the existential dilemma – the isolation of man within nature, and the alienation of man in the modern world. It is a dilemma which could only be exaggerated in its Australian context, where the dream of the lost paradise, the small communities living close to the earth in a beneficent sunlight, was held briefly, and lost most bitterly, and finally forever. (64)

In his approach to love and land Stow displays, as Kinsella suggests, his own version of Blake's contraries. But it is more than this, looking closely at the Hewett statement we see the Romantic Stow and the existential Stow but we also see a third facet – the Australian Stow. Stow's poetry is both mythic and real and further complicated by this fact. In the majority of his work this is not expressed in a poetry of mythic space; instead, it is in his realistic approach to the natural detail of the country. In his love lyrics, Stow searches for individuals, particular relationships, even if these relationships are expressed in the wider language of place and even if through their composition Stow comes to speak of the country and his relationship to it.

John Kinsella says of his own ties to the Western Australian wheat belt, that it helps to have grown where Stow grew, to know the land in order to understand Stow's poetry (50). I too came to Stow through an actual landscape, just south of Geraldton on the Western Australian coast in the town of Cervantes, joined to Stow's work through the dissonance of encountering the ghosts of European shipwrecks as everyday street names in a place of taverns, taciturn weathered men and a wind that turns every metal thing to rust. The great criticism of the idea of an "objective correlative" is whether it is possible for a poem to evoke only a singular, intended, emotional response in the reader. We can know the land Stow knew but we can never know exactly how he knew it, never be "from" or "of"' the same mindscape. Judith Wright said of poetry in Australia that "the writer must be at peace with his landscapes before he can turn confidently to its human figures" (*Preoccupations in Australian Poetry* 5).

In most of the criticism of Stow there is the same sense of unease, a desire to foreground place and thereby perhaps to understand where our own writing comes from. This has led to the bulk of what has been written on Stow's poetry, and to some extent his prose, emphasising landscape to the detriment of other poetic and personal considerations. This essay has played a role in the opening up of Stow's poetry to wider concerns, particularly in light of the availability of new biographical information.

Yet, despite this enhanced biography, we can never know who or what exactly inspired Stow's love poems. In the final pages of her over 700 page biography of Stow, Falkiner writes that an "unanswered question ... for a biographer concerns the identity of Stow's great loves ... The answer is not simple. Mick loved a number of people – men and women – deeply in different ways. Stow's *beau ideal* was a romantic masculine figure, a bushman or Conradian seaman" (725). What we do know is how Stow sought "[t]he feeling, the sense, what a Spaniard would call the *sentiment* of Australia: the external forms filtered back through the conscious and unconscious mind" ("Raw Material" 407). Stow remains a unique figure in the development of Australian poetry, not seeking through poetry to know or capture the land. Instead he simply knew the land and sought through poetry a knowledge of himself, of being human, which necessarily includes aspects of the environment. Hopefully Stow's poetry will continue to be reassessed, not just for its nationhood but for the individual particularities that make it his own.

Works Cited

Beston, John. "The Love Poetry of Randolph Stow." *ACLALS Bulletin*, vol. 4, no. 5, 1977, pp. 12-25.

Carey, Gabrielle. "Randolph Stow: An Ambivalent Australian." *Kill Your Darlings*, no. 12, 2013, pp. 27-37.

Duckworth, Melanie. "Grievous Music: Randolph Stow's Middle Ages."*Australian Literary Studies,* vol. 26, no. 3-4, 2011, pp.102-114.

Eliot, T.S. "Hamlet and His Problems." Bartleby.com, 9 December 2015. www. *bartleby.com*.

---. "Tradition and the Individual Talent." Bartleby.com, 9 December 2015. *bartleby.com*.

Falkiner, Suzanne. *Mick: A Life of Randolph Stow*, UWA Publishing, 2016.

Haskell, Dennis. "Private Letters" *Australian Book Review,* September, 2012, pp. 42-43.

Hassal, Anthony, Edited by *Randolph Stow*, University of Queensland Press,1990.

---. *Strange Country: A Study of Randolph Stow*, University of Queensland Press, 1986.

Hewett, Dorothy. "Silence, Exile and Cunning: The Poetry of Randolph Stow." *Westerly,* vol. 2, 1988, pp. 59-66.

Keller, Lynn. "Post-Language Lyric: The Example of Juliana Spahr." *Chicago Review,* vol. 55, no. 3-4, 2010, pp. 74-83.

Kinsella, John. Introduction. *The Land's Meaning: New Selected Poems Randolph Stow,* edited by John Kinsella, Fremantle Press, 2012, pp. 9-65.

Stow, Randolph. *Act One*, Macdonald & Co, 1957.

---. "Breaking the Silence" Interview with Anthony J. Hassal. *Randolph Stow*, edited by Anthony J. Hassal, University of Queensland Press, 1986, pp. 380-401.

---. "A Colonist with Words" Interview with Xavier Pons and Neil Keeble. *Randolph Stow*, edited by Anthony J. Hassal, University of Queensland Press, 1986, pp. 356-368.

---. "A Conversation with Randolph Stow." Interview with Richard Kelly Tipping. *Antipodes,* vol. 1, no. 2, 1987, pp. 71-74.

---. *A Counterfeit Silence: Selected Poems*, Angus and Robertson, 1969.

---. "Home and Away" Interview with Bruce Bennet. *Randolph Stow*, edited by Anthony J. Hassal, University of Queensland Press, 1986, pp. 369-379.

---. "Mostly Private Letters" Interview with John B. Beston. *Randolph Stow*, edited by Anthony J. Hassal, University of Queensland Press,

1986, pp. 349-355.

---. *Outrider: Poems, 1956-1962*, Macdonald & Co, 1962.

---. "Raw Material." *Randolph Stow*, edited by Anthony J. Hassal, University of Queensland Press, 1986, pp. 405-408.

---. "The Southland." *Randolph Stow*, edited by Anthony J. Hassal, University of Queensland Press, 1986, pp. 410-419.

---. *To the Islands*, Penguin Books, 1962.

Whitehouse, Carl. "Randolph Stow's Outrider and the French Voyager Poem." *Australian Literary Studies*, vol. 18, no. 2, 1997, pp. 116-127.

Wright, Judith. "Australian Poetry Since 1941." *Southerly*, vol. 31, 1971, pp. 19-28.

---. *Preoccupations in Australian Poetry*, Oxford University Press, 1965.

Zwicky, Fay. "Speeches and Silences." *The Lyre in the Pawn Shop: Essays on Literature and Survival, 1974-1984*, edited by Fay Zwicky, University of Western Australia Press, 1986, pp. 23-36.

---. "The Price of Silence: Further Thoughts on the Poetry of Randolph Stow." *The Lyre in the Pawn Shop: Essays on Literature and Survival, 1974-1984*, edited by Fay Zwicky, University of Western Australia Press, 1986, pp. 103-111.

Chapter 10

Les Murray's Mannerist Grotesque

David Musgrave

As Les Murray approaches his 80th birthday it is worth trying to assess the continuity of his achievement over a career that has now entered its 53rd year. In this chapter I approach this through examining, primarily in his later work, what I see as two central, and linked preoccupations — a fascination with distortion, exaggeration and (re)framing, combined with a sense of an abject sexuality. I argue that 'late' Murray arrived relatively early, around the time of his return to Bunyah in the late 1980s, when he was in his late 40s, but also that this 'lateness' has clear and discernible roots in his early lyric poetry.

    I want to explore the relevance of the grotesque mode to Murray's poetry, in terms of his engagement with it and also in terms of his theorisation of it. Elements of the grotesque appear frequently in his poetry as word-play, cryptic riddling, compound words and catachretical metaphors and, in the later work, as part of an exaggerated mannerist style. Most of these instances of the grotesque occur in poems which are not, as a whole, grotesque. As a mode or category, the grotesque is one useful means by which to approach the totality of Murray's achievement, drawing together key aspects of his work such as a preoccupation with the tension between margins and centres (one version of which is the tension between the city and the bush), a fascination with sexual abjection, an epideictic linguistic flashiness and a deep interest in peculiarity (one senses a deep affinity between Murray and the Hopkins of "Pied Beauty": "All things counter, original, spare, strange"), ugliness and suffering.

    I want to start by comparing two poems from different periods, the first being "The Winter Rising" from Murray's first book, *The Ilex Tree* (1965), and the second from *Translations from the Natural World*

(1992), near the beginning of what I argue is Murray's 'late' period. It's worth comparing these quite different poems, one a young man's poem and the other a baroque bravura piece, because of some shared qualities. First, the earlier poem:

The Winter Rising

We lived below the houses of the hill,
Their light, their music were not ours,
Their songs were delicate and French.
          Bowers
Of tin were our dwellings, and terraces
Of weeping brick all down to a frozen river.
At night, the shunting freight trains nagged us
Into nightmares. We learned love shivering
Under the viaducts, down amongst the weeds.
            One day
The idea there was something could be done
To change the tenor of our times arrived
Amongst our houses, youthful, fierce, begrimed,
Not to be trusted.
       But we listened; listened:
It turned our faces and our hatred up
Towards the Hill. And at dawn we enlisted
Knives, torches, beams against the walls
Of the great houses.
        Their fall was enormous,
A flood of crystal, privilege and baubles,
And well-bred corpses, indelicately dead.
            And then,
When all the walls of tyranny were down,
It was still cold. The rivers were still ice,
Our houses tin, and no lights on the hill. (*The Ilex Tree* 26)

The poem fantasises a revolution against a rural elite, juxtaposing the situation of the rural poor ("Bowers/ Of tin were our dwelling"[1]) with the elevated mansions of the well-bred, delivering an ambivalent moral: the call for collective action is "Not to be trusted" and the extinction of the squattocracy (presuming that the poem is in fact set in an imaginary Australia — the tin dwellings would seem to suggest this, but this is not conclusive), does nothing to change the misery of the poor. Curiously, in a poem that simultaneously fantasises and rejects revolution, an abject version of love is depicted: "we learned love, shivering / under the viaducts, amongst the weeds", and it is tempting to ask whether there is a link between the desire to overturn and sexual abjection.

The impulse to overturn an existing order, particularly one that is clearly a European-influenced elite is an example of the rage which Dan Chiasson and J.M. Coetzee find is the dominant tone of Murray's poetry. In this case it is a rage directed against the now familiar targets (cultural elites, whether rural or urban) tempered by a distrust of collective action. It is also a moment of inversion, where the hierarchies of an imagined society are for a brief moment overthrown and turned upside down in a kind of *mundus reversus*; and yet the poem perhaps confusedly echoes Ben Chifley's famous speech from 1949, where "the light on the hill" stands as the epitome of the Labor objective. Both the desire to overturn and a sense of abjection resonate with the grotesque mode, which is not to suggest that the poem is an example of the grotesque. It isn't, although other poems of Murray's are. *The Boys Who Stole the Funeral* (1980) is a phantasmogoric grotesquerie, for example, but the grotesque mode doesn't really fully effloresce until much later, an example being "Mollusc" from *Translations from the Natural World* (1992):

Mollusc

By its nobship sailing upside down,
by its inner sexes, by the crystalline

pimplings of its skirts, by the sucked-on
lifelong kiss of its toppling motion,
by the viscose optics now extruded
now wizened instantaneously, by the
ridges, grating up a food-path by
the pop shell in its nick of dry,
by excretion, the earthworm coils, the glibbing,
by the gilt slipway, and by pointing
perhaps as far back into time as
ahead, a shore being folded interior,
by boiling on salt, by coming uncut over
a razor's edge, by hiding the Oligocene
underleaf may this and every snail sense
itself ornament the weave of presence. (26)

At first glance, it might appear that these are poems by different poets, with the verbal dexterity of the later poem having an epideictic quality absent from the earlier poem. Yet "Mollusc" begins with what could be the image of a member of an elite: a nob, here mock-reverently suffixed with "ship" to denote character, office or skill and, like the nobs of "The Winter Rising", also inverted. The succeeding verb, however, literalises the "ship" as a vessel, calling into question the "nob" of "nobship." When I hear the word nob, I think of a penis before I think of a nabob, and if I think of what a nobship might be, apart from an (in this case) inverted example of some kind of mollusc aristocrat, I imagine the snail as a kind of glistery, slimy penis housed in its vessel, its shell, sailing along with a kind of insouciant splendour. The thing about this reading is that it can't simply be discounted as my perverted take on a snail-riddle, as the linguistic ambiguity, one of the hallmarks of the grotesque, allows it. It is a reading which is further supported by the imagery which follows: the "inner sexes" surely points back to "nob" as penis as much as it leads forward to the adolescent "pimplings", the "sucked-on / lifelong kiss"[2], both of which are inescapably sexual, as is the "viscose optics now extruded / now wizened instantaneously", an image of tumescence and detumescence if ever there was one.

As with "The Winter Rising" the sexual imagery here is primarily abject: slimy, viscose, pimpled, sucked-on, snail-like: the penis is a kind of mollusc, an organ which is only obliquely celebrated here. Yet if this is so, what relation does it bear to the rest of the poem? How is sexual abjection linked to the snail sensing itself "ornament the weave of presence"? The link is, I think, the textile metaphor of "weave". Each clause of this poem is linked by the ablative (or instrumental) anaphora of "by," such that the "weave of presence" which the snail may sense of itself is also the weave of these several clausal strings, namely the "presence" of the poem. "Presence" is a big word, and it is surely meant as a riposte to those intellectual traditions which lament the impossibility of presence or celebrate its endless deferral. "Mollusc" is a grotesque self-portrait of his nibs the poet, playfully but not unawkwardly depersonalised by "its nobship." The grotesquerie of the poem is one of the most revealing in all of Murray's oeuvre as it clearly makes the link between sexual abjection and textual profusion in the emblematic figure of the snail-poet.

The Grotesque

Before I proceed any further it is necessary to examine what I mean by the term 'grotesque' in relation to language or to linguistic art forms. The term 'grotesque' has a long history which I will touch on briefly, as it involves a fortuitous coincidence which is useful for considering one aspect of it which is relevant to Murray's work. The Italian term *grottesche* came to be applied to frescoes that were discovered in the palace of Nero, the Domus Aurea, in the 1480s, as the frescoes were discovered underground. Geoffrey Harpham notes that:

> this naming is a mistake pregnant with truth, for although the designs were never intended to be underground, nor Nero's palace a grotto, the word is perfect. The Latin form of *grotta* is probably

crupta (cf. 'crypt'), which in turn derives from the Greek Κρυπτη, a vault; one of the cognates is Κρυπτειγ, to hide. *Grotesque*, then, gathers into itself suggestions of the underground, of burial, and of secrecy (27)

As luck would have it, the cryptic *is* an essential feature of the grotesque in general. Citing George Santayana, Harpham asserts that "the grotesque occupies a gap or interval; it is the middle of a narrative of emergent comprehension" (15) insofar as the heterogeneous elements of the grotesque must be encountered and reconciled before meaning can take place: a little like solving a riddle. I will return to the cryptic aspect of the grotesque after briefly considering some major theorists of the grotesque and determining which kind of grotesque relates most directly to Murray's work.

Most of the treatments of the grotesque in language have tended to be either iconographic or biased towards the visual. Two of the dominant theorists of the mode in the twentieth century, Wolfgang Kayser and Mikhail Bakhtin, are almost at complete odds with each other. Kayser sees the grotesque as: "a structure. Its nature could be summed up in a phrase that has repeatedly suggested itself to us: THE GROTESQUE IS THE ESTRANGED WORLD" (184), based largely on a study of German modernism. Bakhtin, on the other hand, sees the grotesque in terms of "joyful relativity", based largely on a re-reading of Rabelais (Bakhtin). Attitudes towards the grotesque differ from period to period, as do the uses to which it is put. For example, in the revision of understandings of the grotesque after Wolfgang Kayser's formulation of it as "the estranged world" it is possible to define it anew, as I have done, as "radical heterogeneity" (Musgrave 26); that is, as a combination and recombination which attends to all aspects of the artwork. In the case of poetry, this radical heterogeneity attends to form, diction and icon; however, given the strong tendency towards theorising the grotesque as something which can be visualised, is it possible to define a grotesque in language which is not reliant on the grotesque image, and if so, how are we to do it?

Philip Thomson's *The Grotesque in German Poetry 1880-1933* is the most extensive study of its kind, trying to establish what the linguistic basis for a grotesque in poetry might be. There are a number of threads which Thomson weaves together in his approach to defining the grotesque in poetry, the most important of which is the "conflict of incompatibles":

> the intertwined coexistence of contraries or incompatibles, while it will shock or disorientate—it is usually intended to—is unacceptable aesthetically (or morally, even) only to those who are inhibited by traditional aesthetic schemata. And of course the grotesque is very often designed to disconcert or infuriate people thus disposed. (8)

Linguistically, this can manifest itself in several ways. One is the yoking together of ideas or symbols which appear not to belong together; an example is Murray's "East Sydney":

> I shot an arrow in the air,
> It fell to earth in Taylor Square
> Transfixing, to my vast delight,
> A policeman and a sodomite.
> (*The Weatherboard Cathedral* 23)

Apart from the parody of Longfellow, the grotesque here consists in the comic shock of the actual physical union, parodic of sodomy, of the policeman and the homosexual. The irreconcilability of this grotesque lies not in the possibility that the two figures might be polar opposites, but rather in the delight which the persona of the poem experiences; moreover, this delight is qualified by the adjective "vast" which, as we shall see, is intimately linked with Murray's presentation of himself in the public realm for most of his career. This kind of grotesque relies heavily on the symbolism of two figures joined in an unnatural manner; in other words, it is an instance of a grotesque that is iconographic, rather than linguistic (such as word-play, cryptic riddling, compound words and catachretical metaphors). I will examine in the next section of this chapter the linguistic grotesque of Murray's poetry as an instance of Mannerism, specifically as a form of eccentric self-portraiture.

Murray's own conceptions of the grotesque are worth examining at this point. In "The Human-Hair Thread" Murray touches on a basic tenet which I think forms one cornerstone of his poetics: "in art, and in my writing, my abiding interest is in integrations, in convergences" (*Persistence in Folly* 27). Integrations and convergences, especially where the differences are (and remain) great, is another way of describing the form of the grotesque. The interesting question then arises with regards to Murray's poetics: can the grotesque be a positive mode for his poetry, or is it doomed to negativity? The answer is intriguing. In "Some Religious Stuff I Know About Australia" Murray offers a revealing definition of grotesque:

> In the huge spaces of the Outback, ordinary souls expand into splendid and often innocent grotesquerie which the cramping of urban surrounding might transmute into ugly, even dangerous forms. (*Persistence in Folly* 116)

For Murray, the grotesquerie into which ordinary souls expand is, by definition large (like Murray himself), splendid and innocent. Grandness and goodness seem to be its prevailing virtues. One can infer the operation of fancy in the elaboration of this grotesquerie, so that this passing observation, as is often the case in Murray's prose, really serves as an idealised description of himself. Generally speaking, this seems to be a view of the grotesque peculiar to Murray: one can cite Barbara Baynton's *Bush Studies* (1902) or John Farrell's *How He Died and Other Poems* (1887) and *My Sundowner and Other Poems* (1904) as instances of an "outback" grotesquerie that is far from innocent or splendid. What is interesting is that Murray conceives of the grotesque in terms that lend themselves to another way of conceiving of the mode. The *mundus reversus*, or world upside down posits a world that is radically different from, but also defined in relation to the everyday world. This is not dissimilar to the tension between margins and centre which, in Murray's work is the ever-present tension between urban and outback/rural/bush. In Murray's oeuvre, where these integrations and convergences wholly succeed, we will, perhaps, not find the grotesque; yet the preoccupation with difference, which this abiding interest presupposes, indicates an ever-abiding nearness or proximity to the grotesque, to a radical heterogeneity. Where Murray attempts integration and convergence, we are therefore likely to find ourselves in or near the realm of the grotesque.

Geoffrey Harpham, the third major theorist of the grotesque after Kayser and Bakhtin, is of the opinion that "looking for unity between center and margin, the interpreter must, whether he finds it or not, pass through the grotesque" (38). It is my contention that the grotesque is a mode central to Murray's work, even if most of his poems do not qualify as grotesque (in the same way that many of the poems Thomson discusses in his study have elements of the grotesque in them but do not qualify as wholly grotesque works of art). In fact, one can consider his verse novel *Fredy Neptune* as an allegory of the grotesque.

Another aspect of the grotesque which is relevant to considering Murray's work is Murray's presentation of himself. Kate Llewellyn's reminiscence of her first encounter with Murray at the Adelaide Festival might be typical of anyone's:

> Two years later, more events were held. I went along. I was entranced. Sitting with my son Hugh outside the Adelaide Museum on a lawn, listening to a big man in khaki overalls read poetry in a breathless way ... The man was Les Murray. He was the first poet I had laid eyes on and I had a sense that he wasn't typical. (Llewellyn)

The year was 1964; several years later, Murray

> attracted attention by his size and his dress: he often wore a baseball cap to cover his large balding head, and a vast jumper, knitted for him by Valerie, which appeared to have been designed to use the last of two dozen batches of different wools, and whose dazzling multicoloured stripes ran to the horizon."
> (Alexander 180)

Such horizontal stripes, as any fashionista might tell you, accentuates one's girth. There seems to be a delight in appearing as unusual, exaggerating his size, even if this is not, strictly speaking, an example of the grotesque. For his Heinemann *Collected Poems* (1994), "Murray chose for its cover a Brueghel painting, *The Strife of Lent with Shrove-Tide*, depicting an exceedingly well-fleshed man, with an uncanny resemblance to Murray"[3] (Alexander 263), which, considered together with the young girl embracing the elephant seated next to her on the cover of his Black Inc. *Collected Poems* (2006), confirms this delight in the unusualness of his appearance. In recent years, Murray's presentation of himself in photographs smiling with missing teeth accentuates a somewhat bumpkinish appearance.

But Murray's presentation of his language skills is another matter:

> I was a freak, but happily my freakishness was in language—not, say, in classifying antique crankshafts. We seem to get a word-freak once or twice a century in the Murray family. Sir James Murray of the Oxford English Dictionary was my cousin, for example.
> When I'd argue points in the OED with my Russian fellow-translator at the National University in Canberra, I'd tell him we Murrays owned the damn language! Being some other kind of freak has its attractions, mind you. I envy painting its impasto and sheer colour-play, how it's not held in by that stubborn insuspendable lexicality that words have. I get out into nonsense

as far as I can. Lord knows, though never for nihilist ends ... There's also the wonderful advantage of music and painting and sculpture, that they don't have to be translated. ("Les Murray, the Art of Poetry No. 89")

or as Edwina Hall observes in her interview with Murray:

> Language has been around in the Murray family a lot. 'The bloke who wrote the Oxford English Dictionary was a cousin of ours called Sir James Murray, a Murray language freak comes up every century or so.' ("Les Murray AO")

Even in the absurd argument of "The Bonny Disproportion" Murray asserts that "the proportion of Scots Australians among our poets is freakishly high" (*Persistence in Folly* 63).

'Freakishness' is therefore a central plank not just in Murray's self-promotion but, by his own admission, his poetics as well. Such freakishness can be an argument for excessive value or distinction; it can also be adduced as evidence of a tendency to distortion, exaggeration, even rage, which Dan Chiasson has identified as "the key to Murray" (Chiasson) and which J.M. Coetzee sees as coming out "most nakedly in the *Subhuman Redneck Poems* of 1996, whose very title is a challenge" (Coetzee). It is indeed a challenge, for the subhuman represents another kind of freak. "Subhuman" has a very specific meaning, originally occurring in "Our Man in Bunyah," a column Murray wrote for the *Independent Monthly* between 1993 and 1996:

> If triumphant Lawrentian sex, the kind that stares challengingly out of films and glossy magazines all over the Western world, is a Nazi—and it is if you think about it, with its tall, beautiful blond idol—then those who have suffered erocide along with children and the old, are its subhumans (*A Working Forest: Selected Prose* 78)

Later, he would begin his grotesque poem "Rock Music" with the phrase "Sex is a Nazi" (*Subhuman Redneck Poems* 16). The avoidance of eros, or an interest in sexual abjection is an important element in Murray's work, and an essential part of the 'freakishness' which he identifies as central to his work. In "The Human Hair Thread", Murray declares "I have an abhorrence anyway for our modern uses of sex" (23). While it is not entirely clear what he means by "modern uses of sex" (is it the omnipresence of sex in modern culture, deployed in art or advertising, or is it pornography, or even casual sex to which Murray refers?) one can only presume a discomfort with eros in general, given the absence of the erotic from Murray's oeuvre and the near-absence of love poems. I may appear to have digressed from freakishness to an avoidance of eros, but I will go on to argue that they are, in fact, linked: the exaggeration of 'freakishness' is a distinguishing feature of Mannerism, and asceticism manifests itself as a form of self-display directed towards the 'other.' One feeds off the other in the idiosyncratic manner which characterises Murray's work.

Baroque, Rococo and Mannerism

As I have shown with 'grotesquerie,' Murray is aware of this aesthetic category and has a positive understanding of it. He has also used the terms "baroque" and "rococo," as if interchangeable, to describe his poetics. In an interview with J. Mark Smith, Murray is quite explicit on how both terms underpin his work:

> Father Gerard Manley Hopkins … taught me how to do baroque diction, how to melt language and model tableaux in it. I taught myself later on how to do this under cover. You gave your work a factual plain surface and worked the baroque and the rococo underneath, so that you and your readers were free of the tyranny of modern 'no nonsense' pretensions. ("A Conversation with Les Murray")

And in *The Paris Review* interview, Murray opines that his readers "like some puzzlement, some baroque, perhaps" and goes on to credit Hopkins with giving him "the baroque—highly elaborated and symbolic art—as an instant gift; and that's been a lasting resource for me" ("Les Murray, the Art of Poetry No. 89"). Similarly, in "The Quality of Sprawl" one of the various definitions of "sprawl" is:

> It is the rococo of being your own still centre.
> (*The People's Otherworld* 28)

In "Literary Editor," the work of the editor is dramatised thus:

> but then a magic word stands up
> off the page: *candelaborough* —
>
> it throws him out of kilter.
> *I've been too fine a filter.*
> *Now see: the name of my true home.*
> *It calls me! My native rococo!*
> (*Conscious and Verbal* 66)

Both baroque and rococo are terms from art, with baroque in particular relating to art of the counter-reformation, characterised by its ornate and elaborate style. There is little evidence to suggest that Murray uses either term in any way other than to describe complexity, through elaborate diction and symbolism, except for the fact that in "A Conversation with Les Murray" and the line from "The Quality of Sprawl" he locates the terms as either being internal or under the surface. This is a significant departure from common understandings of either term. This indicates to me that Murray's concern with either category is not just in terms of display but also in terms of structure: extravagance, distortion, exaggeration, excessive ornamentation, clumsily florid, perhaps, in an internalised state. Moreover, the baroque and rococo are a means, paradoxically enough, of being "free of the tyranny of modern 'no nonsense' pretensions," indicating that it is part of a grotesque strategy to subordinate the centre to the margins, one of the key motivations of Murray's work. Here, the interiority of the baroque and the rococo bears a striking parallel to the expansive grotesquerie of the outback; similarly, it can be implied that the cramped ugliness of the urban environment has its parallel in the "tyranny of modern 'no nonsense' pretensions." Given Murray's avowed interest in convergences and integrations, one must presume, after Harpham, that the grotesque is a phase one must pass through when juxtaposing and reconciling the margin with the centre. Giancarlo Maiorino terms this strategy "liminality," which "sets up a position of eccentricity vis-à-vis a given center" (82). In Murray's poetic lexicon, "rococo" and "baroque" teeter, perhaps uncomfortably, into the territory of the liminal grotesque.

A better way of understanding Murray's elaborate diction and complexity, therefore, is to place it in the context of the grotesque, specifically the Mannerist grotesque. Arnold Hauser identifies three key areas of Mannerism in sixteenth century Italian art which are also common to the grotesque mode, and would seem to apply to the later Murray's work: paradox, eccentricity and piquancy:

> the idea of paradox could provide the basis of a definition that attempted to cover most of the phenomena in question and at the same time do justice to their positive and original stylistic traits instead of merely contrasting them with other artistic styles. At first sight, it is an eccentric and piquant quality, never absent in any mannerist work, however profound and serious it may be, that expresses itself in paradox. A certain piquancy, a predilection for the subtle, the strange, the over-strained, the abstruse and yet stimulating, the pungent, the bold, and the challenging, are characteristics of mannerist art in all its phases, and are the hallmark of the most diverse of its representatives. (12)

Here it is important to stress that the eccentric, in relation to Murray, should be seen as 'ex-centric' or from the margins. One cannot understand his baroque and rococo qualities without considering them in relation to an overall strategy to elevate the margin and to de-centre the centre. The paradoxical in the later Murray is to be found nearly everywhere. As Lisa Gorton writes in her review of *Waiting for the Past*, "riddles are at the heart of Les Murray's poetry" and, moreover, "Murray's descriptions are never far from paradox, very often combining a close-up view of something with a sense of its strangeness" (Gorton). Perhaps there is a sense in which the tendency toward paradox and riddling in Murray is a distancing effect. It is also part of the impulse towards ascesis, more of which in the next section, which takes an epideictic form:

> It is often this piquancy—a playful or compulsive deviation from the normal, an affected, frisky quality, or a tormented grimace—that first betrays the mannerist nature of a work. The virtuosity that is always displayed contributes greatly to the piquancy. A mannerist work of art is always a piece of bravura, a triumphant conjuring trick, a firework displaying with flying sparks and colours. (Hauser 13)

The Mannerist grotesque, therefore, is that mode which draws attention to itself through a strategy of inversion or reversal, accompanied by extravagance, exaggeration and paradox. Part of the process of inversion and reversal can be that of the supplanted frame: think of a beautiful picture in a large, ornate frame swarming with grotesque figures—humans and vegetable and animal shapes in fanciful combinations—such that the frame itself overwhelms the painting at its centre. This is close to what I mean by the tension between centre and margin in Murray's work. It is not just a theme, that the rural is superior to the urban: it is a structural principle, a grotesque strategy that brings with it all the accompanying Mannerist techniques detailed above.

A poet's style differs from his or her mannerisms when one considers tensions and extremisms in his or her work, such as a tendency toward riddling, compound words, unusual or recherché diction, as in the case of the later Murray, as mannerisms. Giorgio Agamben takes this distinction further:

> If style marks the artist's most characteristic trait, manner registers an inverse process of expropriation and exclusion. It is as if the old poet, who found his style and reached perfection in it, now forgets that in order to advance the singular claim of expressing himself solely through impropriety. (97)

The Mannerism of Murray's later work, as I will argue below, is in evidence in his earlier work, but not to as marked a degree as in his later work. For this reason, we can designate Mannerism, as opposed to the lyric, as the defining mode of late Murray. Agamben goes on to say:

> In art history, mannerism thus 'presupposes the knowledge of a style to which one believes oneself to adhere, but which one instead unconsciously seeks to avoid' (Pinder). For psychiatrists, on the other hand, the mode of being of the mannerist consists in showing 'impropriety in the sense of not being oneself and at the same time, the will to earn thereby one's own terrain and status (Binswanger)' (98)

Mannerism relies on an exaggerated sense of difference: to oneself and to the 'other' of art. In the early Murray, this exaggerated sense of difference largely took place in response to other poets, the 'other' of the urban elites (imaginary or otherwise)[4]; in the late Murray, this 'other' is his earlier lyrical self. I will examine this proposition through a close reading of poems from his earlier period (pre-1990) and from his later period in the final section of this chapter.

As with 'grotesquerie,' "rococo" and "baroque", "mannerism"

or mannered is part of Murray's critical idiom, although he uses it as a term of abuse. Here is how he has written on Patrick White in his essay "Eric Rolls and the Golden Disobedience":

> We have grown used in recent years to highly mannered forms of prose fiction, many of them derived in this country from Patrick White's method of dabbling small exacerbated qualifications of extreme sensitivity over narrative and character in ways which constantly threaten to snub us if we do not render abashed assent. Few writers, perhaps, have followed White's other trick of inverting ordinary snobbery and transposing it into mystical election ... (*Persistence in Folly* 163)

This essay dates from 1982, several years before Murray gave into his own ascetic imperative after his return to Bunyah from Sydney. In the highly mannered style which has evolved in his poetry since then, replete with riddling and a tendency towards paradox, one wonders whether Murray's take on White's writing could, with a little tweaking, now apply to his own: that Murray's readers must, through solving his riddles and resolving paradoxes, render their abashed assent to his cryptic, mannerist skill, or risk being snubbed.

Murray's Mannerism evolved slowly, although there are many intimations of it in his work before 1990. One earlier poem which stands out as almost purely Mannerist is "The Broad Bean Sermon" (1974); it bears comparison with the Mannerist grotesques of Arcimboldo, where a painting that at first appears to be an agglomeration of fish, fruit, vegetation or books resolves into a human face the further one is from the painting (Maiorino 31-59). The grotesque of such painting does not consist in its affect—delight, not revulsion is the predominant feeling most experience when encountering Arcimboldo for the first time—but in its liminality (Harpham *On the Grotesque: Strategies of Contradiction in Art and Literature* 13-14). Is it a human face or a collection of fish or books? At what point does it become one or the other? In "The Broad Bean Sermon" the copiousness of the broad beans themselves is complemented by the copiousness of the imagery with which the broad beans are described: "mint Air Force dacron, with unbuttoned leaves", "thin-crescent, frown-shaped, bird-shouldered, boat-keel ones, / beans knuckled and single-bulged, minute green dolphins at suck, // beans upright like lecturing", "like templates for subtly broad grins, like unique caught expressions, // like edible meanings", "misshapen as toes." The final image of deformity is a kind of *sprezzatura*, typical of Mannerism (Maiorino 18-19), which foreshadows the coarser textures of the later Murray's Mannerism. Yet here its aptness is celebratory, in what is perhaps Murray's most perfectly realized lyric. I cannot help but be put in mind of E. H. Gombrich's observation when thinking of Murray's poetry in his later period:

> Mannerism comes to its climax at the moment when the inherent ambiguities of the Renaissance ideas of artistic progress become apparent—at the moment when, by common assent, Michelangelo has achieved 'perfection' by realizing 'the highest potentialities of his art' (9).

The Ascetic Imperative

Rock Music

Sex is a Nazi. The students all knew
this at your school. To it, everyone's subhuman
for parts of their lives. Some are all their lives.
You'll be one of those if these things worry you.

The beautiful Nazis, why are they so cruel?
Why, to castrate the aberrant, the original, the wounded
who might change our species and make obsolete
the true race. Which is those who never leave school.
For the truth, we are silent. For the flattering dream,

in massed farting reassurance, we spasm and scream,
but what is a Nazi but sex pitched for crowds?

It's the Calvin SS: you are what you've got
and you'll wrinkle and fawn and work after you're shot
though tears pour in secret from the hot indoor clouds.
(*Subhuman Redneck Poems* 16)

"The goal of all asceticism is perfect union with God," (22) writes Geoffrey Harpham, something to which the dedication "To the greater glory of God" in all of Murray's books since the "little chapbook *Equanimities* (1982)" (Alexander 241) signals as a basic impulse in Murray' poetry: "Perhaps a poet like Murray, who dedicates his volume 'To the glory of God,' has left human style behind" (Vendler). Any account of the Mannerist grotesque in Murray would be incomplete without considering in some detail the strong ascetic impulse that has been evident in his work at least since *The Boys Who Stole the Funeral* (1980), if not before.

A turning point in Murray's attitude to writing about sex appears to have been in March 1988, when he gave a reading at the Taree Rotary Club. There:

> he was approached by a former school fellow, who had been one of his most relentless and subtle pursuers thirty years before. She talked to him for a little, and then, to remind him of those days, dropped into the conversation the name she had used on him so often: 'Bottom.' Murray was stabbed to the heart: though he concealed the fact and continued the conversation, he got away from her as quickly as he could and went home wounded to Bunyah. (Alexander 229)

The severe depression which ensued from this lasted several years and has been documented extensively (*Killing the Black Dog;* Alexander 236-48). Given that the genesis of this depression was in the rekindling of the experience of bullying and sexual humiliation at school, the struggle to overcome the depression would seem to entail a confrontation with the root cause. This manifested itself in an intensification of manner, and an explicit linking of sexuality with the grotesque strategy of seeking to supplant the centre with the margins, thus signalling the arrival of Murray's late style.

Two poems about sex from before and after would seem to bear out this distinction. "The Fall of Aphrodite Street" was originally published as "The Liberated Plague" in the *London Review of Books*, 29 October 1987 and then later, with the same title in *Overland*, no.109, December 1987:

The Fall of Aphrodite Street

So it's back to window shopping
on Aphrodite Street
for the apples are stacked and juicy
but some are death to eat.

For just one generation
the plateglass turned to air –
when you look for that generation
half of it isn't there.

An ugliness of spirit
leered like a hunting dog
over the world. Now it snarls and whines
at its fleshy analogue.

What pleased it made it angry:
scholars Score and Flaunt and Scene
taught that everything outstanding
was knobs on a skin machine.
Purer grades of this metaphysic

were sold out of parked cars
down alleys where people paired or reeled
like desperate swastikas.

Age, spirit, kindness, all were taunts;
grace was enslaved to meat.
You never were mugged till you were mugged
on Aphrodite Street.

God help the millions that street killed
and those it sickened too,
when it was built past every house
and often bulldozed through.

Apples still swell, but more and more
are literal death to eat
and it's back to window shopping
on Aphrodite Street.
(*Dog Fox Field* 9)

This is not a grotesque poem, but it does have grotesque elements: "down alleys where people paired or reeled / like desperate swastikas" is clearly a foreshadowing of "Sex is a Nazi." The equation of lovers with fascism is disturbing, however, indicating a paranoiac equation of liberated sexual behaviour with the repression of National Socialism. "Knobs on a skin machine" is another grotesque (with an unfortunate pun) which is similar, in its grotesquerie of fusing the human form with the inanimate, to the invitation to urolagnia in *The Boys Who Stole the Funeral*: '*Kneel and drink from the tap, cunt!*' (7). While "The Fall of Aphrodite Street" can now be read as an allegory for AIDS, this version is not particularly homophobic: what Alan Wearne and John Fletcher objected to in letters to the *London Review of Books* after its publication[5] has largely been excised from this version. In the original "The Liberated Plague" the second line of the fourth stanza read "scholars flaunt and Vaseline" and the seventh stanza originally read "Sweetness was so brief before contempt—/ the fish above, the bait below—/ but much that stretched like good faith then / is truly rubber now." The reference to "Vaseline" is clearly a reference to lubrication for anal sex, and the punning on "truly rubber," which seems insensitive, can be read as a reference to condom use; the collocation of Vaseline with condoms is a virtual solecism, though, as it was and is well known that Vaseline is not recommended as a lubricant for condom use. The original poem is more grotesque than the amended version and is clearly focussed on male homosexuality. As Fletcher points out, the title conflates "gay liberation" with the perception that AIDS was a new plague (Fletcher, Letter 4 Feb 1988 and 31 March 1988) and Murray's reply to Fletcher and subsequent amendments to the poem, indicates he acknowledged the validity of most of Fletcher's complaints. (Murray, Letter 18 February 1988).

"Rock Music", on the other hand, displays a compression of thought which is problematic from beginning to end. The notion that sex is a Nazi is ill-considered: if it refers to persecution and murder, then it is hyperbole; if it refers to the eugenics of Nazism, then it is as wrong-headed and silly as the argument of "The Bonnie Disproportion," implying that roles and identities which are often socially created can be passed down genetically (as is the notion that aberrance or freakishness can necessarily be passed down genetically). The second last line is of particular interest: it can be read as an allegory for what it is to live in obeisance to fashionable, urban sexual selection (which is also inflected with a sectarian bias, assuming that Calvin Klein is not meant by "Calvin SS"), that one will age ("wrinkle"), be obsequiously servile to that sexual authority ("fawn") and made to work before being "shot". It can also be read in a different way: "wrinkle" recalls an image of male genitals from *The Boys Who Stole the Funeral*: "Damp plum among wrinkles" (7); but also specifically a detumescent penis ("Laugh, who never shrank around wizened genitals there / or killed themselves to stop dying" ("Corniche"); "Snide universal testing leads them to each one / who will shrivel reliably, whom the rest will then shun" ("Where Humans Can't Leave and Mustn't Complain"); the shrivelling or wrinkling can be read as spiritual and genital, giving a different complexion to "you're shot", which can be read as a hinted orgasm, albeit abject, having 'shot one's load'. If we knew the author of this poem to be a 58 year old man, and nothing else, one might be tempted to see a hint of sexual frustration and envy here, rather than as a magisterial denunciation of a human sexual selection which is governed by fashion, fear, cruelty and corruption. Like the recurrence of the word "police" or "policeman" throughout Murray's poetry, which serves as a symbol of enforcement of rules or boundaries by urban elites and their representatives, so too does "Nazi" work as a kind of private shorthand for the cruel consequences of sexual selection at school. The problem with such private shorthand is that the meaning encoded in the cryptic reference is somewhat open to interpretation. Either way, the sexual abjection here is one of the major ascetic impulses in Murray's work. The more he denounces the sexuality, imagined or otherwise, of the urban centre, the closer he moves towards God.

Another example of this tendency is "The Beneficiaries:"

> Higamus hogamous
> Western intellectuals
> never praise Auschwitz.
> Most ungenerous. Most odd,
> when they claim it's what finally
> won them their centuries-
> long war against God.
> (*Subhuman Redneck Poems* 24)

The first line is a quotation from a brief bit of doggerel, doubtfully attributed to William James:

> Hogamus, higamous
> Man is polygamous

Higamus, hogamous
Woman monogamous.

What is interesting in Murray's appropriation of the first line is the link between male polygamy and contrasting female monogamy, Western intellectuals and Auschwitz. This can only be described as bizarre, even if it can be made sense of. The oddity here is that Murray has chosen the second line of the poem which is paired with the rhyme "woman monogamous," but in this poem has substituted "woman monogamous" with "Western intellectuals," suggesting a connection between the two. If Murray had begun his poem "Hogamus, higamous," at least the implied equation between "Western intellectuals" and polygamous males would be consistent with his view of the moral and sexual corruption of urban elites. Instead, is the implication that the supposed monogamy of woman is shared by Western intellectuals, and is a factor in their ungodliness? Surely this cannot be the thrust of the poem's argument, yet the disjunction between the line of doggerel and the rest of the poem asks questions which cannot satisfactorily be resolved. Such is the irreconcilability of the grotesque. Yet it nevertheless clearly does link asceticism (an implied equation of Western intellectuals' sexuality with their "centuries- / long war against God," a struggle from which the persona of the poem remains remote), with the grotesque (claiming that Western intellectuals should be praising Auschwitz, a grotesque logic if ever there was one), forming an irreconcilably uncomfortable whole. "Anti-intellectual" does not begin to do justice to the implications of this poem.

Interestingly, one of the few positive sexual images in the later Murray is closely associated with reading. In "Incunabular", Murray writes:

> The stacks clanged down metal stairs
> to floors below reality,
> to books in dragon-buckram, books like dreams,

> antiphonaries and grimoires,
> philologies with pages still uncut:
>
> my blade made a sound like *rut*.
> (*Conscious and Verbal* 34)

The phallic connotations of "blade" and the onomatopoeic "*rut*" are unmistakable, reinforced by the students who "murmured airily of the phallic / they were going to be marked by" in the sixth stanza. The above lines present an image of priapic confidence, as well as symbolically enacting the breaking of the hymen, intimately linking this with the practise of reading. It is also surreal and chthonic: the "rutting" takes place below ground, "below reality," in a cryptic realm which harks back to the grotesque.

The impulse to asceticism has strong roots in Murray's abjective stance with regard to sexuality (or at least sex as it is not condoned by the Catholic church). The ascetic imperative, however, has wide-reaching consequences for the later Murray's work. One of the fundamental aspects of the ascetic is the denial or retreat from the world, which Harpham has described as "an attempt by human beings to stand 'outside the world' by assuming the character of language" (Harpham, *The Ascetic Imperative in Culture and Criticism* 20). Why would this be the case? Harpham begins his second chapter with an epigraph from Roland Barthes' *A Lover's Discourse*:

> Askesis (the impulse to askesis) is addressed to the other: turn back, look at me, see what you have made of me. (Barthes 33)

As much as ascesis has as its ultimate aim union with God, it manifests itself in a social context through a denial of that context which must be witnessed or acknowledged. Whether the impulse to ascesis in Murray's poetry is a product of, or mirrors personal experience, or is a part of the Mannerism which has developed increasingly in the later work—or both—is not the place of this chapter to decide. Rather, it is there in the work, in the manner I have described, and needs to be read in the broader context of his Mannerist grotesque. As such, it is an integral part of the elaboration of a poetic self. Harpham observes that "both early and late forms of asceticism prescribe methods for becoming self-made men, beings that owe nothing to genealogy or community" (30); the later Murray has intuited this, and through his anti-humanist stance has articulated a complex, even baroque self which displays itself as it removes itself from its communitarian context and displays its trajectory towards God. It seems little surprise that the first wholly new book after Murray's breakdown was *Translations from the Natural World* (1992), which can be read as an incorporation of the world, from which the poet stands apart, into the figure of the poet-as-language. There is no clearer statement of this than in "Corniche", which like "The Quality of Sprawl", can be read as a statement of poetics for its period (the later Murray). The line: "I adore the creator because I made myself" (*Subhuman Redneck Poems* 19) makes clear the relation between self-creation (through language) and ascesis. Such a statement draws us back to reconsider the sexual abjection of "Mollusc" I identified earlier as essentially a symptom of the impulse to ascesis.

Reconsidering the earlier Murray through the prism of the ascetic impulse in his later work can help us understand some poems, such as "An Absolutely Ordinary Rainbow," in a new light. As John Tranter has noted:

> The details, the verbal texture and the conclusion of Seferis's poem 'Narration' are all quite unlike those of Les Murray's poem, though the unusual central drama is interestingly similar. (239)

Here is the Seferis poem:

Narration

That man walks along weeping
no one can say why
sometimes they think he's weeping for lost loves
like those that torture us so much
on summer beaches with the gramophones.

Other people go about their business
endless paper, children growing up, women
ageing awkwardly.
He has two eyes like poppies
like cut spring poppies
and two trickles in the corners of his eyes.

He walks along the streets, never lies down
striding small squares on the earth's back
instrument of a boundless pain
that's finally lost all significance.

Some have heard him speak
to himself as he passed by
about mirrors broken years ago
about broken forms in the mirrors
that no one can ever put together again.
Others have heard him talk about sleep
images of horror on the threshold of sleep
faces unbearable in their tenderness.

We've grown used to him; he's presentable and quiet
only that he walks along weeping continually
like willows on a riverbank you see from the train
as you wake uncomfortably some clouded dawn.

We've grown used to him; like everything else you're used to
he doesn't stand for anything
and I talk to you about him because I can't find
anything that you're not used to;
I pay my respects.
(243)

Tranter thanks Edmund Keeley, the translator of Seferis's *Collected Poems 1925-1955*, for pointing out the similarity and notes that when "An Absolutely Ordinary Rainbow" "was reprinted in Alexander Craig's 1970 anthology it had the words 'Penarth, 1967' appended, which implies the poem was written in Wales during a trip to Europe that Les Murray made in 1967", and goes on to surmise that he may have encountered Keeley's translation during this time (239). Tranter's parody of Murray's poem, "An Absolutely Extraordinary Recital" concludes with the line, "Evading autograph hounds [Murray] hurries off down Pitt Street" (237). As is often the case with successful parody, it accurately identifies one aspect of the work, which is the figure of the weeping man as an attention seeker; however, it equally begs the question as to why the man is weeping in Murray's poem. If the figure is Les Murray himself (and one does wonder about the rhyme of "hurries" with "Murray's" in the last line), then bewailing the loss of his mother during his childhood, the sexual humiliation through bullying he experienced at Taree High would be obvious causes. The showiness of the display, however, could be argued to be part of a movement to ascesis, and the hurrying away at the end of the poem is figurative of the withdrawal from the world, as well as an avoidance of the "belief" of the crowd. Either way, it is a radically uncomfortable rejection of acknowledgement of suffering which is at odds with Seferis's understated conclusion: "I pay my respects" (243). There is an unresolved discomfort in Murray's poem which, it would appear, would require the ensuing decades to be worked out in terms satisfactory to his poetic project.

Early Lyricism vs Late Mannerism

"The Quality of Sprawl" is a candidate for an *ars poetica* poem of the early Murray. It is brash, confidently asserting the power of language to achieve convergences in the manner of "the man who cut down his Rolls-Royce / into a farm utility truck" and be anti-authoritarian. As I have already discussed, the "rococo of being your own still centre" invokes the tension between centre and margins, implying a devotion to excess that is in keeping with "The Broad Bean Sermon". Under a populist aegis, it evokes impractical or impossible ideals of sprawl being "really classless" and getting "up the nose of many kinds of people / (every kind that comes in kinds)", as if it were possible to not belong to a kind (i.e. to be some kind of "freak"). Helen Vendler rightly takes issue with this:

> The populist side of Murray's poetics, the vain dream of being 'classless' that besets the educated poet who knows he cannot, whatever his social sympathies, be a member of the proletariat, shows through in an alarming aside on poetics prompted by a pelican with a defective beak:
>
> > Its trouble looks like a birth defect, not an injury
> > and raises questions.
> > There are poetics would require it to be pecked
> > to death by fellow pelicans, or kids to smash it with a stick
> > ("At the Aquatic Carnival")

Just what is Murray implying? Whose poetics require thuglike acts on defective objects? Does he mean a poetics of "the beautiful"? But every poetics of the beautiful, at least since Aristotle, has allowed for the presence of the distorted, the ugly, and the maimed within the tragic and the sublime, as well as within the comic. Murray's oblique remark sounds sociological rather than aesthetic in reference. There is something in Murray that wants to muddle things—to mix the persecution of the defective (a palpable social evil) with a nameless "poetics" (Vendler).

Murray's poetics from this time strains to embrace the grotesque, wanting an exception to be made for his exceptionalism. It is not until "Corniche" that a poetics of the ascetic imperative merges with his Mannerist grotesque. The adoration Murray evinces for the creator "because I made myself" is partly a reference to the reconstruction of his psyche required by recovery from depressive breakdown: "Back when God made me, I had no script. It was better." (*Subhuman Redneck Poems* 19) The script referred to here is a pun on the medication Murray (largely unsuccessfully) took for his depression (Alexander 233); it also evokes the figure of the newly minted poet as a *tabula rasa* upon which his self would be inscribed as an ongoing poesis: he has assumed the character of language. The shift from "The Quality of Sprawl" is subtle but decisive, with the grotesque now front and centre in this Mannerist self-portrait:

> A Hindenburg of vast rage
> rots, though, above your life. See it, and you feel flogged
> but like an addict you sniffle aboard, to your cage ...
> (*Subhuman Redneck Poems* 20)

There are several other comparisons which could be made between the early and late Murray, but there is not space here to settle on them. Looking at the treatment of breakfast cereal could be one approach. In "The Returnees":

> As we were rowing to the lakes
> our oars were blunt and steady wings
>
> the tanbark-coloured water was
> a gruel of pollen: more coming down
> hinted strange futures to our cells

The far hills ancient under it
The corn flats black-green under heat
Were cut in an antique grainy gold

It was the light of Boeotian art.
(*Ethnic Radio* 10)

There is a clarity here to the convergence between the urban/domestic and the natural ("gruel of pollen"). Compare this with the following lines from "Green Rose Tan" (1996):

Destitution's an antique. The huge-headed
are sad chaff blown by military bohemians.
Their thin metal bowls are filled or not

from the sky by deodorised descendants
of a tart-tongued womb-noticing noblesse
in the goffered hair-puddings of God's law

who pumped pioneer bouillons with a potstick,
or of dazzled human muesli poured from ships
under the milk of smoke and decades.
(*Subhuman Redneck Poems* 13)

William Logan writes of these lines:

I can make sense of this, more or less (the editorializing is pretty thin), but by the time I get to 'human muesli' it hardly seems worth the effort. I find myself rooting for Murray to make his clumsiness a virtue, though it almost never is. (212)

Similarly, Logan makes short work out of "Where Humans Can't Leave and Mustn't Complain":

> Where humans can't leave and mustn't complain
> there are some who emerge who enjoy giving pain.
>
> Snide universal testing leads them to each one
> who will shrivel reliably, whom the rest will then shun.
>
> Some who might have been chosen, and natural police,
> do routine hurt, the catcalling, the giving no peace.
> (*Subhuman Redneck Poems* 12)

observing that

> This seems badly translated out of Old Church Slavonic with only a Bulgarian phrasebook at hand. Poets of such intelligence can seldom be quoted so plainly against themselves. The loutishness may be calculated; but the more you allow contempt to prove your independence from poetic tradition, the less you are free to invoke that tradition when it suits you. Only by incorporating the unpoetic can the poetic move forward, but bad poetry is no defense against rejection (least of all revenge for schoolyard rejection). Poetry can give up many things, but when it loses the reader's trust it becomes hostage to its vices. (Logan 213)

In 1989 James Tulip warned at the end of his lecture on Murray's poetry for the English Association that his return to Bunyah did not augur well for his poetry (Tulip). Since then, other critics have come to agree with Tulip's prescience. Peter Kirkpatrick, for example, writes that

> I should fess up that I'm one of those who thinks Murray's lyrical poetry has declined, become less fully realized over the last two decades, since his return to Bunyah and *The Daylight Moon*. It's one thing to rhapsodize Boeotia from an Athenian distance, and quite another to attempt the same thing from within its cowyard

gates; for, strange to say, Murray's lyrical practice has moved ever further away from the 'colloquial, middle-voiced poetry' celebrated in his prose.

The deeper Murray's gone bush the more he's become, stylistically, a crypto-modernist. (Kirkpatrick 200)

Other critics, such as Coetzee, who suggest that "the time has perhaps come for Les Murray to let go of old grudges" are perhaps missing the point. Murray's Mannerist grotesque and his tendency towards asceticism are what drive his work. The development of an increasingly baroque, mannered style has many aspects: a repudiation (because of a supposed improvement) of the simple lyric of his earlier self; a gradually more complete incorporation of what seems to be a deep-seated sense of sexual abjection, combined with an increasing tendency towards asceticism; perhaps even a calculated pitch to be considered exceptional, in more ways than one. It has not been uncommon for those who ardently support Murray's work to make a case of looking beyond the awkwardness of poems about "erocide" and being bullied at school. But the bathwater can't be thrown out without the baby being in danger of slipping out too. The exceptionalism of Murray includes the peculiar, the bumpkinish as well as the arrestingly adroit linguistic achievement. In Murray's late period (after 1990), the number of poems which hector and rail has increased in direct correlation to the number of mannered, baroque poems: as I have argued, the two are intimately linked. The result is a career in two halves, with the bulk of Murray's future reputation likely to rest on his earlier achievements. In 'late' Murray, the tendency towards distortion and exaggeration has seemed inevitable, is occasionally brilliant but often unbalanced or awkward. One senses that this has been necessary for the poet, as if Murray has come to understand of himself that, like Aubrey Beardsley, "if I am not grotesque, I am nothing."

Notes

1. "Tin is probably mainly the taste of being relegated and scorned, as a country bumpkin, an uncultured yahoo, all that sanctified anti-rural prejudice that goes right back to classical times and which no antidiscrimination law or postcolonial rhetoric ever protects you from—so to hell with those. It's fair to say that anti-rural bias became steadily more vicious in Australia during my lifetime. It only relaxed and returned to a frail new sanity about five or six years ago. I don't trust that respite to last. Tin is a funny word in Australian idiom: tinny means both cheap and lucky, among other meanings. Won the lottery? You tinny bugger!" (Murray "Les Murray, the Art of Poetry No. 89")
2. Interesting recurrence of 'suck' from "The Broadbean Sermon"
3. The painting also depicts "two scrawny and malevolent figures, one of whom is taking a large bite out of his [cheek]. Murray told Philip Hodgins it was a 'pic of me & Fay [Zwicky] & Sr Veronica [Brady]'" (Alexander 263)
4. See my discussion of the early Murray's reworking and overcoming of various poetic influences, including W. B. Yeats, Dylan Thomas, Robert Bly, T. S. Eliot and James Wright (Musgrave "Reading for Publication: Murray, Murphy and Kinsella"). To this list can be added Ronald Berndt's translation of "Song Cycle of the Moon-Bone" of the Wonguri-Mandjigai People and the reworking of George Seferis' "Narration" in "An Absolutely Ordinary Rainbow" (Tranter 236-39).
5. See the Letters in *London Review of Books*, Vol. 9 No. 22, 10 December 1987, Vol. 10 No. 1, 7 January 1988, Vol. 10 No. 3, 4 February 1988, Vol. 10 No. 4, 18 February 1988 and Vol. 10 No. 7, 31 March 1988 for an exchange between Wearne and Murray, and Fletcher and Murray.

Works Cited

Agamben, Giorgio. *The End of the Poem: Studies in Poetics*, translated by Daniel Heller-Roazen, Stanford University Press, 1999.

Alexander, Peter. *Les Murray: A Life in Progress*, Oxford University Press, 2000.

Bakhtin, Mikhail. *Rabelais and His World*, translated by Hélène Iswolsky. Bloomington, Indiana University Press, 1984.

Barthes, Roland. *A Lover's Discourse: Fragments*, translated by Richard Howard, Hill and Wang, 2010.

Chiasson, Dan. "Fire Down Below: The Poetry of Les Murray." *New Yorker,* June 11 2007.
Chifley, Ben. "'The Light on the Hill' Speech to ALP Conference 1949." 12 June 1949. 3/9/2016.
Coetzee, J. M. "The Angry Genius of Les Murray." *The New York Review of Books,* vol. 58, no. 14, 2011.
Fletcher, John. "Letter." *London Review of Books,* vol. 10 no.3, 4 Feb 1988.
---. Letter. *London Review of Books,* vol.10 no.7, 31 March 1988.
Gombrich, E. H. *Norm and Form; Studies in the Art of the Renaissance,* Phaidon Press, 1966.
Gorton, Lisa. "Widespeak." *Sydney Review of Books,* 15 May 2015, 2015.
Harpham, Geoffrey Galt. *The Ascetic Imperative in Culture and Criticism,* The University of Chicago Press, 1987.
---. *On the Grotesque: Strategies of Contradiction in Art and Literature,* Princeton University Press, 1982.
Hauser, Arnold. *Mannerism: The Crisis of the Renaissance and the Origin of Modern Art,* Routledge & Kegan Paul, 1965.
Kayser, Wolfgang. *The Grotesque in Art and Literature,* translated by Ulrich Weisstein, Indiana University Press, 1963.
Kirkpatrick, Peter. "Book Review." *Journal of the Association for the Study of Australian Literature,* vol. 2, 2003, pp. 196-200.
Llewellyn, Kate. "To Adelaide, with Love." *The Age,* March 4 2006.
Logan, William. *Desperate Measures,* University Press of Florida, 2002.
Maiorino, Giancarlo. *The Portrait of Eccentricity: Arcimbolo and the Mannersit Grotesque,* The Pennsylvania State University Press, 1991.
Murray, Les. "A Conversation with Les Murray", edited by J. Mark Smith, *Image,* Issue 64, Winter 2009-10.
---. *A Working Forest: Selected Prose,* Duffy and Snellgrove, 1997.
---. *Conscious and Verbal,* Duffy & Snellgrove, 1999.
---. *Dog Fox Field,* Angus & Robertson, 1990.
---. *Ethnic Radio,* Angus & Robertson, 1977.
---. *Killing the Black Dog,* Federation Press, 1996.

---. "Les Murray AO", edited by Edwina Hall, *Kairos*, Vol. 24, Issue 6, 2012. http://melbournecatholic.org.au/Archive/Kairos/les-murray-ao >

---. "Les Murray, the Art of Poetry No. 89", edited by Dennis O'Driscoll, *The Paris Review*, 2005. https://www.theparisreview.org/interviews/5508/les-murray-the-art-of-poetry-no-89-les-murray

---. "Letter." *London Review of Books*, vol 10. no. 4, 18 February 1988.

---. *Persistence in Folly*, Sirius, 1984.

---. *Subhuman Redneck Poems*, Duffy and Snellgrove, 1996.

---. *The Boys Who Stole the Funeral*, Angus & Robertson, 1980.

---. *The People's Otherworld*, NSW, Angus & Robertson, 1983.

---. *The Weatherboard Cathedral*. Sydney, Angus & Robertson, 1969.

---. *Translations from the Natural World*, Isabella Press, 1992.

--- and Geoffrey Lehmann. *The Ilex Tree*, Angus and Robertson, 1965.

Musgrave, David. *Grotesque Anatomies: Menippean Satire since the Renaissance*, Cambridge Scholars Press, 2014.

---. "Reading for Publication: Murray, Murphy and Kinsella *"Five Bells*, vol. 16, no. 2 and 3, 2009.

Seferis, George. *Collected Poems 1924-1955*, translated and edited by Edmund Keeley and Philip Sherrard, Princeton University Press, 1967.

Thomson, Philip. *The Grotesque in German Poetry 1880-1933*, The Hawthorn Press, 1975.

Tranter, John E. "Distant Voices." University of Wollongong, 2009, Doctor of Creative Arts Thesis.

Tulip, James. "The Poetry of Les Murray" The English Association, 1989.

Vendler, Helen. "Four Prized Poets." *The New York Review of Books*, vol. 36, no. 13 August 17, 1989. https://www.nybooks.com/articles/1989/08/17/four-prized-poets/

Chapter 11

Matters Invisible: J. S. Harry's Lyrical Poems

KERRY PLUNKETT

Anonymity surrounds and shades J. S. Harry and her poetry. Even today, after she has published nine collections and won numerous awards, when I mention the poet J. S Harry, the common response is, "Who?" The reasons for this can, in part, be attributed to the poet herself. Harry was a retiring soul who preferred to devote her time to nurturing animals rather than spending it on the act of self-promotion. This reticence has rendered her almost invisible and publicly her voice only whispers among her more prominent peers. Harry's enigmatic and ungendered pen name is also a contributing factor. But, paradoxically, the most outstanding feature responsible for the sense of anonymity found in her poetry is the absence of a distinctive voice and personality. Instead, Harry's poetry is populated by a diverse range of poetic voices engendered by multifarious poetic forms and styles. Why does Harry choose to be obscure? And what underpins her motive to remain distant? There is an esoteric quality to Harry's poetry in which, I assert, she is actively exploring a variety of complex and interlaced spiritual discourses. Rooted in these discourses is the idea of egolessness, the non-attachment to the ego-self.[1] It is my contention that the sense of anonymity in Harry's poetry is an attempt to depict egolessness, and that it is a motif in her poetry that exemplifies her personal ontology and this essay will be a starting point in its exploration.

It is a critical commonplace to view Harry's poetry as linguistic experiments as applied philosophical concepts, many of which engage with "the significant preoccupations of Wittgenstein's philosophy" (Dray 194). Harry's most conspicuous experiment has been the use of a philosophically enquiring rabbit named Peter, who is the predominant voice in Harry's book *Not Finding Wittgenstein*. Harry has said that she devised Peter as "a way of looking at different kinds of situations and in some ways of inviting readers to look at things from different points of view" (Stasko 2). Peter is the most obvious example of Harry erasing herself from the poetic voice. He is a distancing device, a buffer between the reader and the poet: and she seems to vanish into his shadow. But, it could also be argued that Harry devised Peter as a symbol to stand in for herself, thereby constructing her identity from, and aligning herself with, nature, rather than, and far removed from, a socio/cultural construct. This action sees Harry challenging Wittgenstein's notion that our identity is socially and culturally formed though a shared language. Marjorie Perloff explains that Wittgenstein believed the subject was "a social construct, a cultural construction [because]… languages of the self depend on social context, culture and class" (20). This belief denies the possibility of a discrete identity, a private self. Perhaps, as a representation of nature, Peter is a device that Harry uses in attempt to startle the reader into recognising our cultural conditioning. Or maybe, he is a witty metaphor standing in for Wittgenstein's claim that there is no private self. Ironically, Peter has to use the language of our culture in order to communicate his experiences, and this action, according to Wittgenstein, for anyone, is "absolutely hopeless" ("Ethics" 12).

The impossibility of trying to communicate private experience in a shared language is described to in the following extract, from the poem "They":

Peter's ears twitch – but he has to agree. Goes on.
Struggles – how to explain: "I's written representation"?

It's a picture,
he says   at last, *it's a stand-for*

> *what lives in each of them, its common*
> *to all of* THEM *– as the earth beneath our paws*
> *is common to all of us (including them)*
> *who run, hop, walk,*
> *fall, lie, or die on it.*
> She doesn't know what die is. *It's a word,*
> he says, *like I is: nobody knows what it's like*
> *inside it.* (*Sun* 6-7)

Here Harry is engaging with an element of Wittgenstein's celebrated private language argument where Wittgenstein rejects the idea that language can directly express private experience and sensations; that we can communicate the "I's" inner experience. In his philosophical investigation §293, the "beetle in the box" Wittgenstein asks us to imagine a group of people who each have a box with something called a 'beetle' inside it. "No one can look into anyone else's, and everyone says he knows what a beetle is only by looking at his beetle" (*PI* 101). Everyone's beetle may be different, always changing, or the box may be empty. As such, explains Stephen Mulhall, there is no possible external referent for the beetle that can be validated by others (133). Wittgenstein goes on to question the use of the word 'beetle' in the language-game. He finds that when a word is used to describe an indeterminate experience, the experience drops out of the language-game: "if we construe the grammar of the expression of sensation on the model of 'object and designation' the object drops out of consideration as irrelevant" (§ 293). If we push this idea a little further we find that the expression of an inner experience (Wittgenstein's 'beetle') can only be made meaningful by the 'other.' The expression of inner experience gets lost in transmission because the 'other' can only look at their own 'beetle'; it is interpreted and understood by their own inner experiences. Therefore, the "I" experience is redundant in language. With this idea in mind, it could be concluded that Harry's fluid identities reflect Wittgenstein's reductive account of the discrete representation of the self in language.

However, Harry continually probes and tests the barrier between experience and expression. Colin Dray observes that there is an ongoing quest in Harry's poetry to overcome "Wittgenstein's... restriction of 'private experience'...[by]...examining the bounds of language (203). This boundary, this barrier, is realised in Wittgenstein's renowned maxim, "*Die Grenzen meiner Sprach bedeuten die Grenzen meiner Welt*" – "*The limits of my language* mean the limits of my world" (*T* 5.6 emphasis in original). *Grenze* literally translates to limit or, more importantly, dividing border, which implies the existence of two separate things. In this case; the known, the world of logic and facts that can be described in language; and the unknown, the mystical, "things that cannot be put into words" (*T* 6.522). Within the mystical is the experiencing "I" and that which is inherent to it: Ethics, which is, according to Wittgenstein, "intrinsically sublime and above all other subject matters" ("Ethics" 7).

Wittgenstein describes Ethics as that which is of absolute value, the enquiry into: what is good, or the meaning of life, or the right way to live ("Ethics" 5). Furthermore, Wittgenstein suggests that when we use expressions as "absolute good" and "absolute value" ("Ethics" 7) we are trying to express thoughts as simple as "the sensation when taking a walk on a summer's day...[to]...the wonder of the existence of the world...[and] ...the experience of feeling absolutely safe" ("Ethics" 8). Wittgenstein identifies Ethics as "supernatural", and therefore cannot be put into words because "our words will only express facts" ("Ethics" 7), though he does find it paradoxical "that an experience, a fact, should seem to have supernatural value" ("Ethics" 10). But is this paradox real? For is it not true, as Marjory Perloff points out, that traditionally the private experiences, sensations and thoughts of the poet have been expressed in the language of the lyric? (182-83). It is here, in poetry, that we encounter the distinction between Harry and Wittgenstein; Harry is a poet, one who uses the language of the lyric to "run against the boundaries of language...against the walls of [her] cage" ("Ethics" 12) to express the ineffable.

Critical opinion on Harry's attempts to overcome the limits of language to express inner experience differs considerably. Although he believes that Harry runs hard against the walls of her cage, Dray, like Wittgenstein, argues that this endeavour is futile. For Marie-Louise Ayres, Harry's lyrical poems break free from this limitation but Ayres considers them a one way journey; Harry ""enters the invisible" and tries to recover it" (31), but where she goes is elusive; it is beyond the critics grasp (29). In contrast, Martin Duwell suggests that Harry is able to mediate between, and cross, the borders between the self and the outside world, between the real and ideal though the use of nature symbols (43). Duwell did not explore this particular concept any further; it will however, underpin this investigation.

Through the exploration and analysis of a sample of Harry's nature-based lyrical poems, this essay will follow Harry into the "invisible" to search for the inner experiencing "I". It will argue that she is not alone in this endeavour and will trace the influence Japanese poetics, the Deep Imagists and the Symbolists, who all experiment with poetic devices to convey what is discovered when journeying into the Self, had on the formation of Harry's poetic style. I will begin in Japan, and discuss the significant impact the Haiku and subsequently, Zen had on Harry's poetics.

Harry published a triptych of poems relating to Japan in her first collection *the deer under the skin*. The first, "Kaguya-hime", is a poetic interpretation of a traditional Japanese folk tale the *Taketori-Monogatari*. The second, "waiting for the express, to go north to Osaka." is a love poem that displays many haiku-like qualities and the third, "to Shiki who died of consumption" is an homage to Shiki that displays a close familiarity with his life and work. Shiki is considered to be the father of the modern Haiku who helped instigate change and progress in all areas of Japanese literature (Beichman Preface). Donald Keene tells us that Shiki initiated a revolution in Japanese poetry, by finding "new possibilities of expression within the traditional forms" (12) and as such, he can be considered an exemplar for Harry.

In this brief but beautiful poem, Harry conveys a considerable amount of biographical information on Shiki and fuses the features of haiku, Shiki's own poetry, and her knowledge of his life to create a poem that captures his existence:

> "The hototogisu
>   is said to vomit blood and die
>   after it has sung eight thousand and eight times" –
>
> I do not know
>   how many times you sang,
>   growing thin over haiku and waka,
>   growing thin…
> From your bed
>   through the window
>   you looked into the autumn;
> upon the screen the shadows
>   of the dragonflies grew thin.
>
> (White the papers on your desk
>   the sudden stormwind…):
>
> opening your cool throat so clearly…
>   then burning, "how deep is the snow…"
>   "how deep is the snow…"
>   you sing, hototogisu, you sing –   (*Deer* 30)

The hototogisu is synonymous with Shiki. Janine Beichman tells us that Shiki is a pen name he took from the Sino-Japanese reading for *hototogisu* which is a reference to the Japanese lesser cuckoo bird that sounds like it is coughing blood when it sings (20), which in turn is a reference to Shiki's terminal illness, tuberculosis. Furthermore, Shiki supervised the now famous *Hototogisu* magazine founded in 1897, to which he contributed many short essays and haiku and assisted with the editing.

Shiki became ill in 1889, when he was twenty-two years of age, and thereafter spent most of his life bedridden. His bedroom became his whole world, "From your bed/ through the window/ you looked into the autumn;". The echo of a haiku resonates in these slight, simple lines that Harry uses to depict the confined compass of Shiki's life; likewise, the lines "(White the papers on your desk/ the sudden stormwind ...)" are suggestive of a haiku. Harry mimics the haiku tradition of using a *kigo*, a season word, but deviates from the norm by using two, autumn and winter. The consequence of this manoeuvre is twofold: it aligns her with Shiki the poetic innovator; it also symbolises the forthcoming conclusion of his life. The poem ends with lines from one of Shiki's most famous haiku, from a sequence of four, named "Byōchū no Yuki" (Snow While Sick) ""how deep is the snow..."/ "how deep is the snow..."" Beichman writes that this haiku "suggests a certain longing and sadness. One feels the poignance of the distance between the poem's speaker and the snow, a distance that can be bridged only by the repeated questioning" (66). Harry intensifies the sense of pathos by reproducing Shiki's repetition and adding her own, "growing thin over haiku and waka/ growing thin ..." and "you sing, hototogisu, you sing –". The crosscurrents of poignancy and sadness between Harry's biographical poem and Shiki's autobiographical haiku signal an affinity between the two and suggests that Harry had immersed herself in Shiki's life and work.

Harry returns to the snow metaphor to reproduce a sense of poignancy in her love poem "waiting for the express, to go north to Osaka." This is a gentle, tender poem set in an unnamed station describing the poet's three-hour wait for a train. There is a sense of restraint in the poem coupled with a profound sense of intimacy, which is intensified by the juxtaposition of contrary emotional behaviours. "You did not/ touch my hand/ in the new style," displays a reserved nature and an old-fashioned outlook whereas "but/ the snow/ melted in your eyes" implies a demonstrative expression of feeling. Together these produce a display of emotion that is heartfelt and poignant. The juxtaposition of opposites is an inherent feature in the haiku with the most notable being the coupling of the momentary with the eternal. This notion is captured in the final stanza of this poem, illustrating the reciprocal closeness between this pair:

> Those three hours sat as lightly
> on our hearts
> as the snow upon your sleeve. (*Deer* 29)

Literally these lines describe a period of time spent happily with a loved one; however, the simile hints at the bittersweet nature of the relationship when it evokes both the momentary and eternal by comparing snow with the temporal and emotional experiences they are sharing. Snow melts very quickly, symbolising the ephemeral quality of this magical time, which is momentary and will disappear, but the memory will linger on. The contradiction found in the above simile illustrates another fundamental feature of the haiku, ambiguity. On one hand, the delicacy of the snow evokes a lightness of heart, a joyful, contented relationship; on the other, it alludes to a relationship that is evanescent.

Haiku conventions are subtly embedded in Harry's lyrics. She adapts them to provide a framework in which she is able to write, as she wished, "with the hope that there should be room in each poem for the imagination of the reader to work in" (*Deer* back cover). Firstly, in haiku, nature is the subject and it is used to reflect human emotions and while the previous poem is not a haiku it does rely on nature, in the form of snow, to express the poet's contrary emotions. Harry is adept at using nature imagery in her poetry to evoke potent feelings. A consequence of this is that the poem has an objective quality and the poet, as a character in the poem, recedes, becoming almost invisible. The objective and accessible attributes of this style allow for a direct experience for the reader and a space for their imagination. Secondly, the haiku, as described by Yoshinobu Hakutani, is "only an outline or highly selective parts [of the subject], the reader must complete the vision" (9). Harry believes that when reading poetry "the reader should be involved in the straining and peering" (*APN* 225), so she pares her poems back "the outside cut away, to that bald, sculpt shape" ("Some" 25), resulting in a haiku-like poem. These reductive features may have contributed to the perception that Harry's lyrical poems have little to say. However, they also alert us to the fact that her 'simple' poems are multi-levelled and meaningful, and like a haiku, convey the essence of a moment or intuitive wisdom.

Harry's Zen–like poem, "temple-viewing" (*Dandelion*, 11), is presented by many critics as an example of her lyrical expertise but one that has little to say. Their comments fail to look past the surface of the poem and they fail to recognise its profundity. Rowe and Smith included this poem in their anthology *Windchimes*, writing that Harry's poems "play with multiple levels of meaning to challenge the reader…[and] all of her work is skilful and sensitive" but they describe "temple-viewing" poem as "simply meditative" (264).Martin Duwell identifies this poem as "a true lyric poem," describing how Harry "establish[es] the kind of hushed atmosphere, suggestive of transcendence, which parallels the scene itself" by the "careful use of line endings [and] the manipulation of sound" (41). He analyses the poem quite literally, suggesting that because the doves are from India, the birthplace of Buddhism, they find themselves at home in a Buddhist temple. He also suggests that the doves "behave with humility" because they know themselves to be part of the natural world, and the "Japanese temple which, among human creations, has molded itself to that world with equal humility" (41). These are all valid observations, particularly the techniques Harry uses to evoke the sensation of serenity and transcendence; however, the deeper one delves into the spiritual and symbolic aspects of this poem the more profound it becomes.

The aesthetic qualities of "temple-viewing" correspond to the qualities of simplicity, directness and profundity found in Zen poetry.[2] They also intimate the tenets of Zen; particularly in the way they facilitate the experience of Zen. The poem begins in a simple, concrete manner by presenting the scene of the arrival of a pair of doves and the surrounding garden, and then, after the chiming of the windbells, it becomes more abstract in nature, which suggests a shift from the physical world into the metaphysical.

The title sets the Zen-like tone for the rest of the poem. Harry does not use capitalisation; each word is equal in status and each one in lower case, which alludes to the Zen belief that no part of the world can "be valued above or below the rest" (Watts 52). Neither does she use punctuation; in fact very few language 'rules' are used at all in this poem, which suggests we are in a place outside conventional practices. This corresponds to Zen because, according to Watts "Zen is above all the liberation of the mind from conventional thought" (51). The temple, according to John Lundquist is the place where wholeness is realised and the place where one "experiences the ultimate revelation: the discovery of oneself (114). In Zen, this discovery is made during meditation and Harry uses imagery, symbols and poetic devices to not only allude to the practice of meditation in this poem, but also, to allow the reader to experience a sense of this.

The manipulation of rhythm enables Harry to enact reality. Here the movement is slow and precise, reproducing the movement of walking meditation:

> respectfully
> barefoot
> mute as lovers
> a pair of spotted turtle doves
> enter the green silence (*Dandelion* 11)

The alliteration of the 't' sound interrupts the flow of the words, slowing down the pace and imitating the footfall. The half rhymes of 'fully' and 'foot' and 'lovers' and 'doves' tie these lines together, softening and counteracting the hard 't' sound without it losing its impact.

Harry sets up a contradiction that is suggestive of a 'haiku moment' when she describes the normally loquacious doves as mute. The metrical emphasis on these words and the contrasting methods of articulation, the stop of the breath in 'mute' and the rush of breath and fricative, in 'lovers' further enhances this shock. This startles us by its unusualness and then draws us in enquiringly. Lovers are quiet during moments of contentment and contemplation, which suggests that these lovers are at peace with one another.

The doves enter the garden:

> walking on round
> brown wooden stones
> sunk between
> white pebbles (*Dandelion* 11)

Stepping-stones in a Japanese garden are intended to slow down visitors in preparation for meditation. The doves' movement slows further, which is reinforced by the repetition of assonance and the long resonant 'n' sound, towards a place where the mind can be stilled: the garden. The Japanese garden is a spiritual sanctuary; according to Christopher McIntosh, the purpose of the Japanese garden is "to enable man, following up his meditation, to go ahead along the road of spiritual search leading to Awakening" (29). Perhaps this is the journey the doves are taking.

Harry brings the garden to life, allowing the reader to both see and hear what is there. She plays with the typography of the poem, setting alternate lines to the right:

> the dwarf bamboos
> sway in the wind
> dipping
> > to the soft
> chimes
> > of the windbells (*Dandelion* 11)

which causes the words to imitate the swaying of the bamboo. The placement of the word 'chimes' by itself emphasises both the word and its onomatopoeic effect. The senses are stimulated, the poem captivates, and the reader is drawn in sensuously as well as mentally.

When the windbells announce the arrival of the wind, the supernatural manifestation of divine intervention, an aura of transcendence is evoked providing the final element for awareness to occur. The doves are then seen to:

> nod and bow
> at the ground as if
> they were in accord
>
> with both the customs
> of the place
> & matters invisible (*Dandelion* 11)

The final lines suggest the awareness of unity and harmony between the physical and metaphysical worlds; the doves, the customs of the place, and matters invisible. The doves have reached their goal and, through the practice of meditation, they have encountered the divine and truth has become known. Even though there has been a sense of peace throughout the poem there is an inkling of doubt at the end. The lack of a full stop leaves the poem unfinished and there is a suggestion of uncertainty because Harry has used the conditional: "as if/ they were in accord", rather than a predicate when alluding to the state of harmony. Perhaps, though, the sense of doubt is intended to prompt the reader to ask their own questions, to begin their own exploration. After sensuously guiding the reader into a sacred space Harry leaves it open, creating a space for the reader's own imagination.

Harry contemplates the theme of unity somewhat differently in "Walking, When The Lake Of The Air Is Blue With Spring" (*Dandelion* 14-15). While different in form, this poem bears a striking similarity to W. S. Merwin's sonnet "The Bathers": both poems symbolically exhibit the interrelationship between all aspects of the natural world; they share the same central images of water, birds, snakes, reflections and transformations; and, significantly, they are both making a symbolic journey into the unconscious. Merwin belonged to a school of visionary poets called the Deep Imagists who were involved in a search for spiritual fulfillment somewhere beyond their lived experience, beyond themselves. Overcoming the ego was essential to their endeavour. Like Harry, a prevailing poetic strategy they employed to reify this notion was the absence of an identifiable speaker. Dennis Haskell writes of the deep-image poetics:

> The speaker will frequently exist within the poem but the reader is left with a curious sense that the speaker is not very particular, that the reader knows very little about him, to the point of being hardly aware of his human existence. (149)

Merwin is noted for his "prevalent use of a disembodied narrative agent", which Jane Frazier believes enables "the participation in nature that [he] desires" (341), which opens the path towards spiritual fulfillment because he is rid of the "burdens of the ego" (341-342).

Musings on the ego are featured frequently, though often subliminally, in Harry's poetry. In "The Glorious I Or A Deviation From Relations," she overtly satirises the over inflated ego and her patriarchal culture. The poem is a reflection on the results of a culture in which the ego has become separated from the Self. It plays with the idea that the ego is a construct by using the pronoun 'I' as a noun: "I is finding it impossible." 'I' has become an objective character and it can only be identified with as 'other.' This emphasises its own self-importance, promotes the concept of individualisation, and creates a barrier between itself and others. The world's wisdom traditions assert that this barrier and its resultant consequences produce a society and a culture that cannot identify or be empathetic towards others, both human and nature, and a 'them and us' mentality ensues. Discrimination, oppression, war and the destruction of the environment are all outcomes of this type of thinking and these issues are predominant themes in both Harry's poetry and deep-image poetry.

There is another, rather enigmatic, aspect to deep-image poetry that corresponds with Harry's and is elucidated by Robert Bly when he describes the manner in which they wrote: "We were devoted to writing poetry of the sort – namely allusive, elegant, inward poetry associated with the French Symbolists, whose language longed to intermingle with the spiritual" (1). According to Thomas Gardner, there was "a growing tendency to direct the imagination inward" in the poetry of Galway Kinnell and his fellow deep-image poets W. S. Merwin and James Wright (423). Interestingly, Harry was identified by James Tulip as a poet whose poetry reflected a movement into her own psyche when he first reviewed her work in 1971 and named her the "high priestess of a cult of the inward ego" ("Transition" 187-188). Paul Breslin tells us that the deep-image movement inwards was related to the rejection of the ego. He writes that they had "the desire to recover innocence and faith at any cost, even the abolition of social reality and the conscious self" (129). To do this they needed to transcend the ego self, to go beyond the ideological structures of society that had been assimilated into the conscious self (Breslin 128-9). To distance themselves from the ego the deep-image poets expressed their inner world using symbols from nature, which, Breslin suggests, are often interpreted from a Jungian perspective. Harry and the deep-image poets adopt comparable symbols to express the same preoccupations, which can be seen in the following passages. Kinnell describes the deep-image journey inwards, and its articulation, thus:

> If you could go even deeper, you'd not be a person, you'd be an animal; and if you went deeper still, you'd be a blade of grass, eventually a stone. If a stone could speak, your poem would be its words. (qtd in Breslin 130)

Harry's poem "their common" resonates with Kinnell's description:

> as stones go into water
> as grass goes into ground
> the words containing
> stones and grass
> go into you
>   and sink
>   are gone
> and round or green
> as pebble or blade
> the words in you
> go rolling on
> a changing ground
>   and you move on
> as round or green
> as the stones and grass
> beneath your feet
> as stones fall into water
> as grass grows out of ground
> the words containing
> stones and grass
> grow out of you
> and you are gone (*Hold* 23)

Both poems are also indicative of the transformation Galway Kinnell believes is possible if one could connect with the unconscious. He believes that the poet can find inner liberation "by going so deeply into himself – into the worst of himself as well as the best – that suddenly he is everyone" (Gardner and Kinnell 423). This action is suggestive of Jung's theory of Individuation and the shift in consciousness from the ego through the unconscious into the collective unconscious and the Self.[3]

"Walking, When The Lake Of The Air Is Blue With Spring" (*Dandelion* 14-15) alludes to Jung's individuation process and its consequential revelation. This discovery transpires literally, through an awareness of the connections within nature, and symbolically, during a journey through the three levels of consciousness associated with Jungian theory.

This is a complex poem and its mystery and ambiguity begin in the title. When we imagine "The Lake Of The Air" (14) do we see a sky so blue it reminds us of a lake, or are we viewing the reflection of the sky in the lake? In visualising two things as one, the reflection and the reflector, the idea that all things are interconnected is established. The lake also acts as a mirror that creates reflections and correspondences, which give this poem a visionary quality.

The poem begins simply with the poet noticing a connection between living things. The simile in "A dark chocolate fungus/ soft as the nose of a deer" (14) connects flora and fauna, and another simile connects the two honeyeaters that fly amongst the "flame flowers" as if "held by an invisible string" (14).

The journey into the unconscious begins when the poet turns her attention to the lake.

> Out on the lake
> one solitary pelican:
> when the pelican
> flaps his wings
> his reflection
> flaps back at him (*Dandelion* 14)

Here the colon highlights the fact that the pelican is alone and the tautology of "one solitary" furthers this idea. Then "when the pelican/ flaps his wings/[and] his reflection/ flaps back at him" the notion of dual consciousness is manifested. A separation between the conscious and unconscious is evinced when the pelican sees its reflection. Symbolically a reflection is a representation of consciousness; in this case it portrays an awareness of a conscious self and, because the reflection is in water, a symbol for the unconscious, awareness of the unconscious self becomes apparent.

The unconscious is symbolically entered when the seagull dives into the lake:

> The seagull diving
> into the lake for bread
> breaks into his own
> white reflection (*Dandelion* 15)

It is suggested that this encounter with the unconscious is a magical and sacred experience because the seagull breaks "into his own/ white reflection", white being a symbol for purity, faith, and ecstasy. There is also a double movement here: the seagull 'dives into' the lake and then 'breaks into' his reflection, which tells us that once inside the unconscious he goes further and enters into himself. In Jungian terms, the seagull enters the personal unconscious and then goes further into the collective unconscious where the Self resides. These ideas also allude to a spiritual encounter because the seagull connects with the sacred other within, his Self. This notion is furthered when Harry alludes to the Christian rite of the Eucharist by placing the word "bread" next to "breaks." The bread for the seagull does not represent the body of another; it is his own body, he is divine. It is here, where the Self is one with everything, that the interconnectedness between all things in the natural world which Harry and the Deep Imagists have faith in occurs.

Now that a connection to the Self has been made a transformation can take place and this is evinced in the next stanza:

> Little black waterbirds   /-//-/
> are diving out on the lake   -/-/--/
> vanishing into ripple   /--/-/-
> their necks rise thin as snakes   -/-/-/   (*Dandelion* 15)

The rhythm of this stanza subtly reinforces the ideas being portrayed. Lines one and three begin with a trochee, creating a falling rhythm, and lines two and four with an iamb, a rising rhythm, which mirrors the diving and rising movement of the birds. A 'technical' reflection is revealed in the syllabic count, 6/7/7/6, which corresponds to the concept of reflection being contemplated in this poem. If a line is drawn between this reflection, two images appear. The first is of "Little black waterbirds ...diving out on the lake," Harry creates an ambiguity here, for "diving out on" can be construed as the birds diving, going into the lake/ unconscious, or they could be diving out of the lake and into the air, rising up out of the water/unconscious, which is what is happening in the second half of the stanza. The birds "vanish into ripple" and then, because Harry has used the simile "thin as snakes," the birds appear to transform into something else, snakes, as they rise out of the water.

The connection between these images is maintained through sound. There is the tinkling of the assonant 'i' in "Little/vanishing/into/ripple/thin" which runs throughout the whole stanza. There are also subtle correspondences between the two halves of the stanza created by the assonance of "diving/rise" and "black/vanishing," and the half rhyme of "little/ripple but it is the rhyming of 'lake' and 'snakes' at the end of line 2 and line 4 that is the most forceful connection.

The symbol of the snake is highly ambiguous because it represents many dichotomies such as good and evil, rejuvenation and death. In Christian traditions it represents the cause of the separation from the divine whereas in Eastern traditions it represents the Kundalini, a spiritual energy, that once awakened facilitates a union with the divine. In Jungian symbology the snake represents "powers from the depths of the psyches of others" (Biedermann 313); in other words, it signifies the collective unconscious. The pairing of opposites, in the form of a winged bird and earthbound snake, further the idea that this image represents the transformational process of individuation within the unconscious because only the unconscious can harmonise contradictions and oppositions.

The final stanza moves away from the mysterious unconscious. Instead, it portrays a moment of transcendence and a newly discovered clarity of consciousness that is represented by the animals moving over the hill in full view.

> A crowcoloured dog
> gallops over the hill
> while the voice of his colour
> caws above him   (*Dandelion* 15)

This image depicts a complete interconnectedness between two distinct things. The dog is described as "crowcoloured" and the crow is described as "the voice of his colour": they are made known by the 'other,' and are part of each other. This connection is emphasised by the simple use of alliteration, "crowcoloured/colour/caws. A transformation in consciousness has taken place, the union of the ego and the Self is symbolically represented by the interconnectedness of the dog and the bird and the journey is now complete.

However, Harry does not finish the poem with a full stop, even though she has used punctuation in other stanzas, suggesting that the ideas she is exploring are still unresolved. It is unsettling that the final image is that of a black dog, which has become the symbol of depression (Musgrave 161) and a crow, which in Jungian symbology represents the dark side of the psyche (Biedermann 280-1). Maybe by leaving the reader with a sense of uncertainty, Harry is echoing her own subtle doubts, the questioning of faith by an ego that will not be silenced.

Harry's spiritual peregrinations have led her along the path of meditation and transformation. In "the wanderer" she journeys further: towards peace and safety in the union with the divine. To convey this ineffable happening Harry turns to the mystical poetry of the Symbolists. Arthur Symons, the critic who introduced the Symbolists to the English in 1899, perceptively described Symbolist poetry as " a literature in which the visible world is no longer a reality, and the unseen world is no longer a dream." (2-3). It is a poetry devoted to the metaphysical and, as Christopher Brennan believed, a unique spiritual activity (145). The Symbolists' objective was to devise a way to express these abstract ideas in language and the symbol was central to their venture.

Symbols are a potent poetic device because they are charged with the power of suggestion. They are ambiguous in nature because they inherently contain multiple and contradictory meanings, and the greater the number of meanings distilled into the symbol, the greater its power. Ambiguity also endows the symbol with a suggestive quality and has the effect of producing "concealment and ...revelation... a silence and speech acting together" (Symons 2), which gives the symbol a mystical air. For Symbolist poet Stéphane Mallarmé, the mystery of the symbol increases the pleasure of reading a poem because "the satisfaction of guessing little by little: to suggest it, to evoke it...that is what charms the imagination" (qtd in Wilson 23). And here we can see Harry's personal poetic theory reverberating with Mallarmé's.

Most importantly, the Symbolists believe that symbols have a profound function; they establish a bridge between the phenomenal and noumenal worlds. This bridge, or connection, between the physical and the metaphysical underpins the theory of correspondences associated with Charles Baudelaire and the French Symbolists. A. R. Chisholm explains that this theory "is based on the concept that the realities revealed by the senses are only symbols or correspondences of a deeper Reality, imperfect echoes or reflections of a perfect and eternal unity" ("Forest" 7). According to Brennan, Mallarmé believed that there exists in each person's soul "the instinct of heaven, our true self" (143) which corresponds to the divine, the One, and while one can never be God, we can become one with the universe when a connection is made between the outer and inner divine, the One and the Self. This connection is made real by the symbol (143). Brennan writes that this made the writing of poetry a unique spiritual activity and for Mallarmé it was a religion (145). Also, like the Deep Imagists, the Symbolists believed that symbols create connections between our conscious and unconscious mind. According to Australian critic A. R. Chisholm, the Symbolists believed that the symbol effected a communication between the conscious and unconscious. It touches both personal, and inherited, memories and experiences within the unconscious and then instantly conveys this to our conscious self ("Forest" 12), which perhaps explains why we sometimes understand a poem before we know it.

The theory of correspondences underpins Harry's poem "the wanderer" and Brennan's "The Wanderer" and, even though they initially appear disparate, the strength and nature of the feeling they evoke within the reader reveals a most compelling similarity.[4] Toby Davidson informs us that in his *Poems (1913)* Brennan "employs Western Christian mystical themes of silence, revelation, spiritual progression, and divine union" (24). These themes are mirrored in the journeys that both the wanderers are taking. Harry's wanderer is on a search for the Self, a troubled being's journey home. Brennan writes that his journey "does lead somewhere ... Man the wanderer is on his way to himself" (45); this idea parallels the theme of Harry's poem, but where her journey is one of a positive transformation, Brennan's is one of endurance and remains unfinished.

The poems share atmospheric qualities that evoke powerful feelings, which is a principle feature of Symbolist poetry. In both poems there is recognition of a deeply felt sense of searching; however, the emotion elicited in each is different. Brennan writes that "the directing emotion of a poem ... is always expressed more by the music of the verse than by the logic of the words" (17). The musicality of the poems differ, suggesting that each traveller has a different experience on their pilgrimage. Colin Roderick says that in "The Wanderer" "you will hear the inexorable beat of time; and from the music of the poem you will gather overtones that tell of lives long past" (71), the music emphasising the enduring journey and recalling ancient myths. Chisholm describes the poem as a song of metaphysical exile, driven through rain and wind along a hopeless road, crying out aloud in his misery but never bowing his head. It is the sort of poetry that needs little comment, it invades you like orchestral music, and you live it as you read. (*CB* 31)

In Harry's poem too, "you live it as you read" but in comparison hers is quieter, it induces a sense of relief. A sense of sacred space is created by the slow pace of the poem, which Harry achieves by breaking up the image and looking at each action individually. If, as Duwell comments, Harry is endeavoring "to enact reality…through the method of projective verse" (106), that is using line-as–breath, she succeeds here. The short first line "frail" not only accentuates the fragile and weary nature of the subject, it also emphasises its isolation. As each consecutive line becomes longer so does the breath, thereby simulating this long, tedious journey.

> frail
> as if
> after a long flight
> over mountains & deserts (*Dandelion* 61)

The mood changes in the second stanza where the pace begins to slow and become more even. The short lines become balanced both rhythmically and phonologically: "soft/ ly dropping/ onto twig," the double 'p' sound in the second line matches the double 't' sound in the third, which also echoes the 't' in the first line, and the 'g' sound at the end of these two lines unites them. Harry creates an image that is dynamic, both visually and aurally, when she breaks the word 'softly' and spreads it over two lines; the adjective 'soft' becomes the adverb 'softly'. This division creates a subtle contradiction because on one hand, it suggests the gentle movement of the rain, but on the other, fractures the sense of gentleness. The break also enacts the movement; as 'ly' drops onto the next line the reader can almost see it fall. This technique is not just projectivist in nature, but is also inherited from the Symbolists. Rosemary Huisman writes that it was the French Symbolist Mallarmé who first became concerned with the "meaning–making potential of graphic display" (50) and the idea that a poem could be written as a musical score. It is the spaces and fragments that speed up or slow down our perception of the poem as we scan the written form.

A feeling of delight and peace is conjured by the musicality of the next stanza. The vowel sounds in the line "light as a blue wren's foot" rise and fall, with grace and delicacy, imitating the chirruping of the wren. The juxtaposition of the visual image of the dainty wren with the sound image of a birdsong takes the reader deeper. It is here, in this serene space, that the rain 'settles' and the journey is over.

Harry's use of the natural world as symbol highlights a fundamental difference in the way her symbols relate the momentary with the eternal compared to Brennan's. For Brennan, "the relation of the eternal to the temporal ... cannot be expressed except in terms of time, by a myth" (143). Brennan relies on the myth's ability to tap into a racial memory that connects humankind to the eternal. Harry, on the other hand, expresses this relationship through the acute observation of nature, which is based on the belief that nature will directly evoke the eternal within us.

A sense of peace is found at the end of both these journeys. For Brennan it is a sombre one. When he writes "I feel a peace fall in the heart of the winds", he is suggesting that he has accepted the fact that he cannot stop searching, for the wind will never stop driving him, he has "to endure the long martyrdom of life and loneliness" (Chisholm *CB* 33). The poem ends with a line that is unsettling and contradictory: "'and a *clear dusk* settle, somewhere, *far in me*" (my emphasis). It is not a contented acceptance, more a resignation. There will always be a distance from the Absolute. The peace that Harry finds comes from the sense of refuge provided by the trees, a divine sanctuary. Martin Duwell finds the ending to be unsatisfactory: "This poem is spoiled by its ultimate lack of faith in the strategy of suggestion, for its conclusion baldly explains "'so comes rain/ to a lodge of leaves'" (40). However, Geoff Page believes that the closing lines of Harry's early poems, of which this is one, are "full of implications" (106). Duwell reads this poem as an exercise in the method of projective verse. He does not read it symbolically and therefore misses the affect and significance of this line.

Harry does not just rely on symbolism to suggest the significance of the end of her poem – she also suggests it stylistically. There is an echo of the sonnet form in this poem. A volta is suggested when the poem turns after the word 'settles' and changes from a portrayal to the results of the journey and the poem ends with an unconventional half rhyming couplet that is equalised by stress, rather than syllable count, which has the effect of reinforcing the significance of the ending.

Harry abruptly shifts the focus of the poem from movement to shelter by her use of a colon. The colon not only describes the shelter: "a hut made of bark"; it also signifies the start of Harry's unconventional couplet, which parallels the traditional end of an Elizabethan sonnet to summarise the whole poem:

> a hut made of bark
> beneath a roof of trees:
>
> so comes rain
> to a lodge of leaves (*Dandelion* 61)

The couplet is describing the shelter found at the end of a journey and the importance of this shelter is emphasised by Harry's use of repetition. Firstly, the insects' movement parallels the movement of the rain, both disturbed and looking for shelter and both finding it. This repeated image of movement towards shelter serves to augment the sense of refuge found there. Secondly, there is the repetition of the stress count and then the repetition of sound in the half rhyme trees/ leaves, and lastly the repetition of the signifiers for the notion of shelter: 'hut', 'roof', and 'lodge,' a hut being a simple dwelling often made of natural materials such as logs or grass and a lodge being, again, a crude dwelling made of boughs. Lodge comes from the Old French word 'loge' and originally meaning 'shelter of foliage.' These are all simple, natural shelters, made from nature and reinforcing the sense of sanctuary to be found in nature. Symbolically, shelter is being found under the protection of trees, a very spiritual place. Trees are recognised as intermediaries between heaven and earth, the roots planted firmly in the earth and the branches reaching upwards to heaven. Baudelaire used the spiritual significance of the tree as a symbol in his poem "Correspondences":

> Nature's a temple where each living column,
> At times, gives forth vague words. There Man advances
> Through forest-groves of symbols, strange and solemn,
> Who follow him with their familiar glance. (Trans. Roy Campbell)

The journey is almost over. Once again, Harry does not finish the poem with a full stop. In this case it may allude to the ephemeral nature of divine union; the earthly spiritual path is everlasting. Or, perhaps, as this is common to each of these poems that explore beyond the limits of language, it is a sign for an opening, an aperture between the world and the mystical ...

Harry's nature-based lyrical poems take us on a journey into her inner world. Her simple and gentle lyrical poems belie multileveled, complex and profound significations that are discovered in the evocative language she employs. Once the essence of this language is located a new way of perceiving her poetry is revealed and new themes, influences and philosophical viewpoints are uncovered.

Mysterious and suggestive symbols are the source of this language. Harry uses the qualities of the symbol to perform many functions; binding the momentary with the eternal; diving into the collective unconscious where there is no separation; and bridging the physical and the metaphysical. Symbols also facilitate the evocation of

Wittgenstein's expressions of absolute value, as "the sensation when taking a walk on a summer's day" ("Ethics" 8) can be correlated with "Walking, When The Lake Of The Air Is Blue With Spring" (*Dandelion* 14-15); "the wonder of the existence of the world" ("Ethics 8) may relate to "temple-viewing" (*Dandelion* 11); and "the experience of feeling absolutely safe" ("Ethics" 8) is clearly evoked in "the wanderer" (*Dandelion 61)*. Harry's unique fusion of the poetics of the Symbolists, the Deep Imagists and Zen, allows her to slip through the walls of her cage, to enable her to successfully recover and express Wittgenstein's sense of the mystical for the reader, the 'other'. It is the dissolution of the ego that allows this to occur. Harry's anonymity can be seen as a symbolic gesture that points to the fact that her private experience is irrelevant in this exchange, as Wittgenstein remarks, "it drops out of consideration" (§ 293). What is important is that her poetry, her manipulation of language, her style, has the potential to cause the 'other' to experience the ineffable. It gently urges us to question whether we are more than a cultural construction; whether there is something more, somewhere where there is no division, only unity, somewhere in the "matters invisible" (*Dandelion* 11).

Notes

1. Following Jung, the ego in the context of this enquiry is defined as a consciousness that has a sense of continuity and, most importantly for this discussion, identity (Jacobi 21). For a full discussion on the relationship of the ego and consciousness in Jungian thought see Jolande Jacobi *The Psychology of C. G. Jung*. 5th Edition. Routledge and Kegan Paul Ltd, 1951. pp.19-67.
2. For an overview of Zen poetry see Lucien Stryk, "Introduction" *The Penguin Book of Zen* edited by Stryk, Lucien and Ikemoto Takashi, Penguin Books Ltd, 1977.
3. The concepts of the ego and the Self are abstruse and it is necessary to distinguish the difference between the two. Jung believed that the psyche consists of two autonomous centers of being which he named the ego and the Self.

The ego is the small part of the psyche that is conscious and the Self is the total psyche. The Self is in essence paradoxical because it is comprised of the union of opposites (Essential 265): it is both conscious and unconscious; the individual, which is the ego; and the eternal, which is the archetype Self. The Self is a part of the collective unconscious, which is itself a part of the divine. Jung writes that the individual begins life with a sense of wholeness but as it grows up the individualised ego-consciousness emerges. If the individual is to remain psychically healthy then the ego must constantly re-establish its relation to the Self (Man 128). Wholeness reoccurs when the relationship between the ego and the Self shifts from one of separation to one of union (Edinger 4) and when this occurs the ego is subordinated to the Self (Edinger 3). To make this connection the ego must first journey through the unconscious into the collective unconscious where the Self-archetype exists (Essential 269).

4. In these poems both Harry and Brennan emulate Mallarmé's maxim "Peindre, non la chose, mais l'effet qu'elle produit" (paint not the thing but the effect it produces). Mallarmé ix.

Works Cited

Ayres, Marie-Louise. "Looking for Some Tracks: Hunting with J. S. Harry" *Southerly*, vol. 56, no. 3, 1996, pp. 17-32.

Baudelaire, Charles. "Correspondences" translated by Roy Campbell, *Poems of Baudelaire*, Pantheon Books, 1952. http://fleursdumal.org/poem/103

Beichman, Janine. *Masaoka Shiki*, Kodansha International, 1986.

Biedermann, Hans. *Dictionary of Symbolism*, Translated by James Hulbert, Facts on File Inc, 1992.

Bly, Robert. "An Interview with Robert Bly" *Robertbly.com* http://www.robertbly.com/int_3.html

Brennan, Christopher. *The Prose of Christopher Brennan*, edited by A. R. Chisholm and J.J. Quinn, Angus and Robertson, 1962.

Breslin, Paul. *The Psycho-Political Muse. American Poetry since the Fifties*, The University Press of Chicago, 1987.

Chisholm, A.R. *A Study of Christopher Brennan's The Forest Of The Night*, Melbourne University Press, 1970.

---. *Christopher Brennan, The Man and His Poetry*, Angus and Robertson, 1946.

Davidson, Toby. *Christian Mysticism and Australian Poetry*, Cambria Press, 2013.
Duwell, Martin. "Both Sides of the Curtain" *Overland*, vol. 106, 1987, pp. 40-45.
Dray, Colin. "The Golden Fish: On Reading J.S. Harry" *Australian Literary Studies*, vol. 22 no. 2, 2005, pp. 192-204.
Edinger, Edward F. *Ego and Archetype*, Penguin Books, 1986.
Frazier, Jane. "Writing Outside the Self: The Disembodied Narrators of W. S. Merwin" *Style*, vol. 30, no. 2, 1996, pp. 341-350.
Gardner, Thomas, and Kinnell, Galway. "An Interview with Galway Kinnell" *Contemporary Literature*, vol. 20, no. 4, 1979, pp. 423-433.
Harry, J.S. *A Dandelion for Van Gogh*, Island Press, 1985.
---. *Australian Poetry Now*, Edited by Thomas Shapcott, Sun Books, 1970.
---. *Hold, For a Little While, And Turn Gently*, Island Press, 1979.
---. *If... And the Moveable Ground*, Picaro, 2004.
---. *Not Finding Wittgenstein*, Bloodaxe Books Ltd, 2012.
---. *Public Private*, Vagabond Press, 2013.
---. *Sun Shadow, Moon Shadow*, Vagabond Press, 2001.
---. *Selected Poems*, Penguin Books, 1995.
---. *the deer under the skin*, University of Queensland Press, 1971.
---. *The Life on Water and The Life Beneath*, Angus & Robertson, 1995.
Harry, J.S. and Roberts, Bev. "J.S. Harry – Some Questions and Answers" *Fine Line*, vol. 3 1988, pp. 21-26.
Haskell, Dennis. "The Modern American Poetry of Deep Image". *Southern Review*, vol. 12, 1979, pp. 137-166.
Hakutani, Yoshinobi. *Haiku and Modernist Poetics*. Palgrave Macmillan, 2009. https://doi-org.ezproxy.newcastle.edu.au/10.1057/9780230100916
Huisman, Rosemary. *The Written Poem: Semiotic Conventions from Old to Modern English*, Cassell, 1998.
Jacobi, Jolande. *The Psychology of C. G. Jung*, 5th Edition. Routledge and Kegan Paul Ltd, 1951.
Jung, C.G. *The Essential Jung*, edited by Anthony Storr, Princeton University Press, 1983.

---. *Man and his Symbols*. edited by C. G. Jung et al., Aldus Books, 1974.
Keene, Donald. *The Winter Sun Shines In: A Life of Masaoka Shiki*, Columbia University Press, 2013.
Lundquist. John M. "C. J. Jung and the Temple Symbols of Wholeness." *C. J. Jung and the Humanities*, edited by Karin Barnaby and Pellegrino D'Acierno, Princeton University Press, 1990.
Mallarmé, Stéphane. *Mallarmé*, translated by Anthony Hartley, Penguin, 1965.
McIntosh, Christopher. *Gardens of the Gods: Myth, Magic and Meaning in Horticulture*, I.B. Tauris, 2005.
Merwin, W. S. *The First Four Books of Poem*, Copper Canyon Press, 2000.
Mulhall, Stephen. *Wittgenstein's Private Language*, Clarendon Press, 2007.
Musgrave, David. ""Black Bile and Man's Best Friend: A History of the Black Dog" *Tracking the Black Dog*, edited by Kerrie Eyres, UNSW Press, 2006.
Page, Geoff. "J. S. Harry" *A Reader's Guide to Contemporary Australian Literature*, University of Queensland Press, 1995.
Perloff, Marjorie. *Wittgenstein's Ladder: Poetic Language and the Strangeness of the Ordinary*, The University of Chicago Press, 1996.
Roderick, Colin. "The Wanderer of the Ways of All the World: A Portrait of Christopher Brennan." *The Australian Quarterly*, vol. 23, no. 1, 1951, pp. 67-80.
Rowe, Noel. and Vivian Smith. *Windchimes: Asia in Australian Poetry*, Pandanus Books, 2006.
Stasko, Nicolette. www.*smh.com.au* June 12 2015. https://www.smh.com.au/national/js-harry-a-skylarker-with-language-whose-first-allegiance-was-always-to-poetry-20150612-ghmas8.html
Stryk, Lucien. *The Penguin Book of Zen Poetry*, edited by Stryk, Lucien and Ikemoto Takashi, Penguin Books Ltd, 1977.
Symons, Arthur. *The Symbolist Movement in Literature*, E. P. Dutton and Co., Inc., 1958.
Tulip, James. "Contemporary Australian Poetry: II Transition and

Advance." *Southerly*, vol. 3, 1972, pp. 176-195.

Watts, Alan. "Beat Zen, Square Zen, and Zen." *Chicago Review*, vol. 42, no. 3-4 1996, pp. 48-55.

Wilson, Edmund. *Axel's Castle. A Study in the Imaginative Literature of 1870-1930*, Fontana Library, 1962.

Wittgenstein, Ludwig. "A Lecture on Ethics" *The Philosophical Review*, vol. 74, no. 1, 1965, pp. 3-12.

---. *Philosophical Investigations.* translated by G. E. M. Anscombe, Basil Blackwell, 1978.

---. *Tractatus Logico-Philosophicus.* translated by D. F. Pears and B. F. McGuinness, Routledge Classics, 2008.

Chapter 12

"The Final Subject Has Been Set. I'm Concentrating Hard on Death": The Poetics of Loss in Philip Hodgins's *Blood and Bone*

CAROLYN RICKETT

Yes the signature always has the knack or art of speaking to us of death; that is its secret, it seals everything that is said with this monumental epitaph.
—Jacques Derrida, *The Work of Mourning*

My speech is a warning that at this very moment death is loose in the world, that it suddenly appeared between me, as I speak, and the being I address ...
—Maurice Blanchot, *The Work of Fire*.

Most theorists agree that the work of mourning involves mental processes that ultimately enable a person to separate from this object they have lost, and this involves the paradoxical experience of focussing on the loss in order to finally disinvest in and detach from it. But even Freud, as Clewell argues in her article "Mourning and Melancholia: Freud's Psychoanalysis of Loss", "explicitly acknowledged that mourning might not be as straightforward a business of severance and redemptive replacement as he earlier surmised" (58).

The less "straightforward" mourning that Clewell suggests here, I believe, is foregrounded in Philip Hodgins's collection *Blood and Bone*. What is at work in his first collection is a kind of proleptic mourning, or anticipatory mourning, where a person begins the mourning process before an actual material death occurs. In this instance Hodgins begins to mourn poetically the very real prospect of his own medically predicted death; however, as Egan points out, "While autothanatographers seek cure or remission, no one accepts death" (203). It becomes for Hodgins, as Ricoeur so eloquently describes, an inevitable insistence on "The life of death ... making itself heard. The agony of death, its shining and mournfully loquacious presence" (20).

The Work of Melancholia

Hodgins's work is important because his voice performs and legitimises something other than the pure language of survival—a circumstance recognised by those with terminal cancer. His diagnosis demonstrates that not every writer survives cancer, and not every writer is able to employ (aesthetic) language in a way that will enable loss to be mourned fully. As Hodgins's poetry suggests, a grief reaction to impending loss can remain as a melancholic fixity on death when someone is given a terminal prognosis.

To be melancholic is perhaps to feel the piercing mark of the incomplete. In the last interview he gave before his death, Jacques Derrida confesses:

> ... I never learned-to-live. In fact not at all! Learning to live should mean learning to die, learning to take into account, so as to accept, absolute mortality that is without salvation, resurrection, or redemption—neither for oneself nor for the other. (*Learning to Live* 24)

Learning to live, Derrida suggests, involves the seeming contradiction of accepting a personal and singular death, and that in preparing for this supreme absence one will have learned to surrender any desire for compensation. This trope of watching death's insistent and attendant capacity for wounding and erasure is one that I see haunting

Hodgins's poetry as he discursively keeps watch over and begins to mourn his own inexorable effacement from a terminal disease. While he cannot witness the final act of his own death from acute myeloid leukaemia, his poems function as sentinels that allow him to view (and ultimately grieve) his dying self in situ referring to himself as the "already dead" (*Blood and Bone* 43). When told by doctors at twenty-four years of age that his disease is incurable, Hodgins engages in a kind of proleptic mourning where he can only lament his death before it actually occurs. In many ways, his anticipatory mourning is poignantly rendered in Paul Ricoeur's phrase "To see myself dead, before being dead ..." (10), or what psychoanalyst Adam Phillips refers to as "getting into practice for one's own death" (124).

Involved in this kind of (uncompleted) mourning process is a persistent melancholia that shapes Hodgins's responses to dying, particularly as he feels he has been denied any opportunity to live life to the full. Confronting a terminal condition in his early twenties, his is a poetics where melancholia comprehensively informs and shapes an inwardly directed grief. The poems that I will refer to in this discussion explore his emotional responses to temporality, illness and dying; poems which render a melancholic separation from self, others and language. In these poems Hodgins charts a new knowledge of radical disease. Here a reader finds that "the work of writing is founded on the void, *le nèant* of death"; and it is here where Hodgins makes "visible the absence that death is" (Stamelman 36).

In his work on Philip Hodgins's strategy of "voicing his body" through his cancer poems, Werner Senn highlights the politics surrounding the representation of illness in Western art and literature, and the ways in which Hodgins tries to assert the "self over bodily dysfunction and dismemberment" (240). He enacts a form of resistance "by using various poetic forms and strategies" (239). Senn acknowledges Sontag's widely circulated argument that "the person dying of cancer is portrayed as robbed of all capacities of self-transcendence, humiliated by fear and agony" (*Illness as Metaphor* 17), and while he concedes that "these characteristics are not entirely absent from [Hodgins's] texts" (239), he concludes that "it is generally not true that fear and agony dominate his writing to the extent of robbing their subject of his capacity for self-transcendence" (239). One of the key arguments Senn uses to support this position is the breadth of work Hodgins "produced before and during his illness" encompassing "more than this single experience: travel, art, sports, family and especially country life are also among his themes" (239). Yet, Senn acknowledges that in the poems where Hodgins references his illness, like the exemplars from *Blood and Bone*, there is "a continuous, if not always successful, effort not only to cope with the apparent hopelessness of his condition but to transcend it" (239).

However, my own reading of *Blood and Bone* differs from Senn on this particular point as I believe the overwhelming tenor of this text is one in which Hodgins's terror of dying and sense of bodily abjection is not transcended, and the idea of consolation, if anything, is further problematised because of the prevailing sense that language is not always up to the task of figuring or making sense of his looming death.[1] As Hodgins candidly confesses: "I've been rehearsing death each night, / and still I haven't got it right" ("The Birds" 37). Through this rhyming couplet he announces the inherent paradox of his need to be prepared, and the inability ever to be prepared for an early death. However, this process can never be fully articulated as Hodgins admits, given his age, that "death is new to me" ("The Guest" 45). It is this continued attempt at figuring his present and future losses that dominates the poetic content of the anthology. He acknowledges an intransigent melancholic trace at work in his first text when he concedes that it is "My bad luck to write the *same* poem every time ..." ("From County Down" 51; emphasis added). For Hodgins, to "write the same poem" is to perform compulsively time and again the dejection felt from the losses rupturing his body, beliefs and language. So what is primarily at work in the *Blood and Bone* anthology is Hodgins's unrelenting and unfulfilled desire of "... wanting to say the unsayable ..." (Watkin 13). The "unsayable" for Hodgins might be described by the autothanatographical limits outlined by Linnell Secomb:

> If death is a certainty, then so too, it seems, is the impossibility of testifying to our own individual deaths. We can describe our being-towards-death or a near-death experience but once death has overtaken us, existence is extinguished and with it the possibility of saying to those who live on: I am dead. (33)

Blood and Bone

Freud writes that "Our own death is indeed unimaginable, and however we try to imagine it, we realize that we are actually still present as onlookers" ("Timely Reflections" 183). It is from this liminal space "between a waxing and waning life" ("The Guest" 45) that Hodgins's gaze is fixated on death's approach and his own imminent departure. There is no resting, only a hyper vigilance as Hodgins's choice of epigraph for this anthology signals: "There is … no death … There is only … me … me … who is going to die …". The words appropriated from André Malraux calibrate the reader's expectation that the poems that are to follow will explore the insularity of one man's dying; the *me* of mortality rather than any inclusive sense of community. His heightened sense of vulnerability and alienation brought on by illness can be more readily understood after reading "The Skull Beneath the Skin: Cancer Survival and Awareness of Death" where Miles Little and Emma-Jane Sayers observe that, at times, "Death salience causes us to question meaning in our lives, and to turn inward, rather than turning outward to valued groups for endorsement …" (193). Hodgins is able to employ various rhetorical strategies to represent his melancholic terror. However, this does not allow him to transcend his sense of corporeal and verbal deterioration: rather it forces him to reflect on his embodied predicament where he is effectively writing about and *through* his diseased body. As Andrew Taylor suggests, Hodgins writes the kind of "poetry that springs from that intensely personal sense of mortality that comes when the poet finds himself or herself in the grip of a life-threatening disease ..." (65). I believe Hodgins's poetry registers this sense of death gripping him in a way which makes him feel that he is losing his grip on bodily and linguistic function. Dominating the poems following the epigraph is this ever-present personal threat: "... darkness something the size of death / is just out of focus" ("Question Time" *Blood and Bone* 17). What is in sharp focus though is the prescient knowledge that advancing illness cannot be halted, and Hodgins signals this inevitable route to the reader: "There is no going back / to the body's evanescent harmony" (*Blood and Bone* 19). Again, such a stark statement denies any refuge in euphemism, and syntactically the notional aesthetics of Hodgins's "harmony" is completely undermined by the foregrounding prohibitive "no going back" (*Blood and Bone* 19).

His poems are ones of unhalting negation. Performed here is a principal mode of narration in which he refuses constructions of false comfort or glib consolation; offered instead are candid account(s) of a man *waiting* for "his *slow* death" ("The Cause of Death" *Blood and Bone* 21; emphasis added). The physical and metaphysical terrain of a terminal illness closes off to Hodgins any imaginative mapping of an optimistic future so conclusively registered in the texts of the other authors. Instead, he is left melancholically tracing and retracing his "condemned" embodiment. As Leader astutely points out, "Melancholia means that after a loss, one's image of oneself is profoundly altered" (34-35). For Hodgins, the potency and virility of manhood is interrupted and ultimately usurped by his observations on the physical and emotional ravages of his leukaemia. There is an altered view of his future as a space of boundless opportunity to one that is contracted, contaminated and finally conquered by disease.

What I see operating in *Blood and Bone* is a psychological condition extending Hodgins's grief rather than (re)solving it because of the insistent and melancholic "I" rehearsing unrelieved anxiety and fear. His is a cancer that cannot be envisaged as localised, contained or excised because of the diseased blood contaminating his entire body. Thus, Hodgins's poetry not only courageously records and discloses his literal wounding from a terminal illness, but also the permanent injury to his psyche, so in this sense, as Watkin argues, "Loss is ontological, irreducible and singular" (23). Or put another way, there is a strong sense that Hodgins's early poetry is "about a vanishing world … written by a vanishing man" (James 26). This notion of "the vanishing man" is acutely taken up in the very first poem entitled "Platform Verse":

> a man stands single
> on a railway station platform
> alone with the smell of his own body:
> the sun is low (*Blood and Bone* 1)

In this vivid scene of a man waiting on a railway station, Hodgins's stark evocation of grief is performed by the use of words like "single" and "alone" (*Blood and Bone* 1). His vulnerability is underscored by his exposure to an indifferent public space:

> his shadow is bigger than he
> the wind interferes with him:
> a train comes
> its shadow blocks out the shadow of the man (*Blood and Bone* 1)

The cumulative imagery of the low sun, the interfering wind and blocking shadows creates a sense of foreboding, and adds to Hodgins's self-portrait of fragility, isolation and loneliness. The shadow of a man is "alone with the smell of his own body", and this phrase quickly moves beyond its literality to represent synedochically Hodgins's threatened mortality:

> its smell blocks out the smell
> of his socks and armpits:

the train catches its breath and creaks
and rolls right out of town (*Blood and Bone* 1)

The train "rolling out of town" symbolises not only the permanent disappearance of robust health, but also his freighted journey towards death. The ironic juxtaposition that the train is more animated than the man who passively waits on the platform is not lost on the reader; nor is it ultimately lost on Hodgins as so many of his poems prefigure a radically embodied subject who is primarily consigned to melancholic stasis, and when there is any observable shift it is registered as an inexorable movement *towards* death. The absence of a full stop at the end of his opening poem signifies Hodgins's inability to halt his disease's trajectory, and this figuration is repeatedly registered in his use of minimal punctuation throughout his poems.

While Hodgins uses third person narration as a distancing technique to try and hold death's intrusion at bay, this device proves unsustainable because in the next poem death *personally* hails him in the hospital room where he lies devastated by *his* prognosis. Forced into a position of passivity in Ward 10 West, Hodgins tells the reader that this place is "just a vehicle for death" ("The Shoot" 49). It is here in the cancer ward, death's world, where he is assailed by the full recognition that biomedicine will fail him: "that all this stuff could do no good" ("Room I Ward 10 West 12/11/83" 2). It is in this hospital room that he fully acknowledges his terminal condition: "and now I understand / what one uncommon word has done" (*Blood and Bone* 2). In this particular poem the idea of death is (at first) only alluded to, but then is comprehensively referenced in personal and immediate terms: "Tonight the dying has begun. There is no cure for blood gone bad" (*Blood and Bone* 2). It is also here that Hodgins first introduces one of the recurring melancholic tropes in his poetry; his blood as contagion. The idea of organic growth being linked to the productivity and continuity of life is rejected by Hodgins as his poor diagnosis causes him to fixate on death.

His poetry enacts the struggle to find words to describe the deadly impact of the contamination, the ensuing dialectical tension between silence and saying, and the failure of language to convey adequately the trauma that his body is actually "nurturing its own determined death" ("Ich Bin Allein" 44). Days later, while still in hospital, he continues to compress and rehearse these potent concerns in "Room 1 Ward 10 West 23/11/83". The now all too familiar experience at the hospital is described as "a wordless afternoon" (*Blood and Bone* 5) where people who are not dying have time "to choose the words" they would like him to hear, in contrast to Hodgins, who, "attached / to a dark / bag of blood / leaking near him" can only choose the words that he is "likely to need" (*Blood and Bone* 5). The reader is left with the impression that the leaking blood, which denies any connotation of a life-giving transfusion, is more fluent than the poetry.

In such a portrayal of a room where blood is endlessly leaking, Hodgins creates a sense of the interminable time passing and the heaviness of his approaching death. In this poignantly nuanced scene of isolation, Hodgins contrasts the purposeful language which he now struggles to enunciate with the unimpaired capacity of others to select and freely draw on a vocabulary of words that captures what they wish to say; for him it seems that the more necessary words are to describe his situation, the more elusive they become. And the confounding irony that words are at once possible and impossible is captured in the last stanza of the poem:

> At twenty-four
> there are so many words
> and this one
> death (*Blood and Bone* 5)

This reference to his personal "death" comes into sharp semiotic focus for the reader by Hodgins strategically placing it completely by itself on the final line. It is a word, like Hodgins himself; singular and separated. Despite the prospect of "so many words" the heightened syntactical presence of "death" prohibits any real capacity to describe it adequately or to write beyond it. The cadaverous presence of "death" in this poem literally is, and has, the last word. This message is distinctly underscored by Hodgins's not placing a full stop after the word signifying that death is definitely "loose in the world" and cannot be physically or linguistically stopped by him.

Even when Hodgins talks of "Leaving Hospital" he signals the idea that his dying cannot be expressed in equivalent language. Despite the potential joy that might be associated with him leaving an emotionally sterile medical environment, he says that "Nothing was resolved" (*Blood and Bone* 7). The tensions and terror of dying cannot be consoled by language with Hodgins admitting that "Blood and bone were shot and death had shown / a way with words beyond the usual sophistry" (*Blood and Bone* 7), and he is forced to concede that "it was impossible to match death's vocabulary" (*Blood and Bone* 7). The idea that death's lexicon will triumph over his ability to write a potent linguistic reply is strongly linked to the deterioration of his body. The sense that language is failing him while his body continues to betray him is imaged in another melancholic reflection:

> I thought of how this blood, this
> volition would bring me back here to die
> in stages of bitterness and regret. I turned around.
> The doors are open. (*Blood and Bone* 7)

Ironically the *open* doors work to make *closure* impossible. The doors symbolically function as the referent to an inexorable death, and emphasise a disruptive and ruptured space where Hodgins waits / looks towards extinction. As if such knowledge proves unbearable, he uses the distancing technique of second person narration to mediate trauma when he writes of the experience of receiving the news from his latest medical tests in the poem "The Wait." "You write of what you know" Hodgins says while maximising the white space between the printed words to represent the expansive and domineering space of waiting for an outcome that could "go either way" (*Blood and Bone* 11). Then, through a compressed flurry of remembrance standing in direct contrast to the waiting room full of anxious people, Hodgins transports the reader to "somewhere else" where the "quality of light is different". He temporarily recreates the *mise en scène* of

> Late afternoon. Little men
> playing cricket in football shorts.
> Bodies glowing brown
> like the dirt pitch. And miles away,
> on the treeline, hundreds of cockatoos
> breaking up the light. (*Blood and Bone* 11)

But this evocative return to childhood cannot withstand the melancholic intrusion of death salience: "Either way you write of death. / Your death" (*Blood and Bone* 11). Even when Hodgins's reverie takes him temporarily out of his diseased body, he "manages to invest the rural world with some of the unnameable terror that inhabits his cancer poems" (Ryan 29). This admission that his thoughts continue to be dictated by an autothanatropic fixation denies any real possibility that his imagination can sustain a transcendent state. Following the "your" comes the unavoidable pronominal revision where he returns to the traumatic knowledge of the narrating "I". In a final haunting admission bereft of imagery, metaphor or conceit Hodgins says of his own death: "It will be horrible. I know" (*Blood and Bone* 11). This time breaking up the sentence with a full stop he forces a prolonged contemplation on *his* singular death. Remembrance of the camaraderie of the cricket pitch is structurally supplanted by his anxious foreshadowing of what is to come. So instead of the reverie functioning as a poetic strategy that might enact a sense of imaginative liberation, poetic transformation, or sense of community, Hodgins inexorably and textually returns us to his present melancholic ruminations on death.

One finds this pattern of thinking stylistically repeated in

"Question Time" where Hodgins initially transports the reader to rural paddocks only to encounter imagery there that forces a return to one of the inscrutable questions that I see dominating the anthology; Hodgins's recurring (and unanswerable) question of "How can you not then think of your own death?" (*Blood and Bone* 16). Still employing the often repeated technique of distanciation through his use of second person narration, Hodgins rhetorically externalises his fears surrounding *his* own body's diseased status by a referent to "your" body where cancer is

> ... right through you,
> efficiently out of control;
> running down while always coming up with more,
> aware that nothing can be done.
> The prognosis says
> you will die
> in a paddock which you have been thinking about
> but one which you have not seen. (*Blood and Bone* 16)

The various positioning and repetition of the word "you" work toward trying to create some safety for himself by projecting his active fears onto the reader with the alarming questions of "Do *you* grind your teeth at night?" ... and "what do *you* do with death?" (*Blood and Bone* 16; emphasis added). However, after trying to manoeuvre away from direct references to himself, the poem inexorably returns to the most personally confronting question: "Why was death announced so soon?" (*Blood and Bone* 17). Even though Hodgins works to control his own fear through the absence of a singular personal pronoun, he still inevitably arrives at a place "that has no consolation" in his words, and acknowledges that:

> ... what discoveries
> there are left to make
> will not involve the sense of touch. (*Blood and Bone* 17)

Hodgins's depiction of human suffering that is denied any haptic relief heightens his perception that he is completely alone and without a future. In a space marked by such isolation his questions proliferate. The questions circling his dying work to inform the poem "Ontology" where "death" again "is the subject of poetry" (*Blood and Bone* 18) and the subject of the self. Associated with the physical demise of his body is the metaphysical collapse of any belief in a beneficent being or divine solace: "the universe is going cold, there is no God ... " (*Blood and Bone* 18). The lack of religious belief, psychological warmth and security is further rendered through the melancholic images of "aching stars" and "waxing gibbous moon" and underscored by the conclusion "all have lost their shine since those clear/childhood nights on the farm alive with voices ..." (*Blood and Bone* 18). Unlike "Question Time", the only voice registered in this particular poem is the first person singular whose introspection leads to grieving comparisons between what *once* was and what now *is*. As Jay Prosser reflects: "... what is melancholy except a looking back ... a failure unlike mourning to look forward?" (248). Of course, to look forward for Hodgins means staring even more directly into death's gaze.

What is striking is that Hodgins chooses to conclude the poem "Ontology" with the word "awakening" (*Blood and Bone* 18). However, given the cumulative impact of the previous images of emaciation and separation, the word fails to carry any enduring gravitas or robust illumination. Because Hodgins's "awakening" might be read as the haunting recognition that he inhabits a cosmos where his physical and spiritual losses occur with "no-one notice[ing]" (*Blood and Bone* 18). His choice of aloof and cold signifiers to describe the universe serve as metaphorical markers for his feelings of complete abandonment. Such feelings of unrelenting deprivation inevitably lead him to a distilled bitterness about human beings and their motivation. His diminishing physical state accords with the melancholic perception of Hodgins seeing himself as inhabiting a threatening and incomprehensible world. It is inevitable that these kinds of recurring thoughts lead him to write about "Self Pity" where he tells of

> ... that unsuspecting day when euphemisms
> dropped their masks and the message was
> WORDS CAN KILL. (*Blood and Bone* 20 capitalisation in
> original)

The sober gravity of prognosis and the grim prediction of his fate graphically reverberate in bold uppercase letters that deny him any literal or poetic transcendence of death. For Hodgins, the absence of any euphemisms in biomedical discourse prevents any evasion of the facts, and this forces him to confront repeatedly the unavoidable reality of his body's status. The direct words of a leukaemia diagnosis activate and prolong his melancholic grief, and he admits "the thought of never growing old / is with me all the time" and feeling "cheated ... could / write poems only in the first person singular—" (*Blood and Bone* 20). The absence of any comforting euphemisms in this and other poems highlights, Cathy Altmann argues, that "Hodgins is engaged in what Foucault terms 'parrhêsia' meaning truth-telling, or all-telling, of a most significant kind" (22), and through this kind of vocalisation, Altmann believes, "the poet with cancer is able to tell a story of being wounded" (22). In Hodgins's case, his is a fatal wound because he has been offered no possibility of recovery from cancer. For me, the power of Hodgins's writing lies in his unwavering commitment to engage in the "truth-telling" of his bodily annihilation. In reflecting on our own ability to confront death, Sandra Gilbert highlights that our first impulse is to "evade" such "fearful knowledge" (XVII),[2] which, to me, makes Hodgins's poetic contribution at the age of twenty-four all the more courageous.

Hodgins's melancholic fixation with deadly wounding is focused on again in "The Cause of Death" where he reiterates "suddenly I am waiting for slow death" (*Blood and Bone* 21). The oxymoronic yoking of the oppositional states of "sudden" and "slow" produces a destabilising effect. Hodgins's stasis is starkly contrasted with the activity of the gum trees in the garden, while his own productivity is impeded by the cancer that is corrupting his blood and bone. Connotations of blood and bone working as an organic fertiliser associated with fecundity and growth are again refused here. Instead, his body is presented as the parasitic accomplice of death. The extended vowel sounds produced by the internal rhyme pattern of this poem's final line "The cause of death is in the blood and bone. / It breeds in the past, and feeds on the future" echoes his own prolonged grief of continuing to see his life "frame by frame / with the frighted sight of the condemned man" (*Blood and Bone* 21). There is no attempt from Hodgins to try and valorise or rhetorically reconstitute his corporeality as anything other than damned which testifies to his readers an extraordinary courage in confronting his fate.

Any physical or psychological changes that Hodgins does register are always in terms of fearing his body's further deterioration. On the rare occasions when he consciously positions himself as taking part in rural activities, like riding along the Yabba trail in "The Change", his thoughts continue to be inflected by a representation of bodily deficit. There is a kinetic thought loop that replays the melancholic intrusion: "I wonder what it will be like / when chronic changes to acute" (*Blood and Bone* 32). For a moment, as if this anticipatory loss is too internally painful to process (again), Hodgins temporarily (re)employs the use of the third person pronoun for an effect of distanciation:

> There's so much space at Yabba North
> it's hard to think an early death
> could toss a rider off his horse
> and leave him trampled underneath. (*Blood and Bone* 32)

But immediately following this image of the destabilised, injured body of the Other Hodgins confronts the traumatic and unceasing intrusion of the personal "I" and his own inescapable fate: "And yet the change will surely come— / as sure as *I* am riding home" (*Blood and Bone* 32; emphasis added). Invoked here is an apocalyptic vision that offers no rhetorical comfort, only the obdurate fact that his body will be finally vanquished by disease. Hodgins's crafted use of alternating pronominal positioning between first, second and third person narration throughout his poems registers a deliberate desire to keep death at arm's length as long as he can, yet as he acknowledges (again) "it [is] impossible to match / death's vocabulary" (*Blood and Bone* 7).

It could be said that as this collection progresses, what changes in Hodgins's relationship to dying is the movement from his representation of death as an abstracted silence to the personification of it having a voice that *personally* hails him. In the poem "Death Who" Hodgins constructs a scenario where he and Death are involved in a tiresome exchange over dinner. The clever characterisation of death as the aggressive conversational bully involves the telling of home truths: "He tells you things about yourself / Forgotten things and those not yet found out ..." (*Blood and Bone* 34). However, the ironic humour is unable to moderate the more hostile and sinister aspects of the encounter:

> ... cancer's got you like conviction
> and he's kneeling on your chest,
> glaring over you,
> pushing a cushion into your face,
> talking quietly and automatically,
> the words not clear.
> He's got you and he's really pushing,
> pushing you to death. (*Blood and Bone* 35)

The movement of the poem, which ends with loquacious death as victor, raises again the repeated failure of language to alter, halt or replace Hodgins's fear of erasure. Death's symbolic smothering of his face with the cushion highlights Senn's point that many of Hodgins's poems are haunted by "The fear that the body will prevail over voice" (244). For Hodgins, a young man with potentially so much to say, the source of his profound psychological wounding is that the corporeal will eventually suffocate the verbal. While he cleverly constructs the conceit of a dinner conversation to mediate this fear, his undressed melancholic reactions are framed in the simple and direct statement: "It's just so unjust" (*Blood and Bone* 34). The reader is acutely aware that Hodgins's lament of having "got the only part in cancer's tragic dialogue" ("The Birds" *Blood and Bone* 37) cannot be assuaged by any clever use of words with which he might choose to reply. In fact his body flying "pain's black flag" (*Blood and Bone* 39) is impervious to any soothing linguistic intervention, and this frustration with his body's refusal to hear or negotiate with him is bluntly expressed in his address to his spleen:

> You kept me up all night looking
> for a voice
> to condemn you in
>
> What use was that?
>
> You only listen to chemotherapy
> You listen and then you stop ("Spleen" *Blood and Bone* 39)

Here Hodgins feels that there is no language other than that of self-recrimination that is appropriate for his rebellious body. He sees language not as a means of solace but as an inadequate medium to temper his disease, and his perceived failure of poetic form to capture his angst is starkly evoked in the poem "Ten Things About it". Here Hodgins's thoughts are reduced to an axiomatic list of the associations he has with cancer:

It's a vehicle.

2. Cancer development isn't character development …

7. Pain cannot be imagined, only experienced …

9. It's bad for sleep, bad for dreams. (*Blood and Bone* 40)

However, the familiar trope of choosing not to directly name his disease eventually gives way under the existential weight of death-consciousness with the last entry on his list moving from a broadly generalised list to a specifically located suffering self: "10. I never forget" (*Blood and Bone* 40). The spectre of death continues to inhibit the possibility of using language as a means of (re)imagining or detaching from Hodgins's present and projected future losses.

This thematic predilection for death's predominance over recuperative language is further highlighted in the poem immediately following. In "Walking Through the Crop" Hodgins indicates a desire to list things adopting a disaffected tone as he shuns the natural world that might have afforded him some aesthetic comfort. He says "it doesn't matter any more / the way the wheat is shivering / on such a beautiful hot day …" (*Blood and Bone* 41), and continues with his disenfranchised account of a late afternoon in spring:

> I couldn't care about the sound
> of insects frying in the heat
> or how a flock of cockatoos
> has gone up in a brilliant sheet.

The reader still navigating the poet's discarded synaesthesia eventually arrives at his core lament:

> I had a list I tried to keep.
> Sometimes I even wrote it down.

> It had all sorts of private things
> like images, sensations, sounds ... (*Blood and Bone* 41)

The unfinished thoughts and the elliptically suspended conclusion are suggestive of the way death's incursion will silence his life. The emotional and linguistic vacuum Hodgins feels from this realisation is sharply repeated in the last stanza composed of only two lines: "There's nothing in these dying days. / I've given everything away" (*Blood and Bone* 41). Induced again is the impoverished relationship Hodgins believes he presently has with language and himself. The bald reductionist statements of "nothing" in the starkly beautiful lines of the poem symbolise the deliberate collapse of highly crafted writing, confirming that the aestheticisation of words provide no solace for his bereavement. Yet, what I find so powerful is that despite his assertion of "giving everything" away and his concomitant disappointment with language as a way of halting or altering disappearance, he still continues to write. Ironically, for the reader of this poem, Hodgins's attention to detail and evocation of the natural world suggests a poet who does "care" about language's capacity to represent and record something of enduring beauty amidst demise.

Understandably though, Hodgins's poetry continues to circulate melancholic thoughts which become tinged with bitterness. He confesses that his death sentence undermines any certainty he might have about relationships:

> But fear has seen through this act of being
> philosophical about death
> and it has made you believe bitter things
> about your friends. ("A Bit of Bitterness" *Blood and Bone* 43)

So, the only conviction the speaker convincingly retains is the belief that he is "the already dead," while surrounded by people he is alienated from: "Their faces are too many and too close" (*Blood and Bone* 43). I believe that one of the reasons for Hodgins remaining in this kind of melancholic grief can be causally linked to Little and Sayers' explanation that:

> cancer impairs personal autonomy, frequently reduces competencies, cuts across the sense of continuity on which identity depends, alters relationships between the self and its containing body, and threatens the meaning of an imagined future. (*The Skull Beneath* 195)

The threat that Hodgins's cancer poses to his immediate future is again darkly realised in "Ich Bin Allein" which poignantly translates his recurring sense of aloneness as he deals with cancer contaminating every aspect of his life: "It is in every part. Nothing can be cut off or out" (*Blood and Bone* 44). In response to a body that is breeding its own demise, he says, "I will find out how much pain is in this body" and "I will not behave myself" (*Blood and Bone* 44). Yet despite the gestured rebellion, there is no fully enacted protest staged, only the resignation that his wretched body

> ... isn't fit for poetry
> but since
> poets create their own mythology
> there is no choice. (*Blood and Bone* 44)

While Hodgins notes that he has an impulsive recourse to write poetry about his illness, he does not represent writing as a means for transcending grief as the poem's final lines toll his forlorn observation: "My friends have all gone home. / I'm in the dank half-light. I am alone" (44). Hodgins draws again on the trope that his diseased body is one existing in morbid isolation. In her work on the transfigured body, Amanda Nettelbeck writes of the "the change from the known body into one made unfamiliar by illness" and how this challenges "a previously unconsidered conception of the body as the primary site and guarantor of individual autonomy" (164) when the whole body is disease-ridden by its own blood. Hodgins continues to circulate this kind of reading of his body as one that is losing its autonomy, and also marked by social rejection.

In her influential essay *Powers of Horror*, Julia Kristeva explains that her reading of the abject is linked to the human reaction a person has when meaning is threatened by the loss of distinguishable boundaries between the self (subject) and other (object). Her principal illustration of this is the reaction/horror a person would experience when first looking at a corpse. In such an encounter, the trauma of directly confronting human materiality heightens a person's feeling of vulnerability as the perception of stable and protective borders comes under active threat. As Kristeva notes, "The corpse, seen without God and outside of science, is the utmost of abjection. It is death infecting life. Abject" (4). This breakdown of boundaries, where a sense of order is disrupted by the anarchic and the transgressing of borders in the body, is particularly evidenced in Hodgins's recurring fear that the demarcations between the oppositional states of health / disease and life / death are now conflated. Jackie Stacey, in *Teratologies: A cultural study of cancer,* makes the observation that "The abject ... is both separate from, and yet part of, the subject" (76), and this is particularly the case for Hodgins as his cancer cannot be physically excised as it is a disease of the blood.

So, for Hodgins, and his reader, the unrestricted presence of leukaemia becomes "a constant reminder of the mutability of our borders and the vulnerability of the subject" (Stacey 76). The prevailing sense of personal vulnerability and bodily defilement Hodgins talks of in his poetry feeds his melancholic apprehension that pervasive contamination, and his inability to contain his disease and "leaking blood", is what expels and excludes him from the social. An observation from Anne McClintock, though her work directly relates to race, gender, sexuality and British imperialism, still usefully describes the process that Hodgins experiences when she writes of the cultural and social effects of abjection: "The abject is everything the subject seeks to expunge in order to become social; it is also a symptom of the failure of this ambition" (71). Hodgins is well aware of the fact that he cannot expunge his disease. Even when he wants physically to leave his material surroundings to travel overseas, his cancerous blood sabotages this prospect in the poem "Trip Cancelled" (*Blood and Bone* 47). The word "trip" suggestive of all the possibilities of him existing / escaping elsewhere, is immediately revoked by the word "cancelled". Temporarily, Hodgins enacts a defence strategy of trying to suspend time while the doctor talks to him of death:

> but what I thought of was a day
> back on the dappled farm beneath
> the peppertree a life ago. (*Blood and Bone* 47)

But any transcendental reverie can only be temporary as Hodgins's consciousness is interrupted by "The words of death" being "all too clear. / I write this poem dumb with fear" (*Blood and Bone* 47). Unable to re-write or transform the loss that this residual sense of susceptibility registers, he remains in a state of discursive abjection. And it is in this way the poem points again to the impossibility of converting his melancholia into mourning. His bleak existential position is extended in the poem following entitled "Apologies" where he writes:

> I'll hate this death
> because it gives the meaning back
> to words I never thought I'd have to use.
> I can't explain. The words
> are plain, the images obvious—
> "This was the last work. Notice the crows." (*Blood and Bone* 48)

By employing traditional imagery of crows as harbingers of death, Hodgins indexes the reduced status he affords his body; human flesh no longer dignified and soon to be carrion for birds. There is no inventive depiction of a body nourished or enveloped by loving relational bonds in his illustration, only the remote and dehumanised landscape of refuse. Kauffman provides an insight into the kind of psyche that would cause Hodgins to narrate such an exilic view of dying: "Death and the bond broken by death can be experienced as devaluing the self" (3). As with shame and melancholia, such an experience Kauffman argues can disconnect "a person from the social world and from oneself" (3).

One might argue that Hodgins's disassociated descriptions of his loss of bodily function and the melancholic voice used in this poem to denounce his diminishing selfhood demonstrates the levels of perceived abandonment that dominate his thinking. The notion of him feeling sick to the bone assists the framing of his body as a signifier of refuse. Such a concept is particularly emphasised in "The Passenger" where cancer is analogous to a parasitic embryo that has inhabited, and is growing inside, his body:

> It is a passenger.
> I feel it
> in my marrow—
> lurching and kicking.
>
> Sometimes I think I feel it grow. (*Blood and Bone* 50)

Hodgins knows that this particular "birth will bring me to a corpse" (*Blood and Bone* 50). The confronting image of his rapid conversion of living flesh into a dead body highlights Hodgins's thanatological preoccupation. His melancholic thinking also increasingly tarnishes his view of the natural world. In the poem "From County Down", death's trace is figured in every scene. While the recurring reference to crows makes him "think of mortality" (*Blood and Bone* 51), so do other birds in his critical ken:

> ... Those swans
> are bits of rubbish on the lake
> and I will be not suffering a late death. (*Blood and Bone* 51)

Hodgins's metaphor of the swan song suggests that he is fully aware of a reduced capacity to use poetic language as a means of surpassing the invasive threat of a premature death. The solemnity of this is underscored in this poem by his inscription of the Latin phrase *Timor mortis conturbat me*, frequently translated as "the fear of death disturbs me" (*Blood and Bone* 51). This phrase, commonly used in Medieval literature, moves from an esoteric reference to Hodgins's colloquialised grief: "I never wanted this" (*Blood and Bone* 51). And, noticeably absent again is a consoling postscript. However, this is not Hodgins's last word on what writing poetry might ultimately offer him—and his readers.

Writing as Epitaph

It is important to note that in one of his later poems entitled "Resurrection" Hodgins does momentarily consider the possible therapeutic effects of words. The faces from his past looking at him in a hospital room make him "want to throw my words around" (*Blood and Bone* 52). Yet there is confounding sense as he says that

> I don't know what I've lost.
> The possibilities are over there
> amongst the things that need belief.
> And what is here is unbelievable
> and hard to explain. (*Blood and Bone* 52)

He is continually reduced to the knowledge that in some way his pain "ensures [its] unsharability through its resistance to language" (Scarry 4). But it seems that Hodgins is less resigned to that point in this particular instance, and towards the end of the poem he makes an incremental move away from a total dissatisfaction with language as a medium to explicate his suffering to an anticipation that it might play a role in legacy building. In a measured invocation Hodgins gestures language's insistence to outlive his diseased body:

> These are my physical thoughts,
> and this is my undrinkable blood.
> The thoughts are not my own
> and the blood is making me write
> letters in verse. (*Blood and Bone* 52)

This representation of his blood writing as a visceral compulsion of poem-making signals the newly considered idea by Hodgins that his abject physical body *might* be (re)rendered as a more enduring textual one. Here, the impulse of writing "letters in verse" is not so much about the completion of any work of mourning as it is about the possibility of melancholia enabling some form of memorialisation. For the first time in *Blood and Bone* the reader finds a tentative suggestion that Hodgins might entertain the notion of the utility and durability of poetic inscription as a means of subverting permanent absence. He says:

> I like the way the letters
> might be read by anyone later on.
> I half believe that it's another way
> of coming back. (*Blood and Bone* 52-53)

But any sure confidence that writing poetry will definitely afford him an enduring textual presence is partially thwarted by his sense that time is running out:

> because contracting this serious disease
> gave me a subject on a mirrored plate
> but didn't give me time to find the words

even though they're short, familiar ones.
("Hotel Minerva" *Blood and Bone* 56)

That Hodgins's words will outlive his deteriorating body is by no means guaranteed. And interestingly this idea of a logocentric return from death is not potent enough to completely arrest the melancholic thoughts that continue to intrude. Another instance of Hodgins's ability to assert his agency as a writer is subverted by his vulnerability as a reader:

> ... even if there is a remission
> there is always a follow-up letter
> saying the cancer has started again,
> cancelling what the previous letter said.
> ("Bad News" *Blood and Bone* 59)

This space of repeated negation has shaped him into a vigilant translator of autothanatropic signs: "There's only one more letter to receive. / Perhaps it has already been dispatched" (*Blood and Bone* 59). Hodgins's reply to this final dispatch might be read as his last poem in the anthology which begins with a confession:

> There is so much uncertainty in this.
> Not only do my cells break all the rules—
> they leave me scratching for an epitaph.
> ("The Shortlist" *Blood and Bone* 60)

Words that will live beyond death do not seem to be at his ready disposal. When the inspiration for his inventory does arrive it is through bearing witness to the death of a man whose hospital bed is across the corridor from his. The patient in the room opposite, diagnosed with same disease as Hodgins, performs a prophetic role: "Because his blood had shifted to acute / I had a view of what I would become" (*Blood and Bone* 60). Perhaps because the groaning man is unconscious, Hodgins duly notes, "the words he knew by heart were pain and death" (*Blood and Bone* 60). He also acknowledges that the same two words "pain" and "death" dictate his own "shortlist", and the reader recognises them as the repeated and repeating melancholic motifs of *Blood and Bone*.

In the last lines of "The Short List" Hodgins finally constructs the epitaph that he has been "scratching" for: "That pain will make my life a simple thing, / and death will take the things I didn't own" (*Blood and Bone* 60). He makes no concession that his poems as epitaphs will ever transpose his fear of losing, or that language will ever truly compensate or console his grief of a premature absence. He acknowledges this melancholic impasse as something that appears "insurmountable."[3] When in the process of dying, it is as Hodgins suggests: impossible to write beyond "the quiet stasis of fear" ("Insomnia" *Blood and Bone* 19). Yet despite Hodgins's intransigent sorrow, he does continue to write *towards* something; the something (or someone) maybe imagined as the future readers of his poems. Perhaps even if Hodgins cannot envisage the kind of textual longevity that Nicholas Chare describes,[4] his readers can: "Writing, like the recordings of a human voice, always forms a leaving behind. It constitutes a process of separation, despite also comprising a technology of preservation" (73).

Unknown to Hodgins at the time he was "scratching for his epitaph" was the fact that he would live another twelve years and produce several other volumes of preserved work.[5] Yet, in his final anthology titled *Things Happen* the reader (re)encounters the palinodic presence—a (re)singing over—of Hodgins's tenacious use of autothanatropic language which is best exemplified in the poem "Wordy Wordy Numb Numb" (*Things Happen* 55):[6]

> Death.
> Now there's a word.
> He wrote it down. (*Things Happen* 55)

Again, Hodgins is not just thinking about his death, he is still actively and unflinchingly *writing* it:

> He couldn't remember
> the first time he'd heard it.
> It seemed to have been always there ... (*Things Happen* 55)

For him, there is no transcendent escape to be occasioned through language, only the unremitting embodiment of his disease:

> Later on, when words had passed,
> he backed it up
> by dying. (*Things Happen* 56)

While Hodgins's laconic turn of phrase refuses to embellish his imminent death, it is precisely his pared down aesthetics to which the reader is so powerfully drawn. What is also present is the potential for a double reading of his statement "when the words had passed." In my view, Hodgins is not just simply or singularly lamenting the transience of telling, because the notion of "the passing of words" also strongly conjures the idea of a literary inheritance; that indeed *his* words can, and will, be "passed" onto those who continue to read his poems. In this way, Hodgins's melancholic wrestle with language might be symbolically reinscribed as a legacy where his poetic invocation ultimately offers a textual consolation of a pattern of words other than death:

> "sun, moon, tree, bread, wine, house, love ... "
> (*Things Happen* 56)

Notes

1. I acknowledge here that Senn is writing across Hodgins's oeuvre whilst my primary focus is on Blood and Bone which, to me, represents his first visceral contemplations and protests about dying so young. However, it is important to also note Hodgins's capacity for wry and humorous observation as Senn so effectively summarises about Hodgins's corpus: "Wit and humour are dominant strategies in Hodgins's texts. They appear in flashes in many instances and enable the writer to keep self-pity and despair at bay – though not necessarily enabling self-transcendence" (240). However, the strategies of wit and humour seem to be somewhat overshadowed by the melancholic fixity on death in *Blood and Bone*.
2. Gilbert argues in *Death's Door: Modern Dying and the Ways We Grieve* that a traumatic event like September 11 is an example where "death's door swings so publicly and dramatically open that we can't look away" (XV11).
3. Though not writing about Hodgins's poetry, Jay Prosser in "A Palinode on Photography and the Transsexual Real" writes of melancholic thinking as "insuperable" and "inconvertible" (249).
4. I note here the particular context of Nicholas Chare's work which reappraises the Kristevan view of abjection and the value of this concept when studying Holocaust testimonies. While the comments that I have cited specifically links to ideas on witnessing and representation of the Holocaust, I find Chare's concept of "a technology of preservation" a helpful one in relation to Hodgins leaving something behind in the form of his published poetry.
5. As a way of acknowledging the beauty and power of Hodgins's writing and his significant literary contribution, in 1997 his peers instituted The Philip Hodgins Memorial Medal which is awarded annually to a highly regarded Australian writer.
6. What Hodgins' sings over again in the poetry of *Things Happen* is "his body's palinode" symbolised by the excruciating comprehension: "My half a bucketful of blood/is filled with rumours of an early death ..." (*Blood and Bone* "A Palinode" 6).

Works Cited

Altmann, Cathy. "'To Use a Metaphor at a Time Like This Would Be Obscene': A Study of Cancer, Poetry and Metaphor." *Colloquy*, vol. 15, 2008, pp. 7-35.

Blanchot, Maurice. *The Work of Fire*, translated by Charlotte Mandell,

Stanford University Press, 1995.
Chare, Nicholas. *Auschwitz and Afterimages: Abjection, Witnessing and Representation*. I.B. Tauris, 2011.
Clewell, Tammy. "Mourning and Melancholia: Freud's Psychoanalysis of Loss." *Journal of the American Psychoanalytic Association*, vol. 52, no.1, 2004, pp. 43-67.
Derrida, Jacques. *The Work of Mourning*. edited by Pascale-Anne Brault and Michael Naas, The University of Chicago Press, 2001.
---. *Learning to Live Finally: The Last Interview*. Translated by Pascale-Anne Brault and Michael Naas, Melville House Publishing, 2007.
Egan, Susanna. *Mirror Talk. Genres of Crisis in Contemporary Autobiography*, University of North Carolina Press, 1999.
Freud, Sigmund. "Timely Reflections on War and Death." *On Murder, Mourning and Melancholia*, translated by Shaun Whiteside, Penguin books, 2005, pp. 167-194.
---. "Mourning and Melancholia." *On Murder, Mourning and Melancholia*, translated by Shaun Whiteside, Penguin books, 2005, pp. 201-218.
Gilbert, Sandra M. *Death's Door: Modern Dying and the Ways We Grieve*, W.W. Norton & Company, 2006.
Hodgins, Philip. *Blood and Bone*, Angus and Robertson Publishers, 1986.
---. *Things Happen*, HarperCollins, 1995.
James, Clive. "The Meaning of Recognition." *Australian Book Review*, vol. 254, 2003, pp. 21-29.
Kauffman, Jeffrey, Editors. *The Shame of Death, Grief and Trauma*, Routledge, 2010.
Kristeva, Julia. *Powers of Horror: An Essay on Abjection*, translated by Leon. S Roudiez, Columbia University Press, 1982.
---. *Black Sun: Depression and Melancholia*, translated by Leon S. Roudiez, Columbia University Press, 1989.
Little, Miles, and Emma-Jane Sayers. "The Skull beneath the Skin: Cancer Survival and Awareness of Death." *Psycho-Oncology*, vol. 13, 2004, pp. 190-98.
McClintock, Anne. *Imperial Leather: Race, Gender and Sexuality in the*

Colonial Contest, Routledge, 1996.

Nettelbeck, Amanda. "The Transfigured Body and the Ethical Turn in Australian Illness Memoir." *Journal of Medical Humanities*, 29 (2008), pp.163-72.

Phillips, Adam. *Darwin's Worms*, Faber and Faber, 1999.

Prosser, Jay. "A Palinode on Photography and the Transsexual Real." *Extremities: Trauma, Testimony and Community*, edited by Nancy K. Miller and Jason Tougaw, University of Illinois Press, 2002, pp. 238-259.

Ricoeur, Paul. *Living up to Death*, translated by David Pellauer, The University of Chicago Press, 2009.

Ryan, Brendan. "Vulnerable landscapes: pastoral in the poetry of Philip Hodgins." *Antipodes*, vol. 15, no.1 2001, pp. 26-30.

Scarry, Elaine. *The Body in Pain: The Making and Unmaking of the World*, Oxford University Press, 1985.

Secomb, Linnell. "Autothanatography." *Mortality*, vol. 7, 2002, pp. 33-46.

Senn, Werner. "Voicing the Body: The Cancer Poems of Philip Hodgins." *Bodies and Voices: The Force-Field of Representation and Discourse in Colonial and Post-Colonial Studies*, edited by Meret Falck Borch et al., Rodopi, 2008, pp. 237-249.

Sontag, Susan. *Illness as Metaphor and Aids and Its Metaphors*. Penguin, 1991.

Stacey, Jackie. *Teratologies: A Cultural Study of Cancer*, Routledge, 1997.

Stamelman, Richard. *Lost Beyond Telling: Representations of Death and Absence in Modern French Poetry*, Cornell University Press, 1990.

Taylor, Andrew. "'To Love That Well': Poetry and Autopathography." *Westerly*, vol. 52, 2007, pp. 63-76.

Watkin, William. *On Mourning: Theories of Loss in Modern Literature*, Edinburgh University Press, 2004.

Chapter 13

"But with a general groan": Public and Private Voices in Jordie Albiston and Melinda Smith's poetry

TEGAN SCHETRUMPF

It is no easy task to construct a voice, or voices, that speak to contemporary Australian readers, given the micro-politics of the Australian millennial poetry scene. Since the inception of the Poetry Wars in 1968, many poetic subsets are encamped somewhere between the flags of more traditional lyrical poetry, and the avant-garde descendants of L=A=N=G=U=A=G=E poets. Keri Glastonbury describes these demarcations, bundled together to face the cultural, economic and digital pressures that seem always to be threatening poetry's existence, as "a UNESCO city of literature" (223). This analogy aptly conveys the range of voices, tones and registers that would be required to speak to Australian poetry audiences as a whole.

Jordie Albiston and Melinda Smith are two notable examples of poets without fixed camps, tenacious enough to achieve critical and public success by employing a diverse range of voices. As writers, they are something like spiders: relying on craft and formal skills, even while taking experimental leaps, building textual webs that span the niches between ecologies of poetry, and inhabiting the overlap between public and private textual spaces. Each poet has therefore ensnared a diverse assortment of readers: Jordie Albiston, a Melbourne academic and prolific poet, debuted with *Nervous Arcs* (1995), which won the Mary Gilmore Award, while *Botany Bay Document: A Poetic History of the Women of Botany Bay* (1996) and *The*

Hanging of Jean Lee (1998) were adapted into musical performances that have played at the Sydney Opera House, suggesting their wide appeal. Albiston's study of music is further evident in *Vertigo: A Cantata* (2007), featured on ABC's Radio National. *the sonnet according to 'm'* (2010) won the NSW Premier's Award, and her most recent collection, *Euclid's Dog* (2017) was shortlisted for Premiers' prizes in New South Wales and Queensland. Canberran poet, Melinda Smith, has published five collections, including her debut, *Pushing thirty, wearing seventeen* (2001), the ArtsACT-funded chapbook, *First… Then….:Poems From Planet Autism* (2012), and *Drag Down to Unlock or Place an Emergency Call* (2013), which won the Prime Minister's Literary Award. Smith is also known for collaborative poetry and art projects that encourage audience interaction. Both poets have backgrounds in historical studies: Smith describes herself on her website as an "ex-PhD student in Japanese history". Similarly, Albiston abandoned a PhD involving archival research into Australia's colonial history, from which *Botany Bay Document* arose. It is perhaps their mutual interest in stories that yoke humans together that imbues their poetry with appeal and relevance. Indeed, through a range of public and private voices, both Albiston and Smith pursue 'realness' via historical documentation and confession of personal experience.

Yet, an imagined public voice for the twenty-first century would surely veer away from "realness" into the insubstantialities of present human experience: the banality of textspeak and social media jargon, and the consumerist drive that saturates millennial culture. However, the potential irony of our "on-demand" engagement with the digital tide of un-cached and largely, unstructured information is dissatisfaction with virtuality, transience, instability and "fakeness" – Australia's recent political and economic precarity bolstering this perception. Voices, texts and experiences that are perceived to be "authentic" or "real" may soothe such cultural dissatisfaction – from the steadying chronology of researching one's historical locus via Ancestry.com, to reading or writing poetry that utilises narrative or traditional rhyming forms that foster cultural continuity. Of course, "authenticity" is problematic in postmodern contexts – its positive connotations of tradition and veracity are undercut by the term's implied need for sanction by an authority. The title of this essay references *Hamlet's* Rosencrantz, who makes several reiterations of the idea that "Never alone / did the king sigh, but with a general groan" (Shakespeare 1094). As he speaks in the court, cravenness and a borrowed air of pomposity makes his voice iterative, since Rosencrantz is not really a free participant in the action – just the tool of a corrupt king. Likewise, not all offers of "authenticity" are authentic – dominant mediums such as reality television and social media encourage users to believe that they are participating in a "real" text, yet their engagement – and the text itself – are often manipulated behind the scenes. While the consequences of being duped into voting for a reality-television star are no more than an overpriced SMS, other offers of "reality", such as a return to "real Aussie values" made by xenophobic groups like "Reclaim Australia" are potentially more harmful.

To their credit, Albiston and Smith's poetic voices balance an engagement with the postmodern condition of language and culture with the reader's desire for "authentic" experiences, hybridising an experimental interest in poetic space, gaps within lines and semiotics, with traditional lyrical poetry elements, including rhyme, narrative, imagery and an attention to sound or musicality. Albiston is known for employing traditional forms, such as sonnet sequences, cinquains and chain verse, yet her interest in archival research and biography also connects her to avant-garde poetry. During the University of Sydney's Experimental Poetics Symposium, Jessica Wilkinson, fellow poet and academic, presented a paper on Albiston where poetic practices related to listing, cataloguing, and archival materials – which are analogous to the collage work of "found objects" in the visual arts – were considered intrinsically experimental (Wilkinson 2014). Emulating sources such as government records, school report cards, newspapers, diary entries, ship logs, and family documents, Albiston moves between a variety of text-type registers and vernacular associated with the public and private voices of her poetic subject – demonstrating the power of language to frame the individual. In *the Hanging of Jean Lee*, the predetermined fate of Jean Lee – Australia's last woman to receive the death penalty – is foreshadowed by the alliterative opening lines of "Birth Column":

> Dark delivery in dinky-di
> Dubbo   a red-haired cherub
> with waxen wings   born (3)

Albiston's spacing within the line and her syntax phrase the poem into two readings – first, the musical cadence: "a red-haired cherub with waxen wings", then the lineation, "with waxen wings   born". The first phrasing offers a lyrical juxtaposition between the innocence of the childlike choir of angels and the fall of Icarus, prefiguring Jean's fall from grace. The second phrasing spatially isolates the word "born" and anticipates its antonym – the death that made Jean Lee known to history. The vernacular "dinky-di" meaning authentic or "truly Australian" is undermined by the phrase's sing-song quality, and the mention of Jean's red hair alludes to the contextual belief that redheads were troublemakers – generally believed to reflect prejudice against Irish convicts. The final stanza of the poem echoes the banal, formulaic language of a newspaper column:

> Send your congrats
>
> and best wishes to our
> latest arrival   mother
> and daughter   both well (3)

Society's bland "best wishes" for the health of women behaving traditionally, as mothers or baby daughters, are sharply contradicted by the public censure and fervent media interest directed toward female criminals, prostitutes and murderesses – Jean Lee was allegedly all three. In the later poem, "Interrogation", heightened language and irregular spacing represent Lee's fractured thinking when the public voice of her old Catholic school prayers is interrupted by frantic realisations:

> Hail Holy Mother   There is no Mary
> Our Father Which art   There is no God
> Christ Almighty there's no more Bonnie
>
> or Clyde   Faith falls like scales from
> my Catholic eyes (5)

Lee's sudden disbelief in the biblical figures of her youth and in the media glamour of American criminals, Bonnie and Clyde, invites a cynical reflection upon the reader's own interest in the figure of Jean Lee, and the ease with which historical or fictional women are relegated to Madonna / whore dichotomies. Albiston's poetic voice is at once public and private. In an interview with Kate Middleton about *Botany Bay Document* and *The Hanging of Jean Lee,* Albiston noted, "For me, those last two books are about me as much as they're about the subject at hand: I see it as a question of metaphoricity, and in the case of a full-length book concerning one person, event or theme, the metaphor is simply extended." Refuting any political or feminist impulse in her attention to the biographies of women, Albiston claims, "I write about women because I am one." Whether or not her interest in Lee is pointedly feminist, Albiston locates value in voicing the otherwise unrepresented or lost experiences of non-privileged individuals. Her poems present stories of individuals whose voices are circumscribed by their social or historical moment – a category that is easily populated by women.

Smith has a similar interest in the way the public voices of a culture can privilege or predetermine the fate of an individual. In the opening poem of *Pushing Thirty, Wearing Seventeen,* Smith uses Australian vernacular to playfully describe high school footballers who are lauded and privileged, but ultimately circumscribed individuals. "Legends" is tonally akin to doggerel, ironising the Australian public voice of praise for sport:

> Rowdy, Chooka, Simmo, Roo,
> PJ, Wardy, Macca too –
> they strode the playground, bronzed and tall:
> heroes, lions, legends all. (7)

The fates of these "legends" are less than glamorous: dying in car-crashes, becoming abattoir workers, or being sidelined to barracking for "Dave and Bevan / in the mortal clash of the under-sevens" (8) which evokes a pitying sort of humour. Yet a darker evocation of football as a legitimisation of male violence is offered in the later poem, "Wake Up Call", when the persona wakes up to her alarm clock radio:

> And then I heard another voice
> behind the *isolated showers* –
> a man – or lots of men? – far off.
> It sounds like footy training. (32)
>
> [...]
> WAAAKE UUUP!!!!
> Youse fucken soft-cocks
> WAAAKE UUUP!!!!
> I'll fucken kill the lot of youse
> Come out, youse cunts
> I'll take you all fucken on (32)

The voices intrude on the private space of the persona's bedroom – the weatherman's familiar phraseology, and the violent phallocentric language of the individual outside. The latter register is also a familiar public voice – according to the simile "it sounds like footy training"

– yet in the private space it becomes even more threatening as "his voice / still shakes the walls" (33). The persona calls the police:

> [...] Someone bored
> picks up the phone: 'Location please.'
> I start, but then he interrupts.
> 'Yeah, unidentified young male
> at Murdoch Street, we've been informed –
> car's on its way.' (33)

The indifferent, bureaucratic register of the police response suggests Australia's cultural complacency regarding male aggression, and contributes to the banality of public voices already established by the abuse and the radio. Yet this tone is contradicted by the arrival of active police, who "solve" the problem with yet more aggression:

> [...] Others, now,
> are firing questions, barking orders –
> circling round the first. The cops
> have come. (34)

The predatory imagery of the police "circling" complements the violent verb choices of "firing" and "barking" which suggest police brutality by connoting gunfire – literally or as phallic symbolism – and the pack mentality of dogs. The persona concludes with a rhetorical question: "what other end did I expect?" (34) which intimates the expectation of violence quivering beneath the sporting celebration of aggressive masculinity, and critiques Australian culture which encourages ultra-aggressiveness, then can only respond to what it has created with more dominating behaviour.

Public voices of dominance and privilege are also critiqued in Albiston's *Vertigo: a cantata*. The musical term "cantata" derives from the Italian feminine verb "to sing", and Albiston's multi-voiced poetic version is comprised of recitatives, arias and choruses. Informed by her study of music at the Victorian College of the Arts, Albiston's language play is often suggestive of musical cadences, where sonic devices create rhythm, and the spaced gaps between words indicate rests in the musical score. In *Vertigo*, musicality becomes explicit through the use of musical signifiers, such as barlines and repeat bars, to structure the poetry. Although the narrative is evidently about a contemporary break-up, since the protagonist "packs up her laptop picks up her dog" (7), the wordplay revolves around dominant male Eurocentric voices and references associated with high or classical culture. For example, the recitative "Amaroso" is named for a musical directive: the Italian masculine adverb "to be played lovingly". However, for non-musical Australian readers, it is difficult to divorce the term from the sexual connotations of "amorous" – a connection that is borne out in the poem's close:

> look | even the
> poem is | masculine now: mouthing out
> metaphors one by one | tongue in my
> ear | hand on my thigh! arms astretch
> in muscular lines | I am not inclined || (6)

The double entendre, "I am not inclined" both suggests Albiston's lack of interest in having her poetry overtaken by unsubtle "masculine" language or rhythms, and her lack of sexual submission, since "inclined" can also mean "willingness" or that one is bending over. Another recitative, similarly titled with a masculine musical directive, "Apassionato", describes a Heathcliff-esque Romantic hero:

> he thundered out! of a wild July | sweet
> froth flicking from his steed's hot flesh
> his hollering thrown like | punches to the
> sky his mouth a noose-formed Munch!
> [...]   I
> suppose you thought if he came at all

he would sneak up | stealthily! whisper
seductively! [...]
                    but | No! it was always
violent & nights were worst with him (8)

Aside from satirising the desirability of this species of masculinity, the allusion to the O-shaped mouth of the central figure in Munch's painting, *The Scream*, critiques Romantic perceptions as a kind of violence of privilege, their idealising prescription of nature upheld by a non-inclusive literary canon: the figure is not screaming, but responding to the primitive scream of Nature itself. It is possible to discern Australia's sense of cultural inadequacy underneath Albiston's high culture references, either due to its subordination to overseas literary and cultural practices, or simply arising from contempt for the contemporary. In the following "Aria #7" the fallibility of Eurocentric, patriarchal voices is explored through Shakespearean allusion: "the old Lear sea intoned / in peaks its certainty of change | " (15). The motif continues, "today the sea is brainwashed" (15) until Albiston's ocean spectacularly crashes into the transience and open-ended nature of the digital contemporary:

                              we
mouthed *forever* and knew that we would always

all ways be complete (ah! better delete that final
bit: delete | delete | delete | delete | delete) || (15)

The persona's desire to delete the final lines represents the self-conscious need to censor, or at least ironise, the voicing of sentiment that is forbidden by postmodern cynicism, though it was permissible, even exalted in earlier literary traditions. The lines also require deleting because they are inaccurate: the couple have broken up. In this instance, and others in Albiston's poetry, the desired metaphysical meaning and the less-than-desirable social circumscription enshrined in literary traditions are grappled with, the resulting cognitive dissonance represented in her voice by postmodern fragmentation.

Digital writing technologies don't always represent limitation or censorship to Albiston, however; indeed, during her interview with ABC Radio National, she described the digital screen as essential to her writing process: "Computer itself is a very important medium for me ... you can go as far up or down or sideways as you want to, and so there's no fear of the edges of the page ... there's a real liberty there, which the page doesn't afford me." Albiston's lax employment of capitalisation and punctuation, and her use of Roman numerals and the ampersand (&) associate her writing with the avant-garde. L=A=N=G=U=A=G=E poets have long been interested in challenging the representational quality of language this way, and during Albiston's pursuit of her PhD in literature, she studied with J.S. Harry, who may have influenced Albiston's typographic choices. Yet Albiston's engagement with semiotic signifiers is also reminiscent of digital or online voices. Her use of the "hashtag" (#) to denote "number" in her titles tinges her poems with ambiguity, since the same symbol is used in online tagging, and, in a musical context, signifies a "sharp" or sombre-toned accidental. Albiston's constant shifting between traditional and contemporary registers is evident in the collective voice of "Chorus #4":

> we have prayed to
> the *and* and the *ampersand* | have
>
> walked over water and swum over
> land just to make sure we're alive | (38)

The self-conscious pun suggests the role of public, perhaps *published*, voices in seeking balance or mediation between literary traditions, and the banalities of the postmodern digital. According to John Leonard Press, *Vertigo*'s chorus, "spoken by a barely determinate 'we'

– descants upon displacement as human experience, and the mystery of recovery." Like the chorus of citizens in Greek drama, Albiston's chorus moralises, warns against extremism, and acts as a witness.

The dramatic monologues of Smith's *First…Then…:Poems From Planet Autism* also enact this chorus function, meshing individual perspectives into a collective which approximates the "truth" of autism, which her foreword describes as "a world which is often misunderstood, misrepresented, or ignored." Many poems are reframings of first-hand accounts proffered by individuals active in autism communities on Twitter and Facebook (Smith, n.d). Fragmented lineation and varied uses of poetic space coincide with traditional poetic forms to convey a range of autism experiences. Other poems, from Smith's own perspective, describe her family's struggle after discovering her son's autism. In the titular poem, "First… then…" her son's voice is represented in italics:

> *First stop biting Mummy*
> *Then play with sliding door*
> *First poo *in toilet**
> *Then flush*
> […]
> First joking about 'our little Rain Man'
>   Then realising the joke was on me
>
> First paralysis
>   Then fear
>
> First incomprehension
>   Then overload (10)

Smith's emotional processing of her son's autism happens in steps, suggested by the indented structure of the "First, Then" anaphora. Ironically, her responses – paralysis, fear, incomprehension, and overload – are not dissimilar to some autistic responses to new stimuli. Smith's blend of lyrical poetic devices and language play is significant in the voicing of autistic experiences for non-autistic audiences, since many on the autistic spectrum struggle with aspects of verbal and non-verbal communication. For example, the metaphoric use of synaesthesia conveys the severity of the child's experience in the poem, "Autistic Child with Acute Auditory Processing Disorder", the clinical voice of the title reflecting the inadequacy of medical jargon to describe lived experience:

> [...] *there's a dryer, there's a dryer*
> any second now, someone will set it off
> the sound will be a faceful of boiling water (16)

Smith's poetry speaks in markedly contemporary registers, reflecting semiotic signifiers popularised by digital communication, such as the use of asterisks for emphasis. This is perhaps accounted for by her strong engagement with digital spaces which are simultaneously – and problematically – public and private. Smith "Tweets", has a Facebook account, a personal blog and a website: *Melinda Smith's Mull and Fiddle*, while Albiston has neither social media accounts, nor a professional website. Indeed, one could speculate that Albiston's positive experience of digital writing is due to her less-than-saturated engagement with it. Smith's fluency in digital languages is flaunted in her engagement with "flarf" – poetry constructed from search engine results – and her titling of poems with "hashtag" digital taglines such as "#autismshirtslogans". There is a satirical sting in these allusions that suggests Smith's resentment of the intrusion of such banal language into the human psyche: for instance, the blatant commercialism of the flarf fragment in "I have autism: Google-sculpture 1":

> [...] MTV dares to
> impress with **'I Have Autism'**. The presentation details
> the lives of three very inspiring young men who all have

differing... (41)

The banal bureaucratic language of public rules is similarly critiqued in the close of "Social Stories for Neurotypical Adults #27: No Dogs Allowed":

> I will try to remember to do what the signs say.
> Smart grown-ups obey signs. (29)

Smith's poetry often engages in political or social critique, probably because it is largely audience-focused: previously, the tagline of Smith's website identified her poetic aims as: "educating, informing and entertaining ... but mostly entertaining" (Smith). Her externalised poetic stance may relate to her practice of workshopping with Suzanne Edgar, Michael Thorley, and Martin Dolan, and her prior participation in Canberra's Closet Poets (Smith). Like Albiston, Smith's poetry illuminates the trespasses of public voices that circumscribe private experiences; however, Smith is more blatant in her approach. For example, whilst Albiston evades the title of "feminist", Smith jokes on her website, "My name is an anagram of 'Dismantle Him.' Read into that what you will" (*Mull*). Smith follows this with a hyperlink to a website where readers can make anagrams of their own names, underlining Smith's interest in wordplay, recurrence, riddling, and inclusivity.

Voices of recurrence or with an iterative quality are a fixation for both poets, since repetition can breed either cliché or tension. The potential for individuals with autism, who are vulnerable to the vagaries of verbal and non-verbal communication, to be exploited is made explicit via repetitions in the villanelle, "What I learned at School":

> Again today he said he was my friend.
> He made me spin around 'til I was sick.
> So is that bullying, or just pretend?
> [...]

but after that he made me stand, and bend,
then poked me in the bottom with a stick
So is that bullying, or just pretend?

My teacher told me off: *This has to end.*
By now you should have wised up to this trick.'
Again today, he says he is my friend.
So is that bullying, or just pretend? (20)

The repeated lines of the villanelle dramatise and mimic the autistic child's reliance on structured and unambiguous communication, and their oscillation between competing uncertainties when dealing with others. This experience may perhaps translate readily for non-autistic individuals who struggle to interpret the open-endedness of postmodern texts and culture, and thus gravitate towards poetry that employs traditional or recognisable forms.

The contemporary significance of recurrence in traditional forms is explored further in Albiston's *the sonnet according to 'm'*. As its blurb intones:

> Recurrence is intrinsic to sonnets. They are patterned internally, and often written in series: a perfect form and formation for poems which worry the distinction between the fatal and banal.

The three voices of the sonnets – the three 'm's – are Albiston herself, her maternal grandmother, and her paternal great-grandmother. These poems give snapshots of the domestic concerns of the women, generations apart. The persona of "em (iv)" is Albiston's great-grandmother, and through her numeric listing, reflects Albiston's access to archival information:

first comes william in 55 who dies   then
little Ellen in 57 followed by annie (close
behind at beechworth 59)   this *glad dose
of daughters* would seem to have no end!
when emily then harriet continues the trend
& marion! makes number 5   add to those
one baby Florence   the 'final girl'   whose
birth occurs before the hearth *extends* at

last to boys   & then Great Joy!   another
william (fillan)   & walter arrive   (though
life being life   only six of the above will

survive)   (our emily skinner   as mother
& wife   continues the moments   *through
thick & thin*   holds onto each one   still) (18)

The Petrarchan sonnet form usually ends with a sestet, but is instead split into two three-line stanzas, each with their own volta. The first turn, "at last to boys" signifies the higher cultural value attributed to male babies. This is supported by the italicised verbal irony in *"glad dose of daughters"* and the emphatic capitalisation and exclamation, "Great Joy!" – where Albiston's usual bag of L=A=N=G=U=A=G=E tricks are employed to resemble Victorian typographic style. The final turn in the sonnet is the future tense declaration, "only six of the above will survive". Though ostensibly spoken by her great-grandmother, whose maternal experience confers this predictive ability, the voice is temporally layered by contemporary knowledge of Victorian infant mortality, and Albiston's additional certainty about which children lived to adulthood, due to her existence in the poem's future, which affords her access to family records. The sense of recurrence in these poems suggests the generative nature of women as mothers – indicated by the three generations of her family represented – but also the recurrence, within private voices and experiences, of universal human experiences. The public voice of cliché, *"through thick & thin"* used as a euphemism to cover the private, if commonplace, grief of losing a child, contrasts with the spacing of the final line: "holds on to each one   still" which creates a triple entendre: the mother continues to hold on to her children long after they have died; the child is imagined, unmoving, in her arms, and the evocation of the term "still birth".

There is Victorian repression evident in "em (iv)" – the impulse to hide unseemly grief – yet there can be a similar aversion among millennial poets to exposing the general community to private griefs, perhaps due to the blurring of public and private textual spaces on social media, where the confessional aspect of self-published voices may be considered crass or over-sharing. However, the "m" sonnets from Albiston's perspective convey a very different kind of confessional voice – one more aligned with the traditions of confessional poetry. In "Methinx (I)" and "Methinx (II)", Albiston borrows existential moments from Renaissance humanist literature – Macbeth's "Tomorrow" monologue, which responds to his wife's death, and scenes of real and feigned madness from *King Lear*:

> 2moro 2moro & 2moro
> goes slo frm day 2 day
> cos we dont talk   cos
> text sez wot we got 2 say

> th clox hav stopt th past
> is ded   th lite is off! off!
> @ last   & life goes fast
> 2 fast 2 liv & we go soft

> b4 we eva speak   o can
> u hear me calling u 2day
> 2day 2day 2day?   &
> r u lisnng   hear me say

ths lifes 2 short 4 a hero
(methinx it all means o) (21)

Despite Albiston's embrace of digital writing technologies, she seems sceptical about textspeak's ability to convey weighty human experiences. The persona's pessimism about the digital breakdown of human communication is contrasted with the evocation of Auden's sentiment in *Funeral Blues* "Stop all the clocks!". Textual layers complicate whether this is a public or private space, since Auden and Macbeth's private voices of grief were constructed to be published or performed. Albiston underscores her own confessed existential concerns about human experience in the twenty-first century with Macbeth's nihilistic ruminations on the abandonment of death rituals, the rapid passage of time, and his loss of continuity and meaning. In "Methinx (II)" a confessional voice is similarly borrowed from *King Lear*. Albiston's private voicing of mental illness is a patchwork of Edgar's feigning voice of Poor Tom – a type of half-mad, ecclesiastical beggar, familiar to Jacobean audiences, that shouts his sins in public places – and Lear himself, whose fragmented private voice is now openly uttered:

> wandering upon the suburban moors
> I am cut to th' brains again   o! When
> will th' moon shine through this poor
> head? *While you have your ransom*

> *let me have surgeons then*   let them
> slice through th' mire for their piece
> of th' pie let them operate ad infinitum
> for my mind doth burst with its species

> of madness   & madness doth spill
> from this mind   but while I'm alone
> I am not short on shrapnel   & will

> (if required) send forth stick & stone
> to combat th' front of this ill *I stand*
> *for nought* o! Edgar I nothing am (22)

Contemporary word choices such as "shrapnel" – used here as a colloquialism for money – and "suburban" signal that these voices are really Albiston engaging in metaphoricity. However, her confessional voice is obscured and perhaps made more private through convoluted references, including mathematical motifs. "[T]heir piece of th' pie" suggests Lear's division of his kingdom amongst his daughters, as in a pie chart, but also puns on the idea of Pi, the irrational number needed in circle geometry to find the circumference of a circle – which is also the shape of an 'O' or zero. Albiston builds on Shakespeare's own play with numeric signifiers: during his lifetime, the numeral zero was imported from Arabic mathematicians, and intrigued many a Renaissance wit; it was something that "stood for" nothing (The pun can be taken further, since Early Modern pronunciation makes "nothing" sound like an "O-thing"). Likewise, Edgar, who claims to be nothing, and pretends to be mad, eventually "stands" as a champion. In the play, these contradictions suggest appearances are deceptive; Alibston's references to them caution against simplistic readings of her poem. In fact, Alibston may be confessing to no more than an irrational drive that fuels her poetry – Pi is an irrational number, meaning it cannot be expressed as a fraction: if converted to decimals, however, the calculator will display a "recurring" decimal, which continues forever, or, "*ad infinitum*". Irrationality is also associated with excess by Socrates, in Plato's *Phaedrus*, who claims that poetry requires madness:

> But he who without the divine madness comes to the doors of the Muses, confident that he will be a good poet by art, meets with no success, and the poetry of the sane man vanishes into nothingness before that of the inspired madmen. (493)

Albiston's confessional voice, although published, is made more private through its encoding. That her poem can be read to signify performed madness or poetic inspiration links it to Plathian traditions that suggest a relationship between mental illness and confessional poetry. In her ABC Radio National interview, Albiston spoke about this connection: "I was born with a neurological sleep disorder, and intense insomnia has always played a very large role in my life. So I think the fact that I was quite melancholy as a child and have suffered quite severe depression as an adult has a direct connection … in fact my sleep doctor says that he thinks I became a poet because of my inability to dream." Albiston likens her poetry to the role of dreams in unpacking, sorting and structuring daily events, and it is possible that some of her technical brilliance stems from her thematic interest in recurrence. The cover of *The Book of Ethel* describes Albiston's poetry as "endeavouring to exact a mathematical sense of existence", and though it is a worthy collection in its own right, the collection traces similar territory to her previous books. *Cordite* reviewer, David Gilbey, highlights the recurrences that form Ethel, Albiston's maternal great grandmother, who began life in Cornwall and travelled to and around Australia as a minister's wife and writer:

> Individual squares of verse are like parts of a patchwork quilt… made from fragments of historical documents, letters, diaries and published articles and stories: Ethel Overend's actual works. As well, *The Book of Ethel* has several echoes of an Old Testament hagiography… the poems reposition a marginalised life and sensibility at the centre of the cultural canvas. Individual poems echo traditional lullabies and nursery rhymes in language richly infused with Cornish dialect (see glossary at the end: *gesyow* [joke] and *hwerdth* [sister] seemed almost onomatopoeic to me; *ydhyn* [bird] seemed delicate, melodious in the poem and *zack* [sixpence] was, I thought, an 'Australian' word which I learned as a migrant from England, arriving in Australia in 1960).

There is a mesmeric interlacing of confessional and historical voices in *the sonnet according to 'm'* and *The Book of Ethel*. The experiences of displacement and resilience of Albiston's ancestors resonate with her, with the experiences of Australian readers with migrant ancestry, and indeed, in the case of first-generation migrants like Gilbey, with their lived experiences. Likewise, the travel and return involved in Ethel's journey, and in Albiston's writer's residency in Cornwall, which facilitated *The Book of Ethel*, gives a "realness" to her depictions of the temporal and geographical recurrences in these personal histories, acknowledging the shared reality in voices that witness place.

A similar consideration of shared realities pervades Smith's poetry. Her best-known collection, *Drag Down to Unlock or Place an Emergency Call*, explores millennial tensions between public and private spaces, her poems traversing trains, courtrooms, hospitals, churches and Skype. The format of the collection is glibly arranged into website subheadings, while the collection's title references the smartphone prompt shown when the device is locked, which one must swipe past in order to engage in the act of communication – framing the collection as both banal and alarming. Smith adopts the often disembodied, yet authoritative, public voices of these spaces. For instance, in "Passengers are Reminded" pre-programmed Cityrail announcements intrude upon Smith's anxiety about being late for a funeral:

> This service is experiencing a slight delay due to a sick customer at Town Hall
> I have been carrying the lilies too long
> This service is experiencing continuing delays due to a sick customer at Town Hall
>
> the petal edges fray to a bruised brown, like old lettuce (2)

The euphemistic reference to a "sick customer" (2) glosses over the trauma being experienced by someone elsewhere, the recurrent announcements multiplying the tension of the locked-in space of the train, where the bruised, fraying edges of the flowers symbolise Smith's frayed nerves. In her more confessional poems, Smith's private voice functions as a challenge to the oppression of these authoritative public voices, including voices of stigma about mental illness – blatantly transgressed in poems like "Song of the Anti-depressant". Smith's confessional voice is thus a kind of "authenticity" utilised for public engagement and catharsis, providing a reading experience where fellow sufferers feel recognised, and non-sufferers may gain insight.

Likewise, Smith's sinister appropriation of hymns and children's songs in "Dialogue" exteriorise or "unlock" that which is hidden. It is perhaps an ironic testament to Smith that the poem, which relates the scene of a child being abused by a priest, is included in a collection endorsed by Tony Abbott, who, during his prime ministership, was publicly criticised for deflecting culpability from the Catholic church about this very issue (*The Guardian*):

you smell funny	incy wincy spider
I don't like that	here is my handle, here is my spout
where are my toys?	the Lord's my shepherd, I'll not want (59)

The use of poetic space distinguishes the two voices in the dialogue: the priest's voice is aligned right, the child's, left. The priest, as a figure of authority, speaks in a composite of borrowed public voices, using children's nursery rhymes to disguise and manipulate a child into sexualised behaviour. The small hand of the child is the "incy wincy spider" that "crawls up the water spout". The rhyme changes to "I'm a little teapot" where "here is my spout" encourages the child to touch the priest's penis. The voice then uses Psalm 23, which in this context reads that priests, who are looked after by the authority of God, will not "want" or go without sex.

The child's first statement, "let me out" (59) implies, figuratively or literally, that they are locked in a confessional box:

> I want to go home
> it's dark in here
> I can't feel my feet (59)

Perhaps the most chilling inclusion in the poem is the allusion to "For the Fallen" by British poet, Laurence Binyon, better known in Australia as the ode used in ANZAC day services. The phrase "we will remember them" (59) suggests an entire generation of children "lost" to sexual abuse, and reminds the reader that it is not merely the priest who is keeping the child trapped, but the complicit elements of the Australian public that choose not to voice dissent against religious authority.

The collection also recognises that not all confessional voices are voices of dissent – indeed, confession may disempower individuals in social or digital spheres, allowing them to be manipulated and exploited by data-mining corporations, exposing them to cyberbullying, or otherwise giving others leverage to use guilt or shame as an agent of control. These contemporary issues are best explored in "Confess":

> Information wants to be free
> Tell me
> Tell the priest
> *Pent up. Repent. Released.*
> *We the jury have found*
> Tell a hole in the ground
> Tell yourself
> *Stow the strongbox on the highest shelf*
> I won't breathe a word
> Tell a little bird
> Tell one person at a time
> *Victim, motive, weapon, crime*

> *Guilt by association*
> Tell the whole congregation
> Tell Big Brother
> *Beg forgiveness from each other*
> When push comes to shove
> Tell the one you love
> Tell whoever's in control
> *I promise not to tell a soul* (57)

The italics indicate a public voice or voices that have some dominion over the individual – "*Information wants to be free*" is a slogan attributed to writer Stewart Brand, who noted the paradox that information has a high value when conserved, but that, the more it circulates, the less valuable it becomes. The phrase has also been used in opposition to intellectual copyright or governments' national security agendas. Smith is concerned about the shifting notions of what is "public" and "private" in the digital era, where an individual's personal information is often circulated used or sold without the individual's awareness. Information's stated desire for freedom is therefore morally ambiguous, and in the context of the poem's many imperatives becomes a sinister and exploitative voice.

The reader is expected to identify with the "me" of the poem, and the voyeurism intrinsic to this digital culture of over-sharing, though Smith intimates that salacious confession is only exacerbated by the digital, not invented by it: the staccato process, "Tell the priest / *Pent up. Repent. Released*," reminds the reader that confession and public shaming cycles are recurrent in past and present closed communities. The collective public voice of the courtroom, "*We the jury*", invokes the confessor's judgment by their peers, the poem sifting through the layered voyeuristic, social, religious, literary and legal dimensions of the term "confession". Many of the seemingly straightforward directives require unpacking. Telling a "hole in the ground" suggests talking to a grave, or a dead person, and in conjunction with the imperative, "tell yourself" becomes a colloquial injunction to commit suicide. Furthermore, the cliché, "Tell a little bird", evokes the social media platform, Twitter, which has been associated with cyberbully-related suicides, like that of Australian public figure, Charlotte Dawson (ABC, 2014). "Tell Big Brother" opens more ambiguity, referencing confession-as-entertainment tropes popularised by the reality TV show, *Big Brother*, and the government surveillance prevalent in Orwell's *Nineteen Eighty-Four*. "Tell the one that you love" is suggestive of the final moment of *Nineteen Eighty Four* where Winston Smith comes to love the oppressive, fictional "Big Brother" or "whoever's in control" – an allegory for popular culture's fervent embrace of public confession. The final cliché, "*I promise not to tell a soul*", is an ironic equivocation – although the voice cannot be trusted, the promise is literally truthful – none of the bodies with whom public confession might be shared have "a soul", be they mechanical, digital, a corporation or a government agency. The convoluted ways in which information and power are passed between these voices expresses Smith's anxiety about the social and political networks of millennial culture and what this might mean for the individual.

With deftness and acuity, Jordie Albiston and Melinda Smith use their poetic voices to pursue stories that are not often told – stories almost lost to the past, or fragmented by a disenfranchised and clamourous present. Behind the shield of language play, or claims of being apolitical, there is a politics of emancipation in their voicing of the non-privileged experiences of individuals, and their use of an array of technical skills to painstakingly recreate or reiterate those voices. Although Albiston and Smith offer authentic "realness", their reiterations of public voices complicate the nature of authentic experience at every turn, exposing the limitations and critiquing the dangers of voices imbued with authority and privilege. These poets are not Rosencrantz, stammering at the mercy of the king's authority. In their engagement with public voices, they more resemble the language-savvy Hamlet, who, performing madness, evades and confounds spies with the epizeuxius: "Words, words, words." (1083)

Both poets seem to believe in the public function of storytelling

– particularly the reiteration of personal histories that may offer the reader a sense of shared space, place or experience. In their engagement with confessional modes, some morsel of belief in the authenticity and universal recurrence of human experience still remains. The "realness" pursued in their poetry is a truth – it may necessitate postmodern language play, archival research, and frequent swapping of registers and perspectives in order to approximate that truth, but it nevertheless glimmers with a little post-Enlightenment meaning.

Works Cited

ABC Radio National. "Poetica: Jordie Albiston." www.abc.net.au/rn/legacy/features/pod/poets/albiston.htm

Auden, Wystan Hugh. "Funeral Blues." *All Poetry*. http://allpoetry.com/Funeral- Blues, 1936.

Albiston, Jordie. *Botany Bay Document: A Poetic History of the Women of Botany Bay*, Black Pepper Publishing, 1996.

---. *The Book of Ethel*, Puncher and Wattmann, 2013.

---. *Nervous Arcs*, Spinifex Press, 1995.

---. *The Hanging of Jean Lee*, Black Pepper Publishing, 1998.

---. *the sonnet according to 'm'*, John Leonard Press, 2009.

---. *Vertigo:a cantata*, John Leonard Press, 2007.

Brand, Stewart. "What Does Information Really Want." http://bigthink.com/videos/what-does-information-really-want, 2010.

Gilbey, David. "Yoked with Contrarities: David Gilbey Reviews Jordie Albiston and Liam Ferney." http://cordite.org.au/reviews/gilbey-albiston-ferney, 2013.

Glastonbury, Keri. "Networking, Bumping into, Sucking up to, Catching up with, Meeting, Greeting, Chatting, Joking, Criticising: The Emerging Writers' Community as *Respublica Literaria*." edited by P. Kirkpatrick & R. Dixon, *Republic of Letters: Literary Communities in Australia*, Sydney University Press, 2012.

Middleton, Kate. "An Interview with Jordie Albiston." http://walleahpress.com.au/INT-Albiston.html

Plato. "Phaedrus." *Plato*, translated by H. Fowler, Harvard University Press, 1914.

Shakespeare, William. "Hamlet, Prince of Denmark." *William Shakespeare: The Complete Works*, Random House Publishing, 1997.

Smith, Melinda. *Drag Down to Unlock or Place Emergency Call*, Pitt Street Poetry, 2013.

---. *First...Then...Poems from Planet Autism*, Ginninderra Press, 2012.

---. *Melinda Smith's Mull and Fiddle*, www.melindasmith.wordpress.com

---. *Pushing Thirty, Wearing Seventeen*, Port Adelaide, SA, Ginninderra Press, 2001.

The Guardian. "Tony Abbott Defends George Pell after Criticism from Child Abuse Inquiry." www.theguardian.com/world/2013/nov/14/tony-abbott-defends-george-pell-after-criticism-from-child-abuse-inquiry, 2013.

Wilkinson, Jessica. "Poetic Biography and Archival Limits." Paper presented at Experimental: A Poetics Symposium, University of Sydney, NSW, 7-8 July, 2014.

Chapter 14

Between Housework and Carrying Her Home: Natalie Harkin's Reparative Poetics[1]

ANN VICKERY

In their introduction to the *Macquarie/PEN Anthology of Aboriginal Literature*, Anita Heiss and Peter Minter discern that Aboriginal writing has been in the "foreground of a renewed and particularly successful resistance to state authority" (4). They cite *We Are Going* by Oodgeroo Noonuccal as emblematic of an activist literature that is directed to her own community as well as a mainstream audience. Heiss and Minter situate Noonuccal's writing within the context of resistance literature, a genre which blurs creative and critical genres in being underwritten by "imperatives of radical critique, political action, and social change" (Harlow 2). Just over fifty years later, Narungga writer Natalie Harkin's installation art and first major poetry collection *Dirty Words* follows and extends Oodgeroo's lead. Just as Oodgeroo was partly influenced by the 1960s Black Rights Movement, Harkin's literary activism is shaped by Black feminism of the 1970s and by First Nations movements from around the world. Harkin views herself is part of an intimate conversation between those that seek to make "meaning in worlds steeped in histories of shared deep colonialisms" ("For You, K. Tsianina Lomawaima" 270).

Harkin's poetry and cross-media experimentation is part of a wave of twenty-first century Australian literature that focuses on issues of Indigenous sovereignty, resilience, and repair. Building upon the groundwork of Oodgeroo and Lionel Fogarty, such poetry combines personal and public histories in critiquing narratives of colonialism that have been circulated as 'truths.' Like Tony Birch and

Jeanine Leane, Harkin writes back to the colonial archive[2], yet Harkin's work joins that of Leane and Ali Cobby Eckermann in focusing predominantly on maternal legacies. In doing so, Harkin troubles the trope of domiciliation that often informs our understanding of the archive. Her writing shifts between the official archive as hold or house (a site of containment) and an alternative archive of the poem as home to cultural memories. As Antoinette Burton points out, the home has been frequently used by women writers and is an ideological construction that crosses national boundaries. She adds that critics must be "attentive to the specific languages, metaphors, and tropes through which it is articulated" (6). Harkin's shifts between house and home foreground her negotiation of the structures of the Australian colonial archive and its reconceptualisation as an affective site. In performing these shifts, Harkin undertakes crucial reparative work. This reparative work is, as Eve Kosofsky Sedgwick suggests, "the process of reconstructing a sustainable life in [the] wake" of trauma (Hanson 105).[3] Yet, it also decolonises the archive in extending what might be considered archive, whether a community or individual might be an archive, and redeploying archival documents through creative practice to engender new archives.

Harkin's work might also be viewed in light of literary interventions in the colonial archive that are occurring increasingly around the world. In *Feeding the Ghosts*, Fred D'Aguiar writes of the profit-driven motivations behind a slave massacre on the *Zong* and the ensuing court trial. He imagines a female survivor whose diary is dismissed as evidence and whose testimony is ultimately lost. D'Aguiar argues that there is a crucial need for storytelling, discerning that "the ghosts feed on the story of themselves" (230). Harkin's approach to the archives is perhaps more aligned to M. NourbeSe Philip's *Zong! As Told to the Author by Setaey Adamu Boateng* (2008) in including its silences and foregrounding spectral echoes. Whereas D'Aguiar concludes that, "the past is laid to rest when it is told" (230), Harkin argues for an activist writing that keeps "the past alive through responsibility, respect, and honouring" ("Collective" 31). As Sedgwick suggests, love is a key factor in any reparative reading (128). Harkin's activism is shaped by the work of Alice Walker, Audre Lorde, and bell hooks, all of whom emphasised the historical and lived experiences of black women and celebrated female strengths and solidarity. It would be further shaped by visiting the Point Pearce Mission Station with her grandmother and spending time with her aunties.

Harkin's interest in archives came about when her grandmother wanted to know about her own mother, "the beloved spectral-matriarch of our family" ("Re)Mapping" 1). In the late 1990s, Harkin went with her cousins to the Aboriginal State Records of South Australia (State Records) in search of her grandmother's missing history. The State Records revealed a system of intense colonial surveillance that had tracked the daily movements of Harkin's grandmother in minute detail. Discovering how her grandmother's life had been structured through a perverse lens of objectification, Harkin felt herself to be in a paradoxical position, wanting to immerse herself in the archives even as she was aware of its dangerous subsumption of Aboriginal subjectivity to reductive, often violent colonial narratives.

Following Derrida, Harkin characterises her desire for the archive as a kind of homesickness. Quoting Derrida's *Archive Fever*, she notes how she experienced a "compulsive, repetitive and nostalgic desire for the archive, an irrepressible desire to return to the origin" (Derrida 91; "(Re)mapping" 3). As Derrida states, the place where things begin is also the place where power originates. The archive is an expression of State power, which finds a narrative between present-day power and past authority. For Harkin, there is an alternative power of Aboriginal sovereignty that is yearned for beyond the official archive. While Derrida engages with a paternal pursuit for origins, looking back at Freud's own search for origins, Harkin engages in a maternal pursuit, partaking in her grandmother's pursuit for origins. Significantly, for both, this registers as a form of house arrest. The archive, for the former, is Freud's home in exile within which Derrida becomes stuck with his computer. For

Harkin, it is the Aboriginal State records, the official containment of Aboriginal history. For Derrida, the archive is the dwelling that marks an "institutional passage from the private to the public" (qtd. in Lynch 67).

For Harkin, the archive marks the removal of Aboriginal girls from the private sphere of their family to be institutionalised and rendered public through State 'welfare.' As part of that passage, they were often educated to become placed as domestic servants within white homes. Burton says that the cult of domesticity informs many women writers' use of home, as they explore its material exigencies in the structurally gendered location of the patriarchal household (6). Harkin explores its application in the Australian context, demonstrating how it was inflected through a racial and class discourse in order to assert colonial power and authority.

Harkin turns to Kiowa American N. Scott Momoday's trope of blood memory as a process of Indigenous recovery and repair ("(Re) Mapping" 6). Blood memory names a process by which Momoday imaginatively re-collects and remembers the stories of his grandfather's life and positions his own identity within an ongoing genealogical sequence of the Momoday family. As Chadwick Allen discerns, Momoday renders himself "coincident with indigenous ancestors and with indigenous history—and makes available to readers both that indigenous past and his contemporary identity *as indigenous*— through tactics of narrative re-membering and transgenerational address" (181). In foregrounding living memory, blood memory is an active alternative to the static 'house arrest' of the institutional archive. Following Momoday, Harkin consciously draws attention to place, emphasising historical events as situated and "[s]eething" ("'I Weave Back to You,'" 82).

In "The Poetics of (Re)Mapping Archives: Memory in the Blood," Harkin declares:

> All haunted by what was neither visible nor invisible, neither present nor absent in the flesh (Derrida, in Rivera 2), I needed

what was beyond the so-called-official record, to enter those hidden in-between places full of mystery, pain and possibility, to peel back layers of my memory and flesh and liberate our stories and skin, particularly for the women in my family. (3)

Harkin seeks to examine the "ways in which the past still haunts us and maintains its influence on the present; and particularly how the layers of meanings in events or texts, previously consigned to history's shadows, can be exposed through creative means" ("(Re) Mapping" 5). Through exercising blood memory, she seeks to destabilise and subvert the 'archons' that have formulated narratives of power and constraint over her family. Poetry becomes a means to claim agency. As bell hooks states, writing is never "solely an expression of creative power, it is an act of resistance, a political gesture that challenges the politics of domination that would render us nameless and voiceless" (126).

In "Archive-Box Transformation," Harkin enacts liberation. She notes how overwhelming archival processes can be:

> *Extract. Describe. Interpret. Sort. Catalogue. File.* There is no end to this forensic cumulative-gathering. As one box closes, another one opens with more stories, facts and events to map and authenticate. (103)

The opening stanzas of the poem are set out in box-like prose form, each stanza numbered. Harkin describes feeling as if she is part of a "secondary entrapment," having been "lured" by the State with her ancestors "used as bait" (103). In this respect, she is

> "[c]aptured by what I set out to transform": "I am pressed between the disintegrating folds, about to be locked up. Filed away. GRG51, GRG52. You can find me here" (103).

Yet the latter part of the poem sees a literal unravelling of the text. Harkin actively resists containment by putting forward her "version of a new-/telling" (104). This is a means to escape the logic of the archive yet to take her ancestors with her through memory:

> I tear my way out   remember to weave
>   future offerings
>   that begin
>
>   and never end. (104)

Sedgwick's theory of reparative reading is pertinent to Harkin's engagement with the archive in its emphasis on the complex affects that emerge and the accretive, creative process of assemblage from fragments and traces. Sedgwick discerns that, "Hope, often a fracturing, even a traumatic thing to experience, is among the energies by which the reparatively positioned reader tries to organize the fragments and part-objects she encounters and creates" (146). Besides hope there is also intense mourning: "Because the reader has room to realise that the future may be different from the present, it is also possible for her to entertain such profoundly painful, profoundly relieving, ethically crucial possibilities as that the past, in turn, could have happened differently from the way it actually did" (146).

In "On Collective Unsettled Pride," Harkin talks about the resulting emotion from her encounter with the state archive: "Sorrow, anger, shame, mourning" (31). This is the affective afterwardness (*Nachtraglichkeit*) that characterises trauma. As Ann Cvetkovich notes, "trauma can be unspeakable and unpresentable and because it is marked by forgetting and dissociation, it often seems to leave behind no records at all" (7). She adds that documenting or remembering hidden or marginalised forms of trauma often requires "new genres of expression … and new forms of monuments, rituals, and performances that can call into being collective witnesses and publics" (7). Harkin undertakes this transformative archive through extending her poetry into performance and art installations.

Cvetkovich advocates an "archive of feelings" that challenges "traditional conceptions of history and understand the quest for history as a psychic need rather than a science" (268). Whereas a state archive is one of order, delineation, closure, status, and scientific, an archive of feelings navigates the ephemeral, the fragmented, and the everyday. It addresses "the determination to 'never forget' that gives archives of traumatic history their urgency" (242). Harkin's reparative reading is one that necessarily extends to her readers. For Harkin, listening is as important as the telling in the process of healing and remaking selves. Governor General William Deane noted in 1997 that the legacy of the Stolen Generation "cannot be addressed unless the whole community listens with an open heart and mind to the stories of what happened in the past" (Human Rights and Equal Opportunity Commission 3). Harkin cites Sara Ahmed in suggesting that "embracing a claim to 'national shame' in the quest for justice is the very thing that allows us to move forward; and that keeping the past alive is in fact the ethical way to live and be" (31).

In "On Collective Unsettled Pride," Harkin writes:

> Personal narratives are often shared at considerable risk. But they continue to be shared because of their ability to resonate, to inform something much larger, something beyond the self. They counter Australia's national—at times wilful—amnesia and offer a potential shift toward 'something else'. (30)

As a critic of Harkin's work, I am generating a further filter of observation and translation.[4] Yet as a reader and a teacher of her poetry, I can begin to undo some of the ethnographic dynamics that surround white attention to Indigenous lives and stories and begin the task of listening. While this chapter follows traditional conventions, it was shaped by extra-textual conversations and learning, and can possibly provide some trajectories to extend that conversation.

An example of how Harkin creates alternative archives of feeling can be found in her elegy "Fabienne, Literary Goddess." Dedicated to a community of women, it celebrates the life of Bundjalung writer Fabienne Bayet-Charlton. It narrates collective grieving as family members and Harkin go through Bayet-Charlton's belongings after her death, a "sorting-packing-tea-drinking process" (50). The writing itself generates a calming, ritualistic rhythm: "We rock with the immensity of immersion in her private-world" (50). It performatively pieces together a shared female resurrection of Bayet-Charlton's world and Bayet-Charlton herself: "We sit and gather, all visceral black-women-intuition, and attempt to piece together fragments of an intricate-broken-life with such conviction and intent that we just might make her whole again (50). Bayet-Charlton's presence is felt in the room, and more specifically through the alternative archive of books and photographs: "As we mediate through many boxes of books we appreciate the scope-depth-meaning of this collection as a direct reflection of her spirit, her soul" (52). Harkin sees the act of writing for Bayet-Charlton as a form of breathing, "her lifeblood" with "her Bundjalung breath in every page" (52). Although Bayet-Charlton's house, the once "vibrant-welcome-place she called home" (51), is being packed away, her books retain that sense of home. And through writing Bayet-Charlton's story, Harkin is participating and passing on the blood-memory as Bayet-Charlton has done through her work: "This sacred memory so deep dark and silent where past-present-future haunts" (51).

Harkin also performs blood memory through her membership in the Unbound Collective. Consisting of four Indigenous women artists, Ali Gumillya Barker, Faye Rosas Blanch, Simone Ulalka Tur, and Harkin, the Unbound Collective have performed *Bound and Unbound: Sovereign Acts*, a series of acts exploring being simultaneously bound and free, contained and excluded. Acts I (2014) and II (2015) focused on institutional spaces around the 'cultural precinct' of Adelaide and involved embodied projection as well as roaming performances. The Unbound Collective question what is recorded, preserved or printed, and how spaces and selves have been controlled. An example is Harkin's art installation "ATTENTION" which consisted of a custom-made solander archive box lined with her poetry that lay open on a desk. A lamp projected the following message on the wall: "Attention Record Keepers of the State/We Have You Under Surveillance" ("Act I" 61).

Her "Archive Fever Paradox [2]" uses everyday objects of female domesticity to foreground a feminist critique of institutionalism. While reproducing words about the indentured Aboriginal labour history in her family on tea-towels and a sheet, Harkin also wove the handwritten letters of her grandmother and great-grandmother from the state's archive into a basket. A postcard capturing the act reads: "I weave your words/ your words from these records/ this basket of words/ I weave/ back to you" (*Bound* 20). In recontextualising her grandmother's words, she frees them from the archival record. Her use of tea-towels and a sheet symbolically gestures towards the whitewashing process following the removal of Aboriginal girls from their family and their subsequent 'domestication.' As with "ATTENTION," it foregrounds colonial processes of discipline. Drawing attention to how common objects from Aboriginal homes were ethnologically rehoused in institutions, she reterritorializes institutional space and processes, using them to produce a counter-message. Harkin's poem, "Surveillance" supplements "Archive Fever Paradox [2]" in foregrounding the possessive rhetoric of colonialism: "[T]hey report   describe categorise   observe the colonial girl." As "rarely-named object" and focus of "their imperial fascination," she becomes possessed as "*their Girl*." The end of the poem is a declaration of resistance: "witness the missing/ carry her home" (74).

In Act II, the servitude of many Aboriginal women under colonialism and their alterity to Western culture is critiqued through Baker's print of Tur in the pose of Johannes Vermeer's 1665 'masterpiece,' *Girl with a Pearl Earring*. In placing her digital print on archival photographic paper, Baker further foregrounds what is considered worth preserving. Declaring themselves "not Bound to one country, time, or community," the Unbound Collective enact "our story," a story held by all rather than any single one of them ("Act I" 64). Moreover, in "tearing through and between the lines of the colonial archive," they seek to "repatriate their ancestors through living stories of hope and transformation" and to "untangle and extract ourselves from the ideas that attempt to suffocate us" ("Act I" 61).

Harkin reflects on her experience in "Bound and Unbound: Act II" in the poem "Cultural Precinct." As she discerns, buildings in the Adelaide cultural precinct are residual markers of colonial oppression: the Migration Museum being the old Protector's Office and Rations Depot; the ammunition stores for the Military Police and Aboriginal Records being housed behind the Art Gallery and the Radford Auditorium; and the South Australian Museum being built out of limestone quarried from an old Kaurna campsite. Harkin notes that the Museum itself "boasts the largest Australian Aboriginal Cultures collection in the world" and promotes itself as a "leader [...] in Australian Aboriginal heritage and scientific research." As a "fantasy monolith-archive," it literally mirrors London's National History Museum, being "an uncanny replica." As the "proudest collection," it "wins the Empire's great race." Harkin's poem foregrounds how her family became reduced to "objects and specimens" within the colonisers' "cabinets of curiosity" and how Aboriginal culture was institutionally contained through "maps, early recordings, photographs, [and] field notebooks" of early ethnologists. As with "Bound and Unbound: Act II," the poem offers an alternative vision of place, impelling the reader to:

> strive to navigate / this violent place   be still and listen   there are waterholes here   /   these fresh-water springs   flow a limestone-memory   erode and expose   our truths will appear.

Like the performance art of the Unbound Collective, much of Harkin's work is self-consciously avant-garde yet distinct from a European heritage in seeking to undo institutional boundaries and to articulate Indigenous sovereignty. In creating a series of *Sovereign*

Love Poems for ten bus-shelter posters with the Unbound Collective, Harkin was led by American black scholar bell hooks who was positively inspired when she unexpectedly came across some graffiti on love. Placed in ordinary public sites, the poems become part of the everyday rather than rarefied. This is explored in the poems themselves. "Sovereign Love Poem #2" recalls Baker's revision of Vermeer's *Girl with a Pearl Earring* in featuring the profile of Faye Blanch from the Unbound Collective wearing chandeliers for earrings. The poem is short: "Feel the earth beneath/ your feet leave traces of love/ on paths well worn/ we are on Kaurna land."[5] It is simultaneously a declaration of sovereignty and an affective call for embodied, enacted community.

Harkin's poetry often seeks to bring ancestors into the time of the present. Both "Harts Mill Projections" and "Ode to PolesApart-Tracking" were written in response to her contemporary r e a's video "PolesApart—Tracking" which sought to honour and embody r e a's grandmother and great aunt who were taken away from their families. While r e a's mother became a maidservant loaned to Dame Nellie Melba and never again saw her family, her great aunt would flee and return home. "PolesApart" enacts an Aboriginal woman being pursued by invisible forces, her long black dress recalling not only the period of r e a's grandmother but, along with the blackened forest setting, elements of mourning and aftermath. The video was projected onto Harts Mill in Port Adelaide as part of the *Stop (the) Gap/Mind (the) Gap: International Indigenous Art in Motion* exhibition in 2011. Whereas "Ode to PolesApart—Tracking" is ekphrastic, "Harts Mill Projections" becomes part of the conversation or counter-discourse started by "PolesApart." In it, Harkin notes that the Mill was built adjacent to significant Kaurna heritage sites and is a "poetic place of haunting." Harkin goes on to honour Lartelare, the great grandmother of Aunty Veronica Brodie who launched a land rights movement over the area known as "Yerta Bulti." Against the "glittering neo-/colonial backdrop" of the New Ports Quays redevelopment with its "neon satisfaction" is the river "flooded with stories" and "layers of residual voices." The presence of Harkin's grandmother and great-grandmother "rise from a sediment" and talk about how "they ran away and toward each other."

Harkin's first full poetry collection, *Dirty Words*, opens with an epigraph by Audre Lorde: "Speak loud/speak unsettling things/ and be dangerous". Harkin notes that she started to work on it in 2011 after an exhibition (featuring her basket of letters and poetry) with Ali Gumillya Baker. ("Interview" 98). The cover uses a print by Baker, "Sovereign Fleet: Black", collaged with an image representing the Maralinga bomb testing in South Australia, and another of a shark which represents Narungga heritage. It therefore emphasises the complex, situated work of decolonisation. The preface presents the poems as a "restless offering: an unfolding that may begin on any page" (ix). As Pip Newling points out, *Dirty Words* is, in many respects, a "snapshot" of the period between 1996 and 2014. Harkin reminds readers how a climate of racism and xenophobia was encouraged under the political leadership of John Howard and Tony Abbott and under the pedagogic leadership by those like Professor Barry Spurr, one-time advisor on the National English Curriculum Review. Harkin further notes the resurgence of xenophobic political parties like One Nation.

The collection is structured like a 'subject index' of key words that might be found in an academic textbook or library catalogue. The words foreground the double nature of language in revealing both layers of racialised violence and trauma, as well as possible liberatory meaning. Harkin took her cue from the poem "(Auto)biography of Mad" by Cherokee Two-Spirit and queer writer Qwo-Li Driskill (Interview 92-93). Against taxonomic order is blood memory and an uncanny knowing beyond the official story. For Harkin, poetry is a vehicle to carry "multiple lived-histories" and "other ways of knowing and being in this world" (*Dirty Words*, ix). The dirty words are words like "sovereignty," "treaty," and "land rights" (Heiss), words that disrupt the "floating words" of colonial mythmaking and the one "sweeping narrative *The Aboriginal problem*" (*Dirty Words*

18). As *Dirty Words* demonstrates, language is the vehicle for racist ideology and untruths: "words/like lives/have histories/actions/like knives/cut-deep" (23). Harkin shows how political correctness has been mobilised as a rhetorical "invention/to dismiss progressive/ dissent intent" and how Spurr could dismiss his bigoted comments as "whimsical-linguistic-games." "History Wars" cites a Minister of Education's call for a rebalancing of the national curriculum in light of "a black-armband view of history" that "over-emphasis[es]" Indigenous culture and "blot[s] out" "our British traditions and British heritage" (12). Harkin turns to the Archival Record to question how one might "balance" "invasion 'versus' settlement" (12). In echoing the Minister's repetition of the term "balance," she demonstrates the term's semantic emptiness (12). Harkin also queries the eugenics-informed discourse around "the true essential Aborigine" (9).

Written before and therefore pre-empting *Sovereign Love Poems*, "Sovereignty" lists protest walks for recognition of Aboriginal sovereignty and reconciliation. Each line acknowledges a different walk and creates a further step in the poem itself, although the poem itself brings itself full circle. It both begins and ends with an entreaty to the reader to "take off your shoes/let the land speak heal your feet/feel the earth find your stride/walk with Indigenous sovereignty" (32-33).

The poem "Domestic" cites from multiple sources, including the South Australian Royal Commission on the Aborigines 1913, the Australian Aborigines Progressive Association 1928, and records held by the Aborigines Protection Board on her grandmother: "Committed to Institution till 18 years. Charged 'Destitute'" (6). As Harkin notes elsewhere, this label of parental neglect is countered by the numerous letters sent from her grandmother and great-grandmother to key agents of the state about access to each other, visits, negotiations, and advocacy ("'I Weave Back to You'" 6). The poem also samples excerpts from a 1926 issue of *The Australian Woman's Mirror* where contributors comment on the traits of their

Aboriginal servant girls. The poem begins with an observation by writer and academic Jackie Huggins that

> The stories of Aboriginal women domestic servants cannot be told enough. They illuminate a deeply-rooted racist facet of Australia's history. They tell of the trials tribulations and triumphs amidst the backdrop of oppression. (6)

After the collage of critical, political, and popular material, the poem concludes with a poetic reflection, "Apron Sorrow." This is taken from a shorter poem written for Harkin's friend Kokatha/ Nukunu glass artist Yhonnie Scarce, who made two linen aprons and hand-blown glass bush plums tucked in the apron pockets. Scarce's work would be dedicated to her own nanna and great-aunt, domestic servants at the same time as Harkin's. The concluding "Apron Sorrow" makes present the absent perspective of the Aboriginal domestics, the unsaid being found through "linen-shadows/ that flicker-float with the sun" in "rhythmic sorrow." (7). It reminds the reader that "secrets" that may have attempted to "whisper" from places within "apron-folds and pockets" have found no audience (7). The separation of the three words "pinned   tucked   hidden" foreground the sense of isolation (7). They also refer to identities that have been hidden, yet kept safely tucked in close to the body.

Against the State-orchestrated domestic placements, Harkin generates the kitchen as a place of affect and (ironically laden) empowerment for her grandmother. In "Queen of England," she refers to her grandmother's fondness for the Royal Family and the use of the Queen's image of biscuit tins, "Mother-Country symbols/ of colonialism" (24). She considers the Queen not simply a residual symbol of colonialism but still Australia's Head of State. Within the poem, the use of gaps within lines emphasise not only the circulation of media sound-bites around the monarchy but human absence.

Originally titled "Ode to the Women," "Resistance" is a serial litany honouring six aunties in Harkin's life (Heiss). Harkin notes that the poem was inspired by Alice Walker's "These Days," in which Walker enumerates friends for whom she hoped "the earth would be saved".[6] Like Walker, Harkin writes back to forms of destruction and instils a sense of homage and hope. Initially written while each aunty was still alive, the form of address and use of repetition in opening and closing each acknowledgement instils a sense of the sacred in "Resistance". Yet there is also a sense of intimacy through non-cognitive remembrances, such as the sound of a voice or the holding of a hand. The skills and strengths of each aunty are detailed, whether it be passing on stories, battling for land rights, or "card-shark-shuffling" (26). Harkin cites the role of those like Aunty Irene who have explained the significance of Aboriginal story song and place, and the interrelatedness of country and people across generations. She also cites Aunty Veronica as a "big-hearted-warrior-woman" but also her "other-Nanna" (28). Her homage to Aunty Doreen pays homage to Ngarrindjeri elder Doreen Kartinyeri, a leading force in the protest against the Hindmarsh Island bridge. With her "photographic memory," Aunty Doreen generates an alternative archive on "bright collage family-love pin-up boards" and through her "rhizome-like oral history" (29). As alternative archivist, Aunty Doreen collected the Aboriginal stories and genealogies of Point Pearce and Point McLeay, much of which had been lost due to colonisation, and founded the Aboriginal Family History unit at the South Australian Museum. Through acknowledging these women's maternal power and wisdom, Harkin creates a circle of knowledge and strength. This is reinforced by the final six poetic lines set low on a separate page:

> These days
> I think of the women
> who fought and loved   so hard
> I raise my hand catch   their last breath
> with clenched-fist-resist
> I thank them. (31)

It is a familiar trope in the black and women's rights movement. While *Dirty Words* names local acts of activism, it positions them within a broader platform of resistance. In seeking to be transcultural, it portrays aspects of grief and loss through a global archive of suffering. In light of the uranium used at Fukushima being sourced from Kakadu, Harkin's poem "Apology" foregrounds how its nuclear disaster have made "two lands united" (1). A collective mourning across space and generations is also suggested by paralleling Fukushima with Chernobyl. While Australia's traditional owners reached out in support of the Fukushima disaster, she notes that "Coalition Governments" remained "unmoved" (2). Similarly, "Boat People" aligns the passage of asylum seekers with the passage of the First Fleet and the "hearts displaced" (3). Harkin's use of alliteration performatively adds to the deeply affective movement of the poem in phrases like "horizon's hope" and "what sorrow/seeks refuge" (3). In placing "homes" (3) on its own, she enacts separation. Climate change is viewed as a worldwide phenomenon that will require transcultural support. Dismissed by an Australian Prime Minister as *"absolute crap"* (*Dirty Words* 4), Harkin notes how "whole nations [...] fear extinction" and "distant strangers [...] watch[...] lives/ slip away" (5). The man-made phenomenon echoes the cultural devastation of colonialism. Harkin's use of half rhymes such as "chokes" and "lakes" and ironic compound words like "salt-blooms" suggests the need for new, lateral thinking as a response (4). Deborah Bird Rose suggests that it is important for Indigenous people to "speak on behalf of and with marginalised migrant communities... [w]ith refugees, asylum seekers and those presently incarcerated in Australian detention camps" (116). While she frames this as an act of sovereign responsibility, Harkin also foregrounds the role of care, nurture, and respect.

Citing a history of forced labour, Aboriginal deaths-in-custody, the detention of asylum-seeker children, and violence targeted towards women, non-heteronormative people, and the Indigenous, the poem "Justice" makes links between the removal of basic rights and freedoms in Australia and Canada. Harkin draws attention to Anishinaabe activist Josephine Mandamin whose water walks drew attention to issues of water access and exploitation, and who was mobilised by the prophecy that by 2030, an ounce of water will cost the same as an ounce of gold. Harkin notes the significance of the relationship between aesthetics and life, speaking of the "beauty" (14) of the Samaqan Water Walkers, the "healing-art"(15) of the victim of a hate crime, the music of a victim of speed, and the poetry of those who have died in police custody.

Like "Resistance," "Justice" makes use of ritual invocation and a shared voice in the performative repetition in the phrase, "we will [...] honour you" (14-15). The poem itself becomes a communal space or home enjoining the reader to be part of the "we." It foregrounds action in writing imperatives in the present and future tense: "we choose," "we carry", and "we will" (14-15). While the poem is serial, it does not synthesise in its naming of injustice. The many spaces within the lines of the poem draw attention to erasures or non-recognition in both history and rhetoric. This is reinforced by Harkin not naming individuals, a reminder that those without basic human rights are typically rendered nameless. Accordingly, the poem shifts between presence and absence, loss and retrieval.

Dirty Words foregrounds how archive, nation, and poem are all sites of domiciliation and often interrelated, and how language can domesticate and contain. Harkin works within these structures, stressing mobility and change. In weaving between sources, she disrupts hierarchies of authority while her linguistic play intervenes in ideological orders. In bringing ancestral and marginalised presences into the body of the poem and creating it as a space of honour and memory, she transforms the poem into a home. Deeply affective and highly performative in enacting the relationship between people and place, Harkin demonstrates how the poem can offer a reparative space in Australian culture. At the same time, Harkin understands the role of housework in generating "hopeful futures" ("On Coalitions" 19):

My compulsion to keep writing is firmly grounded in family story; it's a drive that comes from a particular kind of innate creative resilience that I am only now beginning to understand. I come from a long line of Aboriginal domestic workers and know there is still so much work to be done to clean up this Colonisation mess. ("On grandmother stories" 13)

Notes

1. I would like to thank Natalie Harkin for her generous engagement with this chapter and for providing some additional contextual details.
2. See Tony Birch, *Broken Teeth* and Jeanine Leane, *Walk Back Over*.
3. Sedgwick notes that there has been an extraordinary emphasis on knowledge in the form of exposure and suggests that exposure itself is "not a mere hop, skip and jump away from getting [systemic oppressions] solved" (139).
4. See Harkin's discussion of types of encounters in "For You, K. Tsianina Lomawaima."
5. "Sovereign Love Poem #6" is similar: "Winds carry whispers/from a lifetime ago/breathe deep and love/we are on Kaurna Land" (*Bound* 25).
6. Email to the author, 8 December 2017.

Works Cited

Allen, Chadwick. *Blood Narrative: Indigenous Identity in American Indian and Maori Literary and Activist Texts*, Duke University Press, 2002.

Baker, Ali Gumillya et al. "Act I: BOUND AND UNBOUND Sovereign Acts," *Artlink*, vol. 35, no. 3, 2015, pp. 60-65.

Baker, Ali Gumillya et al. *Bound and Unbound: Sovereign Acts II*, Yunggorendi First Nations Centre, 2015.

Birch, Tony. *Broken Teeth*, Cordite Press, 2016.

Burton, Antoinette. *Dwelling in the Archive: Women Writing House, Home and History in Late Colonial India*, Oxford University Press, 2003.

Cvetkovich, Ann. *An Archive of Feelings: Trauma, Sexuality and Lesbian Public Culture*, Duke University Press, 2003.

D'Aguiar, Fred. *Feeding the Ghosts*. London, Chatto & Windus, 1997.
Hanson, Ellis. "The Future's Eve: Reparative Reading after Sedgwick," *The South Atlantic Quarterly*, vol. 110, no.1, 2011, pp. 101-19.
Harkin, Natalie. "Remembering Fabienne, literary goddess," *Southerly*, vol. 71, no. 2, 2011, pp. 50-54.
---. "Harts Mill Projections," *Cordite Poetry Review*, 2013, https://cordite.org.au/chapbooks-features/proteaceae/harts-mill-projections/
---. "Ode to PolesApart—Tracking," *Cordite Poetry Review*, 2013. http://pandora.nla.gov.au/pan/14234/20131220-0005/cordite.org.au/poetry/ode-to-polesapart-tracking/index.html. ---. "The Poetics of (Re)Mapping Archives: Memory in the Blood," *Journal of the Association for the Study of Australian Literature*, vol. 14, no.3, 2014, pp. 1-14.
---. *Dirty Words*, Cordite Press, 2015.
---. "Cultural Precinct," *Cordite Poetry Review*, 2016, https://cordite.org.au/poetry/theend/cultural-precinct/
---. "On Collective Unsettled Pride," *Overland*, no. 222, 2016, pp. 30-31.
---. "On grandmother stories and creative resilience," *Overland*, vol. 223, 2016, pp. 12-13.
---. "On Coalitions for Hopeful Futures," *Overland*, vol. 224, 2016, pp. 19-20.
---. "Surveillance," *Wasafiri*, vol 31, no. 2, 2016, p. 74.
---. "For You, K. Tsianina Lomawaima," *Biography*, vol. 39, no. 3, 2016, pp. 270-73.
---. "'I Weave Back to You': Archival Poetics for the Record," PhD Dissertation, University of South Australia, 2016.
---. "Interview, by Corey Wakeling," *Rabbit*, vol. 21, 2017, pp.90-100.
---. "Archive-Box Transformation," *Rabbit*, vol. 21, 2017, pp. 103-04.
Harlow, Barbara. *Resistance Literature*, Methuen, 1987.
Heiss, Anita. Interview with Natalie Harkin, https://anitaheiss.wordpress.com/2015/07/07/poet-natalie-harkin-on-writing-

dirty-words

Heiss, Anita and Peter Minter. "Aboriginal Literature," *Anthology of Australian Aboriginal Literature*, edited by Anita Heiss and Peter Minter, McGill-Queen's University Press, 2008.

Hooks, Bell. "Talking Back," *Discourse*, vol,8, no. 86-87, 1986, pp. 123-28.

Human Rights and Equal Opportunity Commission. *Bringing them Home: Report* of *the National Inquiry into the Separation of Aboriginal and Torres Strait Islander Children from their Families*. Sydney, Human Rights and Equal Opportunity Commission, 1997. http://www.hreoc.gov.au/social_justice/bth_report/report/appendices_9.html.

Leane, Janine. *Walk Back Over*, Cordite Books, 2017.

Lynch, Michael. "Archives in Formation: Privileged Spaces, Popular Archives, and Paper Trails," *History of the Human Sciences*, vol. 12, no.2,1999, pp. 65-87.

Newling, Pip. Review of Natalie Harkin's *Dirty Words, Mascara Literary Review*, 2016, http://mascarareview.com/pip-newling-reviews-dirty-words-by-natalie-harkin

Noonuccal, Oodgeroo. *We Are Going*, Jacaranda Press, 1964.

Philips, M. NourbeSe. *Zong! As Told to the Author by Setaey Adamu Boateng*, Wesleyan University Press, 2008.

r e a. *PolesApart*. 2009, https://vimeo.com/108870026.

Rose, Deborah Bird. *Reports from a Wild Country: Ethics for Decolonisation*, University of New South Wales Press, 2004.

Sedgwick, Eve Kosofsky. *Touching Feeling: Affect, Pedagogy, Performativity*, Duke University Press, 2003.

Author Biographies

Cassandra Atherton is a widely anthologised prose poet and one of Australia's leading experts on prose poetry. She was a Visiting Scholar in English at Harvard University in 2016 sponsored by Stephen Greenblatt, and a Visiting Fellow at Sophia University, Tokyo, in 2014. Cassandra has published 17 critical and creative books and is the successful recipient of more than fifteen national and international research grants and awards, including a Creative Victoria grant and an Australia Council grant. She has judged poetry awards including the Victorian Premier's Prize for Poetry, the joanne burns award and the Lord Mayor's Prize for Poetry. She is an Associate Professor of Writing and Literature and the current poetry editor of *Westerly* magazine

A.J. Carruthers (also aj carruthers) is an experimental poet and literary critic, author of *Stave Sightings: Notational Experiments in North American Long Poems* (Cham: Palgrave Macmillan, 2017), and the first volume of a lifelong long poem *AXIS Book 1* (Sydney: Vagabond, 2014). Other works are *Opus 16 on Tehching Hsieh* (Oakland: Gauss PDF, 2016), and excerpts from AXIS appeared in *The Blazar Axes* (Calgary: Spacecraft Press, 2018). On the way is a book on avant-garde Australian poetry and literary history, and some continuing stanzaworks under the rubric of 'dissonant prosody' and the 'prepared page.' In 2017 he was appointed Lecturer at the Australian Studies Centre, SUIBE, in Shanghai.

Toby Davidson is a senior lecturer and Australian literature researcher at Macquarie University. He is the editor of Francis Webb's *Collected Poems* (UWA Publishing) and author of the critical study *Christian Mysticism and Australian Poetry* (Cambria Press). His first poetry collection is *Beast Language* (Five Islands Press).

Martin Duwell taught for many years in the School of English, Media Studies and Art History at the University of Queensland. He edited *Makar* magazine and ran its associated press in the seventies and eighties. He has published a number of books including (with R.M.W Dixon) two anthologies of Aboriginal song poetry. He has written extensively on contemporary Australian poetry and, since 2006, has published a monthly review on the website *Australian Poetry Review* (www.australianpoetryreview.com.au).

Andy Kissane has published a novel, a book of short stories, *The Swarm*, (Puncher & Wattmann, 2012) and four books of poetry. *Radiance* (Puncher & Wattmann, 2014) was shortlisted for the Victorian and Western Australian Premier's Prizes for Poetry and the Adelaide Festival Awards. His essay on the Indigenous poet, Dennis McDermott was the winner of the inaugural BTG-*Blue Dog* Poetry Reviewing Prize. He is currently working on a verse novel and a short story cycle.

Martin Langford has published seven books of poetry, the most recent of which is *Ground* (Puncher &Wattmann, 2015). A collection of aphorisms, *Neat Snakes*, was published in 2018. He is co-editor (with Judith Beveridge, Judy Johnson and David Musgrave) of *Contemporary Australian Poetry* (Puncher and Wattmann, 2016). An essayist and critic, he is the poetry reviewer for *Meanjin*. He is the Deputy Chair of Australian Poetry Ltd.

Lyn McCredden is Professor of Literary Studies at Deakin University, Melbourne. She writes criticism and poetry. Her latest books are *The Fiction of Tim Winton: Earthed and Sacred* (SUP, 2017), and a volume of poetry, *Wanting Only* (Ginninderra Press, 2018).

Caitlin Maling is from Western Australia. She has published poetry and non-fiction throughout Australia, the UK and the US, in places such as *Best Australian Poems, Prairie Schooner, Australian Poetry Journal,*

Australian Book Review, cordite, Westerly, The Australian, Stand and *The Threepenny Review*, among others. She holds an MFA in poetry from the University of Houston and is a previous recipient of the Marten Bequest in Poetry, the Harri Jones Memorial Award and the John Marsden Poetry Prize. Her poetry collections include *Conversations I've Never Had*, which was shortlisted for the Mary Gilmore Award and in the WA Premier's Book Awards, and *Border Crossing. Fish Song* her third book of poetry is due in 2019.

David Musgrave teaches English and Writing at the University of Newcastle. He was a co-editor (with Martin Langford, Judith Beveridge and Judy Johnson) of *Contemporary Australian Poetry* (Puncher & Wattmann, 2016). He has published six collections of poetry, the most recent being *Anatomy of Voice* (GloriaSMH, 2016) which was awarded the Arts Queensland Judith Wright Calanthe Award for Poetry, and which is being published in the UK and USA by Eyewear Publishing in late 2018. He founded Puncher & Wattmann in 2005.

Kerry Plunkett is currently completing her PhD at the University of Newcastle. An unexpected resonance between the poetry of J. S. Harry and a little known seventeenth century poet, Lady Hester Pulter, led to her interest in the history of female aesthetics. Her present research is centred on early modern female creativity, specifically the diverse and creative ways that women poets interpreted and applied contemporary literary theory in the construction of their poetry.

Carolyn Rickett is an Assistant Dean (Research), Senior Lecturer in Communication and creative arts practitioner at Avondale College of Higher Education. She is co-ordinator for *The New Leaves* writing project for people who have experienced a life threatening illness. Her research, teaching interests and peer-reviewed publications focus on: trauma and bereavement studies; writing as therapeutic intervention; memoir and autobiographical writing; medical humanities; journalism ethics and praxis; literary and poetry studies; the psychosocial and spiritual care of patients. She also works as a chaplain at Sydney Adventist Hospital.

Tegan Jane Schetrumpf is a poet and academic. A firm believer in interdisciplinary study, she has a Bachelor of Medical Science and a Master of Letters in English from the University of Sydney. In 2015, her postgraduate research into "New Traditionalism" in millennial Australian poetry won the Dame Leonie Prize. Her essays and poetry have been published in *Antipodes*, *Axon*, *Meanjin*, *Southerly*, and *The Australian Poetry Journal*. Previously the Creative Editor for the postgraduate journal, *Philament*, Tegan is currently the Creative Editor for *Alterity Studies and World Literature*.

Ann Vickery teaches Writing and Literature at Deakin University. She is the author of *Devious Intimacy* (2015), *The Complete Pocketbook of Swoon* (2014), *Stressing the Modern: Cultural Politics in Australian Women's Poetry* (2007) and *Leaving Lines of Gender: A Feminist Genealogy of Language Writing* (2000). She co-authored *The Intimate Archive: Journeys through Private Papers* (2009) with Maryanne Dever and Sally Newman and co-edited *Poetry and the Trace* (2013) with John Hawke.

www.ingramcontent.com/pod-product-compliance
Lightning Source LLC
Chambersburg PA
CBHW031420150426
43191CB00006B/333